Supervision
in
Early Childhood Education
A DEVELOPMENTAL PERSPECTIVE

Joseph J. Caruso

M. Temple Fawcett

TEACHERS
COLLEGE
PRESS

Teachers College, Columbia University
New York and London

Published by Teachers College Press, 1234 Amsterdam Avenue, New York, N.Y. 10027

Library of Congress Cataloging in Publication Data

Caruso, Joseph J., 1943–
  Supervision in early childhood education.

  (Early childhood education series)
  Bibliography: p.
  Includes index.
  1. School supervision — United States. 2. Education,
Preschool — United States. 3. Child development —
United States. 4. Educational surveys — United States.
I. Fawcett, M. Temple, 1928–   II. Title.
III. Series.
LB2822.7.C37 1986   372.12   86–5749

ISBN-0-8077-2802-0

Manufactured in the United States of America

91 90 89 88 87   2 3 4 5 6

Contents

PART II.   A DEVELOPMENTAL PERSPECTIVE

PART IV. STAFF DEVELOPMENT IN PRACTICE

Preface

This book about supervision in early childhood education addresses supervisory issues and methods pertinent to personnel working in both public and private settings. It is meant to fill a gap in the supervision and the early childhood literature, which thus far has failed to take into account the special needs of supervisors and staff in programs for young children.

Many readers will be directors, coordinators, head teachers, and consultants to group programs for young children who recognize a need to expand and improve their supervision. Other readers who will find this a useful book are college and high school supervisors, administrators in public school systems adopting preschool programs, and supervisors of individuals working with young children in hospitals, museums, social service, and community settings. Persons preparing for early childhood leadership, administrative, and supervisory positions should find the text informative and meaningful.

This is a book about working with adults from a strong developmental perspective. We believe that the personal and professional development of the adult is basic to formulating supervisory strategies. Through supervision, staff members can receive continuing support in their development as professionals and paraprofessionals, and thus become better providers for children. Although supervision may well encompass more than staff development, we have chosen to focus this book on that aspect of supervision. We also stress the importance of the supervisor's own ongoing development and learning.

The content of this volume is intended to be both descriptive and practical. We have administered surveys and conducted many interviews in order to incorporate the thoughts, feelings, dilemmas, and concerns of early childhood personnel into the text and to clarify supervisor and supervisee roles and responsibilities. We provide the reader with specific suggestions for improving supervisory skills when working with individual staff members and with groups.

This volume has four major sections. In Part I, some supervisory myths are challenged in order to ease the burden under which supervisors carry out their work. Then the various types of early childhood programs and the people who work with them are described from the perspective of the supervisor's role.

The development of supervisors and supervisees and its implications for planning supervisory approaches is explored in Part II. Part III offers some basic information and suggestions for observing, holding conferences, and evaluating staff within the context of a clinical supervision approach. Several significant issues that affect staff morale and effectiveness are examined in Part IV, followed by suggestions for designing various types of staff development and training, and some specific tools for putting these plans into practice.

Throughout this book, we use the term *supervisor* to mean those persons who do supervision as part or all of their jobs. These may be administrators, supervisors, or teachers. The terms *teacher, staff member, caregiver,* and *child care worker* are used interchangeably.

The reader will certainly sense the diversity of programs, roles, and titles characteristic of the early childhood field, which is still striving toward greater professionalization. We hope this book contributes to the attainment of that goal and to the common mission that brings early childhood professionals together — that is, to support the growth and development of young children and their families.

Acknowledgments

We are grateful to the early childhood supervisors who eagerly talked with us at length about their jobs. Many of these individuals, from various parts of the United States, attended the annual Wheelock College Advanced Seminar in Day Care Administration. Others, in the metropolitan Boston and Providence areas, took time from busy schedules at their centers to share their concerns, frustrations, hopes, and triumphs with us. Excerpts from these interviews appear in various chapters in this text. Students in our supervision courses at Wheelock College and Roger Williams College also contributed many ideas. Especially helpful was the feedback about earlier drafts of our manuscript from students of Patricia Ramsey at Wheelock College and Abbie Gordon Klein at Cleveland State University.

Busy directors, coordinators, head teachers, and others from many states who took time to complete our surveys deserve special recognition.

We are appreciative of Gordon Klopf and John Correiro, of Tom Bucar and Bill Fricke, and of other friends and colleagues for their support, encouragement, and forbearance.

Anne Coolidge was enormously helpful and giving of her time to assist us in the design of a national survey from which we obtained significant data appearing throughout this book. Anne's help was indispensable.

The feedback from numerous colleagues who read and commented on chapters was greatly appreciated.

Lorrie Smith and Sheryl Madeira, our typists, were very accurate and very patient.

Lastly, we are indebted to Lisa Carlson who, unknowingly, encouraged us to write this book in the first place.

Part I

THE SUPERVISORY CONTEXT

1   Myths About Supervision

Myths influence, shape, and are often used to justify behavior. Myths about supervision come from expectations supervisors have about their jobs and their past supervisory experiences, training, and education. Myths can also arise from the attitudes toward supervisors held by staff members and others. Some of these beliefs are simply not true. Others are partially true. Nevertheless, they can create internal stress for supervisors and bring about pressure from others.

What are some of the myths about supervision in programs for young children?

Almost anyone can be an early childhood supervisor.

If the individual hired to be a director, educational coordinator, or head teacher of an early childhood program has had children, is a nice person, and has taught in the classroom, then few other qualifications are thought necessary to be a good supervisor. After all, parents have raised children for years without formal training, so why would a director need any special skills or knowledge to supervise babysitters? And anyone who has taught understands teachers' problems and can, therefore, supervise teachers effectively.

This kind of thinking—perhaps more prevalent in the minds of the public at large than in the child care field—certainly contributes to the feelings many supervisors have that their work is not valued. Such thinking is based upon a lack of knowledge about the process of working with adults and about the cognitive, social, emotional, and physical development of young children and their needs. It fails to recognize the importance of the environments in which children learn and of the interactions between children and adults in those environments.

Supervision cannot be carried out without careful thought, planning, and skill. Not all adults are competent to work with other adults or with children. Some who work well with children have to make many adjustments to work effectively with adults. Other adults work best alone, or with machines, or

3

behind a desk. They may not have the stamina or sensitivity to interact with people daily in small settings.

Persons holding supervisory positions in early childhood programs usually have more than one role to fill and are responsible for working with all types of people. Those who strive to provide quality supervision to their staff members do so because they understand its positive effects on children. They carry on with conviction and determination, despite the perceptions people may have about the nature and importance of their work. The myth that anyone can supervise tends to be held by those unfamiliar with early childhood programs, not by those who work in them.

There is one best supervisory approach to use with everyone.

Life would be easy for supervisors if they could read a book or take a course that would guarantee them one workable method of supervision that would almost always succeed. Frustrated by many problems and desperate for immediate solutions, this panacea can be appealing to supervisors.

Supervisors work with people. The problem with adopting a "package" to solve one's supervisory dilemmas or clinging to a home-grown method is the human factor: caregivers are unique. They have varying personal and professional needs and different levels of ability and skill, which require various supervisory strategies.

Experienced supervisors know that some supervisees need to be shown what to do and how to do it in a direct and detailed way. Yet others can develop their own solutions to problems or take the initiative to do what needs to be done without direction. Some people prefer to interact with authority figures with whom they can establish a personal relationship; that is, they prefer supervisors who are warm, expressive, sensitive, and who model appropriate behaviors for them. Others object to overly attentive supervisors. They prefer to develop their own solutions to problems and appreciate a supervisor who is formal, serious, and impersonal.

The reasons why supervisees respond to one approach or to another may have to do with cognitive style, cultural background, intelligence, personality, experience, developmental level, or other factors. Supervisors need flexibility when working with caregivers: the size of the settings, the number of supervisees for whom they are responsible, the individual differences among their supervisees, and their own personality and style all affect the supervisory strategies to be considered.

Supervision is a process involving the many variables of human behavior. Negating this process by looking at supervision with "tunnel vision" and adopting a single supervisory method will not resolve the complex problems supervisors face and will not help change caregiver behavior.

Supervisors have all the answers.

The myth that supervisors must have all the answers is one that creates continuous pressure on supervisors, who live in fear that someone might discover they don't have a solution to a problem or don't even know how to go about solving it. They fear that others will think less of them or will suggest that they are incompetent and shouldn't be in a leadership position if they cannot step in, take charge, and resolve a pressing problem in short order.

This assumption is based on the belief that supervisors are omnipotent, that they are more than human. This viewpoint makes it difficult for supervisors to be honest with themselves and with their staff members. It fails to recognize that some organizational problems or people problems take time to resolve—sometimes several years. This myth also discourages collaborative problem-solving between a supervisor and a staff member, for a collaborative mode acknowledges that others have expertise, perhaps in areas in which a supervisor is weak. Through the dialogue, interaction, and give-and-take of the problem-solving process, supervisors and supervisees can grow professionally.

This myth is reflected in behavior in which supervisors feel obligated to tell caregivers how to resolve a problem or how to teach better. Supervisors may feel guilty if they cannot do so and may tend to react too quickly to a supervisee's questions or doubts by continually talking and offering solutions. The youthfulness of early childhood supervisors and the turnover rate among them may increase pressure on supervisors to prove themselves. Providing all the answers is, after all, what an expert, a *super*-visor, is expected to do.

Learning to listen to a staff member and to ask questions takes practice. By thinking through problems and developing solutions with a supervisor instead of simply being told answers, supervisees can be encouraged to move toward greater independence. By relieving themselves of the burden of having quick remedies to complex problems at their fingertips, supervisors can relax and explore the subtle circumstances and details of an event.

Supervisors are human. They have strengths and limitations. Although they have control over some of the variables affecting their programs, they have little influence and control over others. Supervisors who can be honest and realistic about themselves can create a group spirit in a program without losing supervisory credibility.

Direct confrontation with staff is non-supportive.

Many supervisors, particularly those in the early childhood field, have great difficulty confronting employees about situations, behavior, and habits that may negatively affect a program. They are reluctant to "lay it on the

line" with a caregiver who, for example, is always late or who is creating
strife among staff members. A direct approach is deemed a non-supportive
one.

Avoiding explicit supervision, a supervisor may deal with a problem indirectly: by raising the issue in a delicate way during a conference, by hint-
ing at possible new behaviors, or by manipulating other variables to reduce
the tension a particular situation has created. These strategies make a supervisor feel better. After all, how can one be so petty as to confront a caregiver
who is earning so little money or who really needs the job? Leveling with
a supervisee seems so anti-humanistic, so uncaring. The direct approach has
not been given much credence in early childhood training.

Attempting to resolve a problem indirectly is often appropriate, but
sometimes supervisees do not "hear" the message or do hear the message but
choose to ignore it, so that problems continue to multiply. In situations such
as these, stating the problem openly in a factual and honest way enables the
issue to be acknowledged and dealt with.

Such a direct approach is exactly what some supervisees need. Although
a caregiver may have recognized a problem, he or she may not have adequate self-discipline to solve it or the courage to go to a supervisor or other
persons for help. On occasion, a teacher may not even be aware that he or
she is not performing appropriately. Getting the concern out in the open
can be revealing and cathartic, often laying the foundation for a trusting,
supportive relationship.

Caregivers appreciate honesty in supervisors; they don't like "beating
around the bush." They want to know what they are doing right and what
they are doing wrong. Airing concerns in a straightforward, fair, and sincere
manner prevents problems from deepening and feelings from intensifying.
It allows supervisor and supervisee to start fresh without resentments from
lingering unaddressed concerns. Evading issues will not improve relationships among people or increase program effectiveness. Problems create tension for supervisors, but confronting problems is part of the job and can actually relieve tension.

Skilled supervisors never engage in manipulation.

The notion of supervision as manipulation is a difficult one to discuss.
No doubt there are supervisors who unfairly control staff members to satisfy
their ego needs, to feel more powerful, or to serve their own purposes.
Manipulation, for example, can take the form of paternalism on the part
of supervisors who always know what's best for their supervisees and never
permit them to voice opinions, feelings, or ideas about an issue. Such supervisors simply make major decisions about the worklife of their teachers, "con-

vincing" the staff and themselves that a particular action is best for a supervisee, even though sometimes it may really be best only for the supervisor. Often, issues of class, status, politics, and culture underlie this type of manipulative behavior.

Supervision as skilled management through which caregivers improve performance and grow professionally is distinct from that which is self-serving and paternalistic. Some supervisors fear that if they make use of skills that enable them to influence a supervisee's behavior, they are being manipulative. Concerned about disrespecting and controlling others, they question the ethics of using these techniques. Supervisory behaviors like praise might be considered manipulative in some situations, but such techniques that shape the behavior of staff members are often appropriate means for building self-confidence.

An example might be a beginning teacher who presents a lesson for the first time. The lesson has many flaws in it, but the teacher is fragile and insecure. In the follow-up conference, the supervisor's feedback may be positive, despite the many problems with the lesson, because the supervisor decides that the emotional state of the teacher requires positive feedback at this time so that he or she can gain confidence and continue to grow and develop professionally. In a sense, this is manipulation on the supervisor's part; yet the truth would have been damaging. In this case, the teacher was inexperienced and still in the process of developing teaching competencies. The supervisor's conscious means of guiding the teacher did not have a selfish motive, nor did it abuse supervisory power. If this had been an experienced teacher, the supervisor's strategy would have been straightforward. In critiquing the lesson with the teacher, most likely all of its flaws would have been openly discussed.

Let us acknowledge, then, that some supervisory situations can be interpreted to have manipulative overtones; however, assumptions that suggest that staff should not be trusted, that they must be constantly watched and controlled, need to have decisions made for them, or should be "used" to the advantage of the supervisor do not have validity as a basis for supervision.

Good teachers do not need supervision.

Supervisors sometimes assume that those staff members who perform their duties in an excellent fashion or who are very experienced in their roles require little or no supervision. This myth may allow problems to go unresolved, may diminish team spirit among staff members, and may cause excellent staff to feel neglected, undervalued, or excluded from the group.

Effective teachers, however experienced, require supervision. Like all staff members, they appreciate attention. They like to be recognized and to receive positive reinforcement. They want to know that supervisors are interested in their work and are knowledgeable about the scope of outstanding work. To do an excellent job without your supervisor being aware of it can be discouraging and can create anxiety and stress.

Good teachers sometimes have work-related problems with other staff or with particular children. Their competence as teachers does not mean they always have the right answer or the skills to resolve every problem. Often, they need someone else to validate their instincts about how to resolve a problem.

Some good teachers "burnout" over time and become bored with their work and eventually uninterested. They may be stimulated by a supervisor who can give them new ideas, allow them to take a new role within a program if there is one available, or encourage them to take leadership roles in the field outside the program.

Effective teachers also value criticism. They want constructive feedback. One reason for their excellence may be their ability to analyze their performance and to accept input about their work so that it constantly improves.

Good teachers have expertise that can be shared with a supervisor and others. A supervisor who neglects competent staff has lost a valuable resource. Excellent and motivated teachers can be a great help to supervisors by modeling behaviors for other staff, by teaching colleagues, and by providing ideas and suggestions to supervisors.

Directors who fail to supervise highly competent staff members risk losing the very people who provide strength to their programs.

Supervision is an objective process.

Supervising is a complex activity that cannot be totally objective. Supervisors come to the educational arena with "colored glasses." The ways in which they view their staff members are affected by their own childhood, their education, their life and work experience, and the philosophy and values they have developed. A supervisor's beliefs and values cannot easily be set aside as he or she works with staff members — nor should they be set aside. They should, however, be recognized.

If, for example, a teacher doesn't implement a lesson the way the supervisor would have, then the supervisor may question whether or not it was done correctly. But the lesson may have achieved its goals even though it did not reflect the supervisor's values. Supervisors are caught in a balancing act. They have their own goals, philosophy, and values, which they would like to see reflected in their programs; yet they wish to respect caregivers' values without being heavy-handed or forcing their personal styles or approaches on teachers.

It is perfectly legitimate for a supervisor to direct a program toward a particular philosophical orientation, but this does not mean that all staff members must think the way their supervisor thinks. It does suggest that supervisors who operate with a high level of consciousness about self can strive to be aware of the "tinted lenses" through which they view their programs and can recognize how their biases might affect the supervisory process.

The process of observing teachers is one that can become more objective through the use of various tools for gathering data. These instruments bring focus to an observation, generate information about teaching behavior, and raise questions of purpose and philosophy (see chapter 11). Evaluation, however, is judgmental and therefore inherently subjective. Supervisors are expected to judge the competency of teachers in their programs as fairly as possible. Because they have expertise and experience, supervisors are qualified to judge and should not feel guilty for doing so.

Supervisors are always calm.

In writing about myths that bind teachers, Herbert Greenberg has described the myths of calmness and moderation. These myths apply to supervisors as well. Supervisors are expected to be model educators. Despite the many pressures they face — frustrations due to working conditions and feelings of impatience with staff members, parents, or government officials — they are always expected to be cool, calm, and collected. They are supposed to be able to respond to pressure in a low-keyed, logical, and emotionless manner. Greenberg notes that this belief is based on the assumption that the "mentally healthy" person does not have problems that cannot be dealt with mildly and does not experience strong feelings.[1]

This myth can create a sense of fear and guilt in supervisors: fear that if they are caught off-guard and show emotion they will lose power and status and their supervisees will think less of them; guilt because they have demonstrated imperfection by losing control for a moment and revealed human weakness.

Supervisors who believe they must be "super" at all times carry a burden that rejects reality and denies their humanness. Teachers who see human qualities in their supervisors often gain greater respect for them. Supervisees respond to, empathize with, and demonstrate greater willingness and enthusiasm for following a leader when they realize that they share certain qualities with that leader.

EXERCISES

1. Discuss how one or more of these myths have affected your own view of supervision and your work as a supervisor.
2. Discuss how these myths might affect a staff member's expectations of the supervisory relationship.
3. Describe other myths that can affect the supervisory role or supervisor-supervisee relationships.

2 Early Childhood Programs and Their Implications for Supervisors

The field called "early childhood education" is remarkably diverse. There are programs for infants as young as a few months and for school children as old as eight; settings designed for children who are present for a few hours a day, two or three days a week, and ones that serve those who come for many hours every day. Goals for early childhood programs may be limited to making social experiences available to children who have many advantages already, or may encompass a rich educational program together with health and social services for those who have very few advantages.

Staff needs are similar in most programs, but staff supervision is affected by such factors as size, hours, staffing patterns, source of funds, children and families served, and educational goals. The differences between an infant/toddler center and a half-day nursery school, or between a Head Start program and a family day care system can have a considerable effect on the way supervisors function, on the kinds of problems they encounter, and on the expectations they have for staff members. The descriptions of early childhood programs offered here, therefore, are intended to highlight the program characteristics that affect supervisory practices, responsibilities, and relationships.

DAY CARE PROGRAMS

The place of day care as a substitute for and supplement to parental home care for a large segment of the day has many implications for children, parents, and staff. The long hours in particular affect both program planning and the social-emotional needs of children and staff. Family day care homes and center-based day care, whether for infants, toddlers, preschool,

11

or older children, have some characteristics in common. Each type of care, however, does have unique features that affect the supervision of staff.

Center-Based Day Care

Center-based programs are usually licensed to provide full-day care (more than thirty hours per week) for six to eight or more children. Although both the program goals and client population of day care have changed a good deal in recent years, there continues to be a public image of such programs as providing only custodial care for low-income children. In reality, there are now many center-based programs that serve middle- or upper-middle-income families, and the number is rapidly increasing. Most now include educational programs for children, and many emphasize developmental goals.

Even with these changes, the majority of those who make use of day care are low-income families.[1] The centers that serve these families are for the most part nonprofit, receiving federal funds administered through state social service departments in the form of direct grants or through vouchers for individual children. This funding supports children of families receiving Aid to Families with Dependent Children (AFDC) who are in work incentive or training programs. Children are also placed in centers for special services, as in cases of abuse or neglect. Financial support for nonprofit centers may also be available from cities and states, churches, social service agencies, and the United Way.

"Profit-making" centers are of two major types: relatively small, individually owned programs, sometimes with several sites, and corporate-owned chains. The individually owned programs are similar to private nursery schools, the main difference being the hours of operation. The "profit" in such centers is principally in the form of salary for the owner-director. The goals and policies of these programs depend almost entirely on the views of the individual owner.

Chains of child care centers are set up by corporations as money-making enterprises. Like privately owned centers, they are usually located in suburban areas and have middle- to upper-middle-class clientele. Kinder-Care, which in 1983 had nearly 800 centers in forty states, serving 62,000 children, reports that their clientele is "typically college-educated couples whose combined salaries total $28,000 a year."[2] In most chains the corporation owns all the centers, although a few sell franchises to individuals who own and operate them within company guidelines. The systems usually have standardized buildings, equipment, and materials. The goals, policies, and curriculum for each center are predetermined by the corporation, often specified in great detail.

Centers sponsored by industries, hospitals, or universities fall into a somewhat different category — not profit-making but also not fitting the definition of nonprofit. They are designed specifically to serve the needs of the people working or studying at these institutions. Companies usually consider them an employee benefit, although fees are commonly charged.

Infants and Toddlers.   Center-based infant and toddler care is not yet widespread in the United States. It is still somewhat controversial because of concern for the possible adverse effects of caring for babies in a group setting. Nevertheless, both the need for such care and the number of centers providing it have grown rapidly in the last decade, and the trend will undoubtedly continue.

Administratively, centers for very young children are similar to other day care programs. Some limit themselves to infants and/or toddlers, while others are part of larger programs for older children. Children may be as young as six weeks, although some programs do not take them below five or six months. The upper limit is two or three years, the age often influenced by licensing standards. Because the children are so young, group sizes tend to be smaller. Larger numbers of staff are needed to maintain desirable adult-to-child ratios.[3] More staff in infant/toddler centers may be paraprofessionals than in programs for older children.

School-Age Children.   School-age child care is often part of a day care program, and some of the issues are similar. Such programs provide a place before and/or after the school day for children of working parents to take part in a varied program on a five-day-a-week basis for as few as two hours or as many as eight hours per day.

Some after-school care takes place in family day care homes, but more and more it is being organized by, or at least housed in, Y's and public and parochial schools, or is an extension of a preschool day care program. Funding comes from a variety of private and public sources, often with a mix within one program.

The age-range of children in extended day programs is from five to about fourteen, although many programs have a younger cut-off point. With such an age span, it is not unusual to have several children from the same family or children who attend the same center year after year.

IMPLICATIONS FOR SUPERVISORS

Of all the types of early childhood programs, day care probably presents the greatest challenge for supervisors. Within the long day and year-round program, routines such as eating, tooth-brushing, napping, and toileting take a prominent place. Individual and family-like activities for children are desirable, as is private time for both staff and children. Privacy and individual attention require flexibility, but there is not always enough staff available to achieve these goals. Communication with parents is of great importance in day care, but this too is sometimes hard to establish, since most parents are at work during the time their children are at the center.

Because centers must be staffed year-round for ten, twelve, or more hours a day, staff members usually work on staggered shifts. This makes it difficult for supervisors to find time to meet with staff. Meetings often take place during nap-time, thus excluding some people, or in the evening, creating extra burdens on caregivers. A feeling of continuity and cohesiveness among staff members is not easily reached when they are not able to meet together to work on common goals.

When a day care center is part of a larger system, such as a social agency, an industrial firm, or a day care corporation, decisions may be made at a central office and may reflect a different order of priorities than those of the local center. Administrators or boards of family service agencies or community action programs, for example, may not understand the educational goals and equipment needs of day care. Or the goal that a chain maintain a uniform curriculum may stand in the way of the flexibility needed to best serve a particular group of children. On the other hand, central administrators can be sources of support and back-up because of the resources at their disposal.

Nonprofit centers have available to them supplemental employees from a number of government-funded sources, such as job training programs, Youth Corps, and the Foster Grandparents Program. Supervisors will have to integrate these additional staff into classroom teams and to offer training and support directed toward the special needs of each group. In large day care programs, supervisors in administrative positions are also likely to have supervisory responsibility for support staff including cooks, custodians, and health and social service personnel. Supervision of staff with such varied duties calls for greater diversity of skills on the part of such administrators.

In infant and toddler centers, the issues confronting supervisors and staff are directly related to the developmental needs of very young children. As William Fowler put it:

> During the first year, infants are so immobile and dependent on adults that the repeated cycle of eating, movement, sleep, elimination, and clothes changing, and the problems of providing access to toys and other forms of stimulation make infant care especially demanding.[4]

Caregivers thus may not easily see that their role has dimensions beyond that of responding to babies' physical needs. Toddlers, on the other hand, are extremely active. They need both freedom to explore and limits, along with help in negotiating social exchanges with their peers.

The group situation can obscure a young child's individuality. It makes it difficult to provide the stimulation that is so important for babies and to allow for the active exploration that a toddler requires. Training in infant and toddler development and in observation and recording skills equips care-givers to see and appreciate the differences in children and the ways they change from day to day.

Research indicates that a familiar caregiver is a significant factor in facilitating an infant's daily separation from home to center and in a child's ability to cope with fearful situations.[5] Thus finding ways to assign care-givers to children in order to maintain continuity of care is a major issue for supervisors. At the same time, however, the possible over-attachment of caregivers to babies or babies to caregivers can also become a matter of concern.

Relationships between caregivers and parents is an issue that is impor-tant at any age, but may require even more nurturing by supervisors of in-fant/toddler center staff. Caregivers are not immune from the feeling that parents should not place very young children in day care, especially if they believe the mother can afford to stay home with her child, and the caregiver may play upon the guilt often felt by parents. Supervisors may have to spend both individual and group staff development time helping caregivers to deal with their feelings and to find ways to develop a partnership, rather than a rivalry, with parents.[6]

The caregiver-parent relationship becomes particularly important as a child grows toward toddlerhood and acquires greater self-control. Parents will have strong feelings about feeding, toilet-training, and discipline, which become more important at this time. Staff members who have developed skill in communicating with parents will be able to discuss such matters in an atmosphere of mutual respect, which encourages an exchange of ideas, feelings, and expertise about what the child is doing.

With school-age children, the important issues are the age range of the children served and the fact that the children have been (or will be) in school for a good part of the day. Accommodating the different social, emotional, and intellectual needs of five-, ten-, and fourteen-year-olds is a major goal of staff. As children move up through the elementary years toward adoles-cence, they become more autonomous and independent and their peer-relationship needs and skills increase. Although children's needs differ with age, school-age day care may be one of the few planned situations in today's world in which children can interact with others of different ages. Planning both same-age and multi-age activities therefore can be appropriate.[7]

Helping staff organize for and feel comfortable with a program that is flexible enough to provide contrast to a sometimes highly structured school day is another issue for supervisors. A staff with many abilities is required for a program that includes recreational activities such as formal and informal sports and games, music, crafts, field trips, and neighborhood excursions, along with homework assistance, tutoring, and language help for bilingual children. Staff training in these skills and in the developmental needs of school-age children may be necessary. Staff need time to meet to discuss the special needs of children who are away from home for long periods of time. These meetings can enable staff to arrive at creative solutions; for example, a program arranging times for "adult conversations" especially for junior high school children.[8]

School-age care is a new field with little training, academic or otherwise, available for staff. Teachers and directors are likely to be young, to come from a variety of backgrounds, and to have little experience in the field. Since many programs are small, directors may also serve as teachers and work as colleagues alongside the staff for whom they are responsible. These factors may lead to uncertainty and lack of direction on the part of supervisors and their staff. On the other hand, they can contribute to an atmosphere where creative programming flourishes, especially if a supervisor builds a team approach among staff and searches out colleagues in nearby communities as a support system.

Family Day Care

Family or home day care is care for children in the home of a non-relative for up to twelve hours a day, five or more days a week. In most states where such care is licensed, the number of children in one home is limited to about six. By far the greatest percentage of the care of children outside the home takes place in family day care settings, much of it through private arrangements between parents and caregivers in the immediate neighborhood of the home.

Day care homes are even more likely to serve low-income families than other day care programs. Subsidies are available to providers who take care of children of low-income parents who work or go to school, and abused or neglected children.

Although most states now license day care homes or have a voluntary registration process, many homes are not licensed. Providers are often reluctant to go through the process of becoming licensed because of the limits imposed by the regulations, many of which seem irrelevant or overly stringent. In many states licensing is required before providers can advertise or take subsidized children.

The ages of children cared for in such settings range from infants to elementary school children, although most are of preschool age. Infants and toddlers are more likely to be cared for in day care homes, in part because infant and toddler centers are not yet widespread, but also because parents value a home-like atmosphere.

Family day care providers have many different backgrounds, income levels, and reasons for involvement. They include mothers and fathers with young children of their own or whose children are all in school, and grandparents whose own children are no longer at home. Mary Keyserling found that in contrast to early childhood staff in general, home care providers had "considerably less education, on the whole, than the average American woman." Only 25 percent said they had four years of high school, and only 1 percent were college graduates. Very few had early childhood or teacher training, although most voiced eagerness for training.[9]

Financially, most providers care for children mainly to supplement their incomes, since it is difficult to earn a living this way without taking in more children than the law allows.[10] Programs to help AFDC recipients become day care providers have been developed in some communities. Some of these have been quite successful, but incentives to continue are considerably lessened because of limits on the amount of outside income caregivers may retain without reductions in their grants.[11]

IMPLICATIONS FOR SUPERVISORS

At the present time, supervision and training reach only a small percentage of home day care providers. When training exists, it is usually provided by licensing agencies or colleges or other organizations that have received federal or state grants. Formal and informal associations are becoming more common as vehicles for providing caregivers with support and self-help, as well as assistance and training from professionals. The Day Care Neighbor Service developed in Oregon is an example.[12]

All caregivers need to know how to provide developmentally appropriate programs for children, but family day care providers have some unique needs. They are probably the most susceptible of early childhood caregivers to society's view that child care is "only babysitting." Thus a supervisor's first priority may be to improve the self-image of day care providers and help them see themselves as professionals who do indeed have, and can further develop, special skills for working with children and parents, and who are carrying out a socially valued job.

Other supervisory issues grow out of the fact that care is given in the provider's own home. The intimacy of the setting may affect parents' expectations about care. Misunderstandings can develop, especially where there are differences in standards and values, unless open communication systems have been developed. Relationships with the provider's spouse and own children, too, can be strained by the presence of day care children.

Family day care providers are especially vulnerable to feelings of isolation because they spend so much time at home. Group training sessions with other providers are often eagerly attended because they give caregivers the opportunity to get out of the house and to share personal and professional concerns. Other issues not encountered by center-based caregivers are home safety, meal planning, handling finances, and using community resources. Peer groups can provide help in these areas as well.

Because of the large number of day care homes and the difficulties involved in setting up monitoring systems, supervisors will find a great deal of variation in the quality of care. In spite of this, Keyserling found that "Most are warm, responsive women who love children and who want to serve mothers in need of day care."[13] Even when their level of education and training is not high, most providers are people who have great potential. Supervision and training designed for their specific needs can be extremely productive.

HEAD START

As of fiscal year 1984, there were 8,700 individual centers in 1,200 Head Start programs across the country, designed to provide comprehensive services to low-income preschool children and their families.[14]

Head Start programs are funded and administered by the federal Agency for Children and Youth (ACYF) of the Department of Health and Human Services (H&HS). Grants are awarded by H&HS regional offices and by the Indian and Migrant Program Division (IMPD) to public agencies, private nonprofit organizations such as Community Action Programs, and some school systems. These agencies in turn operate individual Head Start programs.

Most Head Start children take part in a center-based preschool program for three to five hours per day, four or five days per week. Today Head Starts usually include home-visitor programs (originally called Home Start) that provide health, social, and educational services to children in their own homes. Other options are bilingual-bicultural programs, in which curricula have been developed to provide instruction in two languages where there are significant numbers of Spanish-speaking children; Parent and Child Centers, which serve children from prenatal through three years of age and their families; and full day care. At least 10 percent of the enrollment in Head Start must be handicapped children. These children receive both regular Head Start services and individualized special services.

Although children's cognitive development has always been a major goal of Head Start, health, nutrition, social services, and parent involvement all receive equal emphasis in program goals and implementation.

One of the most important premises of Head Start is that parents, as the "responsible guardians . . . and prime educators of their children,"[15] must be included as paid workers or as volunteers in classrooms and must be assisted in designing parent education for themselves. They are also to be given opportunities to participate in program decisions through committees and the policy council, which is the governing board of each Head Start program.

Staff training is also a key element of Head Start. Individual training needs are to be assessed and in-service training and college-based course work made available. All staff are encouraged to develop competencies that enable them to move vertically (e.g., from aide to teacher) or horizontally (e.g., from social service to education) within the program.

Another distinctive feature of Head Start is its built-in system for ensuring that comprehensive early childhood services based on Head Start goals are actually being delivered by each local program, while allowing for flexibility at the local level. Two procedures assist this effort:

1. The Head Start Performance Standards, which clearly define minimum performance expectations for all Head Starts. The standards "were very carefully drawn to mandate program quality without being prescriptive in terms of program design."[16]
2. A mandated self-assessment system through which grantees are required to "systematically reexamine their program design in relation to documented community needs and priorities, and their performance in relation to the program standards."[17] This yearly self-assessment is supplemented by a procedure known as the In Depth Validation (IDV), which takes place approximately every three years and includes an on-site visit from an outside team. The local program's own self-assessment is "validated," and where it is found to be out of compliance with the Performance Standards, it is given from three months to a year to correct the deficiencies.

IMPLICATIONS FOR SUPERVISORS

Each of the elements discussed above has an impact on the supervisory process, both for program directors and for educational coordinators. First, administrators will find that program goals that are mandated and closely monitored by the funding source (in this case, the federal government) can have both advantages and disadvantages. Accountability through various levels of bureaucracy can be confusing and frustrating. Newcomers to Head Start are confronted with a dizzying array of terminology and acronyms. Paperwork can seem endless. Policies or their interpretation may change with little time for staff preparation, and questions about whether the local program is in compliance with the Performance Standards are not always easily answered. These concerns can be especially unnerving when it comes time for the In Depth Validation.

On the other hand, the structures Head Start has created provide supports within the system that can be very helpful to supervisors. The Performance Standards, which serve as the basis for all program decisions, provide clear goals within a developmental early childhood perspective. They serve as common reference points for all staff, from aides and volunteers through the director. Supervision, training, and curriculum development all start from this point, but enough flexibility is allowed so that staff and parent input can make a difference. In addition, the In Depth Validation, in spite of the tremendous amount of work it requires, furnishes valuable information on strengths and weaknesses on which to build for the future.

Other supports built into the Head Start system are funds for training and technical assistance and for college courses and Child Development Associate (CDA)[18] training; state and regional organizations of Head Start directors and supervisors; and regional office personnel.

The emphasis on the involvement of parents has a number of implications for supervision and training. Staff members — and supervisors themselves — may find it difficult to adjust to untrained parents as decision makers or to find ways to work through differences of opinion on important issues. Staff development that emphasizes communications skills and an understanding of the concerns of low-income parents can help teachers to work sensitively with parents in the classroom, in conferences, and in home visits. Effective orientation and training programs for parent aides and volunteers also contribute to staff-parent understanding.

Finally, in any program with a predominantly low-income clientele, some staff members may find it difficult to deal with the very real problems facing some of the children, parents, and even other staff. Racial, class, and cultural differences can also sometimes create barriers to communication and understanding (see chapter 13). Young, middle-class teachers with little or no experience with low-income children are especially vulnerable, though this is by no means universal.

NURSERY SCHOOLS AND RELATED PROGRAMS

Nursery schools have been, except for kindergartens, the most widespread type of early childhood programs. Small size, part-day programs for three- and four-year-olds with different children and teachers in mornings and afternoons, and alternate-day-attendance options are characteristic of most such programs. A number also include kindergartens. Full-day options for children of working parents are becoming more common.

Nursery schools are almost always either privately owned or sponsored by a church, synagogue, YM or YWCA, or similar organizations, rather than being publicly funded. An individual school may be an independent enterprise for an owner-director, or it may be parent sponsored and managed.

In formally organized parent cooperatives, there is a paid director, who most likely teaches, and sometimes one or more paid teachers. But a large part of the responsibility for the teaching and care of the children is carried out by the parents. Mothers and fathers may also contribute their required hours of service per week through secretarial, maintenance, or other needed work around the school.

A laboratory school that is associated with a high school, vocational school, college, or university is established primarily as a place for students to observe and practice working with children as part of early childhood training. Laboratory schools usually have a nursery school format. Day care programs, increasingly available in colleges to provide care for children of faculty, staff, or students, may also be used as a laboratory setting, but usually training is a secondary, rather than a primary, objective of these programs. In both types of centers, major teaching responsibilities are borne by the students in training or by work-study students who serve as paid assistants.

IMPLICATIONS FOR SUPERVISORS

Although nursery schools have traditionally been thought of as places for children to develop social skills, today there is often at least an equal emphasis on providing an educational program. Pressure from parents to train children in academic skills sometimes makes it difficult to resist including activities that may be inappropriate for preschool children.

The small size of most nursery schools makes supervision an informal process. Directors may find it difficult to even think about "supervising" an assistant or a teacher whom they think of as a colleague or friend. In this intimate atmosphere problems can be hard to deal with. It is also difficult for teacher-directors who have responsibility for a group of children to find ways to observe teachers who work in adjacent rooms. Even in small programs, however, staff members can benefit from opportunities for peer evaluation and from assistance in improving their teaching.

Staff in nursery schools often have difficulty finding time when all can meet together, particularly when different teachers work in the morning and in the afternoon. Teachers and directors are frequently not paid for nonteaching time. Convincing boards of directors to pay teachers to attend staff and parent meetings, for time to set up classrooms before the school year officially begins, and for in-service training time during the year can be frustrating for supervisors. When funds must come out of an owner-director's own pocket, obtaining money for such "extra" time may be even more challenging.

In parent coops, training and coordination are major issues for supervisors. Not only are there likely to be many different individuals working with the children over the course of each week, even in a small school, but there also may be an almost entirely new group of parent-staff members each year. Most of the classroom staff, therefore, will have little or no training in early childhood education. A clear understanding that staff development sessions are part of the parents' responsibilities helps to set a positive climate for such training.

Differences in philosophy about discipline and about curriculum and methods are bound to arise from time to time between parents and staff. As in Head Start programs, one of the supervisor's tasks is to work out processes for resolving such differences, so that parents are really involved in decisions while the professional knowledge of the staff is still respected.

Other issues that frequently surface in coops are fairness in balancing one person's time commitment versus another's, especially where there are variations in tuition depending on the hours worked, and questions about whether parents should work in the groups to which their children are assigned. Supervisors may find that many of these concerns are more easily resolved in a coop that is newly formed than in one that has existed for several years. The enthusiasm and sense of purpose of the founding group of parents may not carry over to subsequent groups.

In a lab school setting, one of the most important supervisory issues is balancing the need to create real learning situations and support for education students while at the same time ensuring that the children receive skilled care and teaching. A supervisor's attention — and loyalties — are perhaps more divided between the needs of children and of caregivers (including paid staff) in a lab school than in any other early childhood setting.

Maintaining good communication and coordination with all those who teach and supervise students is more complicated when course instruction is the responsibility of a separate faculty, when a supervising teacher is not directly involved with the children, or when lab school staff do not have faculty status. In schools associated with private colleges, the director may have to devote time to justifying the school's budget or very existence.

Ensuring adequate staff coverage can be another problem for supervisors. Sometimes children may be overwhelmed by too many caregivers. At other times, class schedules of education students may conflict with periods when staff are needed the most, or students may want time off during exam weeks, even though student and faculty parents still need care for their children. Helping education students understand the importance of their presence to children's well-being, therefore, becomes a key task for the supervisor.

KINDERGARTENS AND PRIMARY
GRADES

Kindergartens may be part of a nursery school or day care program, or they may be based in public, private, or parochial schools. The majority at this time are half-day, five-day-a-week programs. In contrast to many nursery schools, the same teacher usually teaches both morning and afternoon sessions.[19] Full-day programs comparable to an elementary school day are in effect or being considered in many public school systems and are not uncommon in private schools. Other organizational patterns, such as a full day on alternate days, are also being tried. Some kindergartens have extended-day programs for children of working parents, with the second half of the day having a nonacademic focus.

Although the educational preparation of preschool teachers varies, teachers in kindergartens approved by state departments of education must be certified with bachelor's degrees and specific teacher training experiences. This training may or may not be at the early childhood level.

Kindergartens in many communities have considerably more children per class than do preschools, often with as many as 25 to 30 students or more. In some states an aide is required if there are more than a certain number of children. These large numbers mean that a teacher may be responsible for as many as 60 or more children per day.

There is a great deal of variation in kindergarten goals and curriculum, even in public school systems. Some kindergartens are an extension of a preschool developmental model in which play is considered a major means of learning for the child. Others focus on having each child accomplish specific skills before he or she may move on to the first grade at the end of the year. In these programs, readiness activities, especially for reading, begin early in the year and may include using workbooks as a daily routine. Goals may be group-oriented or individualized, based on detailed behavioral objectives, but play is usually not seen as a major vehicle for learning.

Most kindergartens probably combine elements of both of these models. In public schools, the curriculum and sometimes the methodology are prescribed, or at least recommended, with some systems allowing greater flexibility than others. Curriculum issues, especially centering on the early teaching of reading and math, are becoming more important as an increasing number of children enter kindergarten with one, two, or even more years of preschool experience.

Primary grades—that is, grades one, two, and three—are sometimes classified at the early childhood level at teacher preparation institutions and by states establishing certification requirements. Teaching usually becomes more formal in these grades, and academic concerns predominate.

IMPLICATIONS FOR SUPERVISORS

Supervisors of kindergarten personnel in public schools are likely to have different roles than supervisors of preschool teachers. As school principals or system-wide supervisors, they usually have responsibility for teachers at several grade levels. Because elementary school principals rarely have training in early childhood education or have experience teaching kindergarten, they may be reluctant and uncomfortable about supervising kindergarten teachers, or they may create unrealistic scheduling or curricular requirements for teachers. This last problem may become more pronounced in the years ahead as state legislatures mandate public preschool programs. Administrative duties or absence of a policy encouraging or requiring support and supervision of staff may also make it difficult for principals to spend much time in this role.

In primary grades, the supervisory roles and concerns are similar to those for kindergarten. Supervisors who understand the developmental needs of children at these ages can support teachers' efforts to respond to them, to lay conceptual foundations before moving on to specific skills, and to focus on children as individuals. Supervisors can encourage staff to communicate with other teachers at their own and different levels, which helps teachers integrate learning from one grade to another. Supervisors are also in a position to recognize and support the continuation of the strong parent-teacher relationship that has often been established at the preschool and kindergarten level.

For directors and principals of preschools, kindergartens, and primary grades who do not have a background in early childhood education and cannot take courses right away, the following books are recommended. They introduce basic early childhood principles from several perspectives.

> Dorothy H. Cohen. *The Learning Child*. New York: Pantheon Books, 1972.
>
> David E. Day. *Early Childhood Education: A Human Ecological Approach*. Glenview, IL: Scott, Foresman, 1983.
>
> Mary Hohmann, Bernard Banet, and David Weikart. *Young Children in Action: A Manual for Preschool Educators*. Ypsilanti, MI: High/Scope Press, 1979.
>
> Katherine H. Read and June Patterson. *The Nursery School and Kindergarten: Human Relationships and Learning*, 7th Edition. New York: Holt, Rinehart and Winston, 1980.

CONCLUSION

The programs we have described in this chapter are the traditional ones in which supervisors and early childhood teachers work. There are other group programs for young children not discussed here, which raise special issues for supervisors and staff: bilingual/bicultural programs, special needs settings, and specialized curricula for Montessori or religion-affiliated schools.

The program differences we have described affect the way supervisors function because they form the context within which supervision takes place. Nevertheless, when it comes to the needs of children and staff members, the similarities are greater than the differences, for it is individuals who are being supervised.

EXERCISES

1. For the program in which you work, describe the characteristics that affect supervision of the staff. Include all the factors that (a) give clues to the kinds of areas where staff are most likely to need help, (b) might have a positive effect on your ability to carry out effective supervision and staff development, and (c) might interfere with or make supervision and staff development more difficult. If you cannot do this based on your own experience, interview the director of a local program.
2. Share this information with people who work in similar programs and with those who work in different programs. Compare and contrast your perceptions and discuss ways that problem areas might be alleviated.

3 Supervisors and Staff: Roles and Responsibilities

The roles and duties of persons in supervisory positions and of those whom they supervise are as varied as the early childhood programs described in the previous chapter. There is at present little uniformity in the titles used for these positions, but as the field moves from semi-professional to professional status, we are beginning to clarify for ourselves what these positions should be called and the qualifications necessary to fill them.[1] Our purpose in this chapter is to describe the most common positions supervisors occupy at the present time, the responsibilities associated with these positions, and the roles and duties of the people whom they supervise.

SUPERVISORS

Practitioners with supervisory responsibilities range from executive directors in central administrative offices of large agencies to those whose main responsibility is to teach children but who also supervise other teachers, aides, and volunteers. Some of the most common positions involving supervision are executive director, program director, educational coordinator, head teacher, teacher, college supervisor, and consultant. However, these jobs have many titles. Individuals in them often have more than one major role to perform. Rarely is supervision the sole component of their work. Positions that carry multiple roles and responsibilities, such as owner-manager, head teacher, or supervisor-bookkeeper, create consequences not always foreseen. Supervisors may experience role ambiguity, conflicting expectations from their supervisees, and overload, stress, and disenchantment with their jobs as they discover that they do not have the time or resources for all their roles.

These circumstances raise a number of questions. How well do supervisors understand each of their official roles? Can they execute each role at a quali-

26

ty level, or do they carry out some superficially? Can individuals move effectively from one role to another and still maintain sufficient clarity about what they are doing and who they are? Are they adequately trained for carrying out the responsibilities that each role requires?

Training and Experience

Many supervisors come into their roles directly from the classroom ranks. Persons in supervisory positions, particularly those in Head Start or other community-based programs, often begin work as aides. After receiving on-the-job training, a high school equivalency degree, a Child Development Associate Credential, or even an associate's or bachelor's degree while working in a program, they are good candidates for supervisory positions because of their understanding of the needs of children and families.

Others, initially hired as teachers or even aides, move into coordinator's or director's roles because of their exceptional skills in working with children or sometimes because they are the only staff with a degree in early childhood education or specific training in supervision. There are also early childhood supervisors with backgrounds in elementary or special education, or such related fields as counseling, nursing, social services, and recreation. Still others have job experience in completely unrelated occupations including advertiser, photographer, mill worker, and tavern worker.[2]

Some early childhood supervisors hold only high school diplomas. Others have earned college degrees, ranging from associate and bachelor's degrees to master's and even doctorates. Supervisors holding associate's degrees tend to have majored in early childhood education, child development, or child care,[3] but many other supervisors have educational backgrounds in vocational, religious, special, art, music, and physical education, the liberal arts, or human services.

Some supervisors have had no formal preparation in supervision; others have had minimal amounts in the form of workshops and college-level course work. For many supervisors, their work with children and the model provided them by their own supervisors were the most helpful experiences in preparing them for their roles.

The multiplicity of supervisory roles; the variability of background, experience, education, and training among supervisors; and the necessity of fulfilling duties outside of supervision are in a very real sense indicators of the evolving nature of early childhood education. As early childhood professionals upgrade their skills and strive to make the field more professional, job qualifications, titles, and responsibilities are likely to become more uniform. With less ambiguity, some of the sources of stress may be removed, enabling supervisors to attain greater satisfaction from the rewards of the job.

Representative Job Titles and Descriptions

EXECUTIVE DIRECTOR

The executive director is usually the chief administrator of a large child care agency and reports directly to a board of directors. Although the organizational charts of such agencies vary, the executive director may supervise an assistant, the coordinators of several social service programs within the agency, program directors at various sites, and all other employees through a central chain of command. Supervision is usually one aspect of an executive director's responsibilities, along with administrative and fiscal duties. The executive director is likely to supervise upper level staff directly but may have little personal contact with the staff who are responsible for children in the agency's various centers.

PROGRAM DIRECTOR

Program directors are administrators who are responsible for running a program. In large day care agencies, they work within the larger organization but do not administer the organization as a whole. Most Head Start directors and public school principals are in this category since their programs or schools are one of several in the organization.[4] In small, private, or nonprofit independent child care centers or nursery schools, directors manage programs that are somewhat more autonomous. Some program directors administer more than one center.

The responsibilities of program directors usually include administration, supervision, board relationships, and community relationships, and, for many, teaching as well. Among their duties are maintaining compliance with applicable laws, recruiting staff and children, budgeting and fund raising, supervising and evaluating staff, conducting annual program evaluations, working with parents and outside agencies and institutions, planning curriculum, reporting to and working with a board, overseeing the maintenance of the facility and of equipment, and planning meals with the cook.

Because program directors are on site and work directly with classroom and non-classroom staff, supervision is a larger part of the job than it is for executive directors. Program administration or teaching can take up much of their time, however, and can overshadow supervisory duties.

Directors come in regular contact with a host of people, each of whom has a set of expectations about what the director should do and how he or she should do it. These include the director's supervisor, employees, and others with whom the director works closely. Together these people make up what sociologists call a *role set* (see Figure 3.1).

Members of a role set communicate their expectations to the director, who responds in certain ways based on his or her understandings and perceptions of the messages received. For example, representatives of community ser-

FIGURE 3.1   *Role Set of a Program Director*

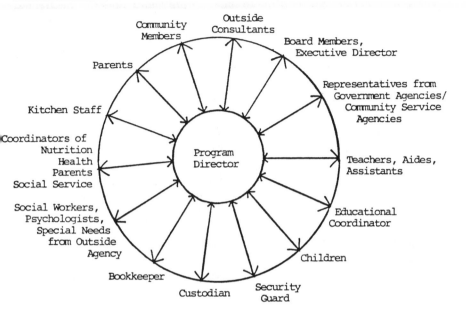

vice agencies may believe that the program director should be more active in dealing with families with serious problems. Or the executive director may think that the director should do a better job of linking with coordinators and other program directors, and in completing paper work on time. Teachers may feel that the director should give them more help in working with hard-to-manage children. And the cook may be unhappy because the director is too involved in weekly menu planning.

Thus, members of the director's role set "push" and "pull" the director, competing for time and attention and creating multiple demands. This pressure may be more intense when the administrator fills more than one official role, a common occurrence as we have already seen. Program directors with clear priorities, goals, and philosophy of education will be better able to formulate realistic expectations for the job and for supervision.

As Figure 3.1 indicates, the program director is also a member of the role set of teachers, children, kitchen staff, and others, and has a responsibility to them. In reality, however, teachers may relate more often and sometimes more immediately to social service or other staff than to the director.

EDUCATIONAL COORDINATOR

The educational coordinator's role is narrower and more focused than the program director's. The coordinator's responsibility is to oversee the educational component of an agency or program to ensure that classrooms and staff are functioning according to the program's guidelines for the greatest benefit to children. The educational coordinator works in the areas of staff development, training, and curriculum, with time alloted for these purposes.

Supervision forms a large part of educational coordinators' work. In smaller programs, educational coordinators supervise staff who work directly with children and are supervised by the program director. In large day care or Head Start agencies, educational coordinators provide emotional and technical support to program directors, as well as to classroom staff, often traveling to various program sites. The coordinators' duties may include observing teachers and children; planning and conducting staff training; conferring with staff; developing curriculum; serving as a liaison with health, nutrition, special needs, and social service coordinators; modeling good teaching behavior; ordering classroom supplies and equipment; working with psychologists; and providing directors with guidance and support.

Coordinators, too, have a role set (see Figure 3.2). Those working in multiple settings are particularly susceptible to situations involving interpersonal conflicts. With their time divided between central office and various sites, they may not have the opportunity to build relationships to the extent they would like or to engage with staff in the process of clarifying and defining each other's roles and responsibilities.

FIGURE 3.2   *Role Set of an Educational Coordinator*

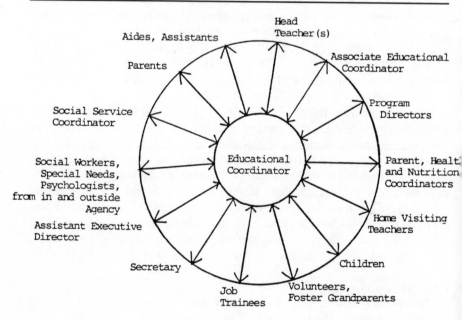

Educational coordinators are usually free from a daily routine and have some flexibility in organizing their day's work. The job of coordinator can be a lonely one, however, as there is usually no one else in the organization with the same role to share common problems and successes.

HEAD TEACHER

Unlike program directors and educational coordinators, who work mostly with adults, head teachers have a primary responsibility for working with children. Usually because of experience, education, training, and/or demonstrated expertise, classroom teachers become head or lead teachers. Head teachers usually oversee the functioning of one or more classrooms, supervise several other teachers, and are supervised by the educational coordinator or program director (see Figure 3.3). As head teachers attempt to meet the dual responsibilities of teaching and supervising, they are likely to experience a certain degree of role conflict.

Among the specific duties of a head teacher are arriving before class to prepare and arrange materials for the day's activities, keeping daily attendance and observation records of children, assisting in planning parent programs, attending evaluation meetings with social service agency representatives, arranging yearly conferences with each parent, making special

FIGURE 3.3   *Role Set of a Head Teacher*

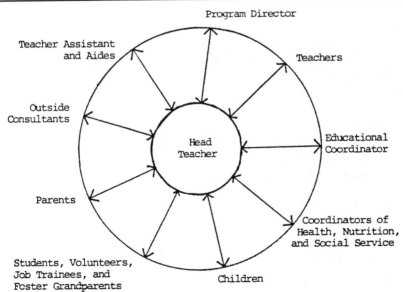

referrals, supervising other team members, teaching children, and planning and leading team meetings.

TEACHER

Unlike public school teachers who rarely supervise other adults in the classroom, preschool teachers often supervise an assistant, paid or volunteer, in addition to educating and caring for young children. Teachers are usually supervised by a head teacher, coordinator, and/or program director.

COLLEGE SUPERVISOR

The college supervisor is a faculty member of a college or university who is responsible for training and supervising those individuals aspiring to work in early childhood programs. Sometimes they supervise experienced caregivers who are working in a special program or for an advanced degree. They often supervise undergraduates who plan to work with young children.

CHILD DEVELOPMENT ASSOCIATE TRAINER

The CDA trainer may be part of a Child Development Associate Training Program or may work on a freelance basis with classroom staff preparing to be assessed for the CDA credential. A CDA trainer is often associated with a college, university, or teacher center but may be a staff member from another preschool or an independent consultant. (See chapter 14 for a description of CDA.)

CONSULTANT

Consultants from teachers' centers, resource centers, or coordinating agencies sometimes work on site with a program as a whole or with individual teachers. They may work with staff members through one-to-one or group supervision. This is a typical form of supervision for family day care providers.

These positions are the most common ones in the early childhood field with important supervisory responsibility. Although the titles we have used are most typical, there are many other job titles for both supervisors and staff in different programs (see Table 3.1).

STAFF

Early childhood supervisors work with staff employed in a variety of jobs. These include providers of direct care, education, or services to children in classrooms, as well as non-classroom staff who help the program run

TABLE 3.1 *Job Titles of Personnel in Center-Based Early Childhood Programs*

SUPERVISORS	CLASSROOM STAFF	NON-CLASSROOM STAFF

SUPERVISORS

Owner-Operator
Director
Owner-Administrator
Teacher-Administrator
Owner-Administrator-Teacher
Assistant Director of Education
Lead Teacher
Administrator
Administrator-Owner, Chair of the Board
Lecturer-Head Teacher
President
Executive Director
Education Coordinator
Teacher
Pastor-Director
Child Care Coordinator
Supervisor and Bookkeeper
Recreational Leader-Program Director-Supervisor-Head Teacher
Minister of Music and Church Growth
Director-Master Teacher
Owner-Manager
Supervisor of Infant/Toddlers
Teacher/Director of Pre-school
Teacher/Director
Education Specialist
Unit Director
Toddler Director
Pre-primary Director
Assistant Administrator
Business Manager

CLASSROOM STAFF

Teacher/Caregivers

Teacher
Lead Teacher
Day Care Worker
Special Ed Teacher
Group Teacher
Group Leader
Foreign Language Teacher
Infant Caregivers
Potty Training Caregiver
Co-teacher
Caregiver
Pre-school Teacher
Head Teacher

Administrators

Pre-primary Director
Toddler Director
Site Director
Unit Director
Supervisor of Infant/Toddlers
Manager
Teacher/Director
Program Coordinator
Teacher/Director of Pre-school
Assistant Director
Center Coordinator

Paraprofessionals

Feeding Aide
Foster Grandparent
Helping Teacher
Teen Assistant
Volunteer
Cook/Teacher Aide
Secretary/Aide
Floaters
Program Aide
Helper
Classroom Assistant
Classroom Aide
Paraprofessional
Teacher Aide
Assistant Instructor
Recreational Assistant
Assistant Teacher

Other

Assistant Professor
RN Caregiver
Nutritionist
Home Visitors
Nurse
Education Specialist
Graduate Assistant

NON-CLASSROOM STAFF

Provide Support to Staff, Family, Children

Family Worker
Parent Advisory Committee President
Coordinator of Handicapped
Health Coordinator
Family Counselor
Home-Based Visitor
Family Service Health Assistant
Parent Volunteer Coordinator
Outreach Specialist
Fieldtrip Director
Community Developer
Faculty Director
Faculty Advisor
Helpers
Volunteer
Social Worker
Speech Therapists
Psychologists

Security, Maintenance, Food, Transportation

Security Guard
Custodian
Cook
AM-PM Bus Monitor
Bus Driver
WEP Kitchen Aide
Food Service Manager
Maid
Housekeeper
Cleaner
Yard Supervision
Landscaper
Painter

Clerical/Administrative Services

Secretary
File Clerk
Office Manager
Bookkeeper
Personnel Dept. Worker
Office Assistant
Assistant Bookkeeper
Purchaser

Source: Joseph J. Caruso, "Characteristics of 184 Early Childhood Supervisors and Their Settings," paper presented at the Rhode Island Early Childhood Conference, Rhode Island College, Providence, RI, April 1982.

smoothly and/or support children by working with families or outside agencies. Program settings, the age levels of the children served, and the range of services provided influence the names we use to identify early childhood staff.

Historically, practitioners have made a distinction between teacher and caregiver and between those in professional and auxiliary roles. Nursery schools have been viewed as serving mainly an educational function, while day care has been seen as having a caregiving/nurturing function. Thus, practitioners in nursery schools have been thought of as teachers and those in day care centers as caregivers. Supervisors and teachers were considered to be professionals. Teacher aides, volunteers, and assistants have been viewed as auxiliaries.[5] Today, the distinction between teacher and caregiver is not quite so clear, nor is there any agreement as to whether those in "professional"roles actually have the status of professionals.[6]

As we can see from Table 3.1, the names we give to caregivers illustrate the variety of roles and responsibilities they have. Their titles range from assistant professor and head teacher to helper. Some of the titles remind us that classroom staff have part-time, non-classroom roles such as secretary or cook; that directors, coordinators, and assistant directors continue to work with children in classrooms despite their administrative functions; and that lead teachers and group leaders have some supervisory functions as part of their roles. Finally, there are those job titles that indicate very specific competencies or responsibilities, such as foreign language teacher, special education teacher, potty training caregiver, and feeding aide.

Training and Experience

Several researchers have examined the educational preparation of child care staff members. The results show variation due to differing sampling procedures, the size and types of programs surveyed, the expectations of child care staff from region to region, and state licensing requirements.

Keyserling[7] found the educational attainment of staff members in day care and Head Start to be variable. Those in proprietary centers were not highly trained, while staff members in nonprofit centers funded by public and philanthropic monies were more apt to have formal training. While 19 percent of staff members in Neugebauer's[8] study of 35 day care centers in New England had no formal course work in early childhood education, 20 percent of staff in small centers, 47 percent in medium sized centers, and 60 percent in large centers had ten or more courses. Gould[9] found that 45 percent of the teachers in her small New York sample had bachelor's degrees, and 64 percent of teacher aides had a high school diploma.

Seventeen percent of classroom staff in the Caruso study[10] of programs in ten states had less than a high school diploma, while 64 percent held bachelor's degrees. Fully 78 percent had received at least one year of training to work with children under five years of age, 25 percent held a CDA Credential, and 20 percent held an early childhood certificate.

In contrast to caregivers, 48 percent of non-classroom staff held only a high school diploma. Those with bachelor's and master's degrees were most likely in such professional roles as social worker or psychologist. Interestingly, about one-fourth of non-classroom staff had at least one year of early childhood related education/training specifically to work with children under five, and about 1 percent held a CDA credential or early childhood certificate.

The results of the National Day Care Study also showed variation in the educational preparation of caregivers as "31.4 percent of the head teachers and 29.3 percent of the teachers held bachelor's degrees . . . "; in contrast, "8.6 percent of the head teachers and 15.9 percent of the teachers held no degree at all including a high school diploma."[11]

This wide range of educational attainment is confirmed by the NAEYC's 1984 national survey of child care salaries and working conditions for aides, assistants, teachers, directors, owners, and others.[12] Its findings, however, point to a promising trend toward bachelor's and master's degrees in early childhood education.

Nonetheless, supervisors cannot be guaranteed that staff members will have a college degree or any specific education or training in early childhood education. Several studies, however, have indicated that college-educated caregivers do not necessarily provide better quality child care. In a review of the research related to day care, Greta Fein and Alison Clarke-Stewart found only two studies supporting the notion that a college degree is needed in order to be an effective preschool teacher. They found more research indicating that individuals without college degrees can be effective teachers or aides in early childhood settings, and that paraprofessionals trained to use specific curricula can be as effective as more highly trained teachers.[13]

College preparation in itself if unrelated to child care shows little relationship to higher quality care, but individuals specifically educated and trained to work with young children do raise the standard of care. The National Day Care Study is very clear on this point:

> Education/training in child-related fields such as developmental psychology, day care, early childhood education, or special education is associated with distinctive patterns of caregiver and child behavior and with higher gains in test scores for children.[14]

These conclusions do not support the widely held view among the general public and some professionals that a person who is a certified elementary teacher holds all of the qualifications necessary to be a preschool teacher.

This view is based on the assumption that the kinds of knowledge and skills one learns to teach older children can be applied directly to work with preschool children or that methods and activities teachers use with older children can be used with younger ones in an easier or simplified way.

There are, of course, common elements in teacher education programs that apply to children of all age levels. Yet neither certification programs for elementary school teachers nor experience at that level emphasize a number of factors essential for working with young children: the importance and meaning of play in learning; the developmental characteristics of children under six; and the understanding of and skills necessary for communicating with program staff members, families, and community representatives. Thus, although individuals prepared in elementary training programs can bring valuable competencies to preschool settings, they may require continued education and retraining.

Experience in group settings with children under six is also frequently considered a valid substitute for formal preparation in early childhood education, a notion reflected in state licensing standards and in program job descriptions. Research suggests, however, that supervisors should not expect teachers or aides with several years experience to have skills equivalent to those of staff with early childhood training. Many teachers can learn much through observation if a good role model is available and the observer knows what to look for.

We do not mean to suggest that experience with young children does not contribute to a caregiver's understanding of and ability to work with them. Supervisors in our interviews often stated that staff who are parents or who have had other experience with young children are better able to understand and apply the training they receive than those who do not.

Representative Job Titles and Descriptions

Classroom staff have a major responsibility for working with children and often have secondary obligations in other areas. Marcy Whitebook and her colleagues found that head teacher-directors, teachers, and aides all have the same range of duties, although head teacher-directors spent more time on parent communication and clerical and administrative work. All did curriculum planning and implementation, meal preparation, and maintenance.[15]

CLASSROOM TEACHERS

Responsibilities of teachers usually include planning and carrying out the program for children, arranging classroom areas for activities, observing and recording children's growth in various skill areas, preparing for snack and lunch, and supervising outdoor play. Caregivers working with infants and toddlers spend a large amount of their time feeding, changing, playing with, and observing children. Part of a caregiver's day also includes communicating with parents about the psychological well-being of their children, not only at the center but often in home visits. Sharing information and ideas with speech or physical therapists, nurses, social workers, and others is also a typical part of the regular routine.

Although teachers may be supervised by a head teacher, director, or coordinator as we noted earlier, they have supervisory responsibilities themselves. They usually have at least one aide or assistant, and many programs have parent and other volunteers, student teachers, foster grandparents, and job trainees. Classroom staff also informally supervise peers who are new to a program, providing emotional support and suggestions. Although the latter form of supervision often happens spontaneously, supervisors can support and train caregivers to work with other classroom staff who have little or no training.

CLASSROOM AIDES AND ASSISTANTS

The job of aide or assistant in a classroom is also important but can be misused. The terms *aide* and *assistant* usually describe the same job, though there are sometimes both positions in a program.

In general, the position of aide is an entry level one with few qualifications other than sensitivity to children and willingness to learn. In some programs, especially those for low-income families, aides may not be required to have a high school diploma, often beginning work as a volunteer and later advancing to paid positions. Nora Gould found that 36 percent of the teachers in her survey had "moved up the ranks" from such jobs.[16] Not surprisingly, she also noted that aides were less experienced, less educated, and less likely to stay on the job than teachers or directors.

Aides assist the classroom teacher in carrying out such duties as teaching, performing clerical or housekeeping chores, preparing for snack time, and ensuring that the environment is sanitary and healthful. They are usually expected to attend staff meetings, training sessions, meetings with other professionals, and meetings with parents. Aides also provide general supportive help in family day care homes, allowing caregivers time for other duties.

NON-CLASSROOM STAFF

Sometimes taken for granted, non-classroom staff are central to a program's efficiency and success. Non-classroom staff come into contact with children and support and serve them and the program in peripheral yet important ways, but their responsibilities do not encompass the direct and ongoing care and education of children.

Non-classroom staff can be grouped into several categories (refer to Table 3.1). Cleaners, painters, and landscapers perform maintenance functions. Secretaries, bookkeepers, file clerks, purchasers, and office assistants are primarily involved with paperwork and administrative tasks. Cooks, security guards, and bus drivers may have more opportunities to interface with children, while community developers and outreach workers may get to know families. Home-based visitors work with both children and families, though for the most part outside the center. Some individuals, such as a health coordinator, coordinator of the handicapped, and faculty advisor, have supervisory functions with adults. Professionals who work on behalf of children and families on a consultant basis, for example, social workers, speech therapists, and psychologists, might also be considered part of the non-classroom staff of a center. As with supervisors and classroom staff, non-classroom staff may be expected to carry out more than one role.

Non-classroom staff members can be indispensable to supervisors and caregivers. They may orient a new director or teacher to a program, "be there" for a director to lean on when there is no one else with whom to discuss pressing problems, or fill in during an emergency. Non-classroom staff should be considered integral members of the program "family."

CONCLUSION

Supervisors and administrators in early childhood programs often have more than one significant role associated with their jobs. Their preparation for supervision varies greatly as do the competency levels, ages, and stages of professional development of the staff members they supervise.

Because of the many demands for supervisor time, attention, and energy, and because of possible insecurity about supervising, sometimes supervision may not take place at all unless it becomes a conscious goal with time set aside to confer with and observe staff on a regular basis. This is a point we would like to underscore.

Individuals who prefer certainty, predictable routines, and clarity of expectations may find the fluidity and complexity of early childhood settings overwhelming. Persons who are more adaptable may be happier and more effective supervisors. Knowledge of early childhood development as well as an understanding of how adults grow and develop can make supervision more satisfying.

Lastly, those who can analyze themselves in relation to their settings and who are realistic about what can be accomplished are likely to be more successful as early childhood supervisors.

EXERCISES

1. Write a job description for your present supervisory position.
2. Given the nature of supervisory jobs in early childhood education, what qualities and competencies should early childhood supervisors possess?
3. Who are the members of your role set? What expectations do they have of you?
4. What are the procedures for hiring staff in your program? What qualities in staff are the most important for your program?
5. Develop job descriptions for classroom and non-classroom staff in your program. Include staff members in this process.
6. Review the qualifications of each of your staff members. As a result of this process, what implications are there for staff development and training? See chapters 14 and 15 for more information.
7. What can you do in your community or at state and national levels to improve working conditions for early childhood staff?

Part II

A DEVELOPMENTAL PERSPECTIVE

4 The Developmental Dynamic

Supervisor, supervisee, and the context in which they work are three components of a complex, dynamic process in which development occurs. Supervisor and supervisee grow and change in an environment that also changes. The interaction between these two individuals and the context in which this takes place can create energy, force, and power for their continued professional and personal growth.

A major assumption of developmental supervision is that there is no single best method of improving the performance and facilitating the professional growth of supervisees. By assessing the developmental characteristics of their staff members, supervisors can select and use an approach that best matches the supervisee and a specific problem or concern. This diagnosis takes into account the supervisees' cognitive abilities, their level of professional development, and their stage in life. The ability to "read" staff members and determine which strategies to use with them and to shift from one mode to another is basic to this notion of supervision.

Knowledge of self is also fundamental to developmental supervision. By understanding themselves and the impact of their own early life experiences, supervisors increase the control they have over their own behavior and can more easily modify and redirect it when necessary. The literature on developmental supervision thus far has focused primarily on teachers. Our intention is to show that the supervisor's perceptions of self, life situations, and levels of competence change too, and that these changes affect the supervision and teacher development that takes place.

Supervisor and caregiver interact within a context. They work with people; they confront problems; they feel pressures that affect the dynamics of the supervisory process. The situation and setting in which they work make up the third significant variable in the developmental dynamic. Figure 4.1 illustrates these three components, which will be discussed further in this chapter.

FIGURE 4.1 *Supervisor, Supervisee, and Context: Three Components of the Developmental Dynamic*

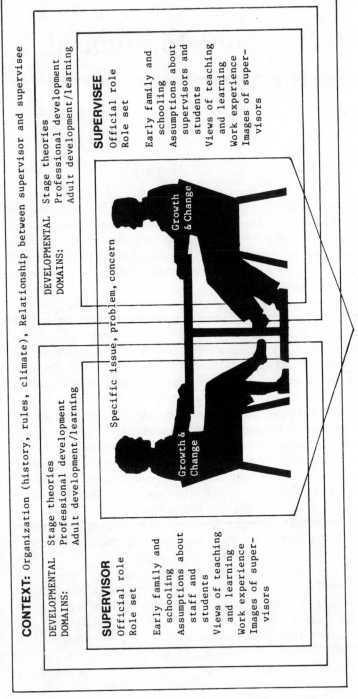

CONTEXT: Organization (history, rules, climate), Relationship between supervisor and supervisee

DEVELOPMENTAL
DOMAINS:
Stage theories
Professional development
Adult development/learning

DEVELOPMENTAL
DOMAINS:
Stage theories
Professional development
Adult development/learning

SUPERVISOR
Official role
Role set

Early family and
schooling
Assumptions about
staff and
students
Views of teaching
and learning
Work experience
Images of super-
visors

Specific issue, problem, concern

Growth &
Change

Growth
& Change

SUPERVISEE
Official role
Role set

Early family and
schooling
Assumptions about
supervisors and
students
Views of teaching
and learning
Work experience
Images of super-
visors

OUTCOMES

INFLUENCE OF BACKGROUND AND BELIEFS

As supervisor and teacher work together, each brings to the encounter an accumulated set of experiences, perceptions, beliefs, and values that make them who they are, shape their behavior, and influence supervisory outcomes. These include early childhood experiences, images of supervisors, assumptions about people, and views about how individuals learn.

Early Childhood Experiences

Supervisors and supervisees live with emotional remnants from their early experience with authority figures. Family training, education, and socialization experiences play a part in how they see themselves and how they express their own authority with others. Two supervisor/teachers illustrate this point in describing their backgrounds and their styles of supervision:

> I grew up in an ethnic community where hard work was deemed important, and I attended parochial schools. As a result of my cultural background and education, I have always had a strong orientation toward personal and group discipline. I have learned to expect little help from the outside and to use my internal resources.
>
> I have served as Executive Director of a day camp, a coordinator of student-teaching, and as a commissioned officer in an Army military police unit. I was also a counter guerilla unit leader.
>
> I perceive my supervisory style as that of a facilitator. Once I perceive what needs to be done, I work to insure that those I supervise are given the means with which to accomplish the task. Depending on the situation, I can remain aloof as an objective mediator or dig in with everyone else to solve a problem with perseverance and perspiration.

> My father expected immediate action following a command. My parents usually fought in front of us over authority issues. Teacher was boss and unfair at times, not listening to my reasons.
>
> As a teacher and supervisor, I try to right the wrongs which were done to me; however, I often fall back into the pattern of wanting things done immediately from kids and of being didactic to staff.

Philosophy of Learning

Assumptions about human nature also affect how supervisors and teachers work with children and adults. Supervisors who see staff members as basically good, honest, and trustworthy are likely to display behavior patterns that are quite different from those of supervisors who regard their supervisees with distrust and suspicion.

A supervisor's or teacher's point of view about learning is another significant factor in determining how they interact with others. Some individuals believe that behavior can be caused and shaped by outside forces. Supervisors and teachers with this orientation select goals and objectives for the learners, organize the material to be learned, and develop ways to reinforce the learners as they strive to attain the established goals. This direct mode of teaching can help the learner organize skills and knowledge essential to specific tasks, and it can shorten learning time since the learner does not have to go through the process of discovering new concepts. Direct teaching tends to work best with students who prefer dependent learning behaviors; but it can foster a cycle of dependency between instructor and student.[1]

Other individuals believe that learners need the freedom to explore and discover knowledge through a natural self-directed process. Supervisors and teachers favoring this view strive to be open, trusting, and non-evaluative. They work in a facilitative mode.

Facilitating helps the learner to discover and create new meanings, skills, and structures from experience. It requires that the facilitator be a catalyst, resource, reflective mirror, and co-inquirer. The structure, objectives, and direction of the learning materials are negotiated, although the context, in the form of personal meanings, comes from the student.[2]

Interaction between the individual and the environment is central to yet another view of learning, which emphasizes collaboration between teacher and student. Supervisors and teachers with this point of view are likely to get learners involved in mutual problem solving and to encourage them to be self-directing and risk-taking; yet teachers also confront, challenge, persuade, build confidence, and provide feedback. Collaboration requires that the learner and teacher jointly engage in the processs of discovering and developing new understandings, skills, and strategies. As co-learners, they act interdependently, dividing tasks on a mutually acceptable basis. This approach helps to build a "community of learners."[3]

Views about how people learn and the connection between a supervisor's or teacher's personal philosophy of learning and personal style of working with others are, of course, not quite as simple as described above or as distinct in practice. An underlying premise of developmental supervision, however, is the recognition that humans learn through self-exploration, collaboration, and conditioning. We believe approaches to teaching and supervision that build on these views of learning are valid and can be used appropriately with adult learners depending upon their needs, the context, and the setting.

CRITERIA FOR DETERMINING
SUPERVISORY APPROACHES

Related to the modes of teaching described above are three orientations to supervision identified by Carl Glickman in his monograph on developmental supervision. He has labeled these three orientations directive, collaborative, and non-directive.[4]

A supervisor with a directive orientation tells teachers what needs to be done. The task is defined, standards are set, and actions are reinforced. Directive behavior is less controlling when it is informational, when the supervisor makes various suggestions about what can be done. A collaborative orientation includes negotiating, problem-solving, and listening behaviors, which result in an agreement between supervisor and supervisee about the next steps for instructional improvement. Supervisors with a non-directive orientation are facilitators who listen, clarify, and encourage the teacher to take the major responsibility for improvement. One orientation is not viewed as better than another; each is valid and is part of a supervisory behavioral continuum. The degree of control a teacher has varies, depending on which orientation a supervisor uses.

Teacher Characteristics

Glickman recommends that supervisors determine the strategy they will use with teachers by assessing two of their developmental characteristics: their level of commitment to the job and their ability to think abstractly.[5] Teachers with high job commitment demonstrate concern for students and for other teachers and devote extra time and great energy to their work. Teachers with high conceptual ability can think about a problem from many perspectives, generate alternative plans for solving it, and choose a plan and carry it out. These teachers benefit most from non-directive supervisory styles.

Staff members who have a low level of commitment to their work, who become easily confused about a problem, and who do not know what can be done to solve it are most likely to profit from directive supervision. Richard Bents and Kenneth Howey suggest that supervisors organize their information and methods for working with these teachers, state their expectations explicitly, and give specific examples for applying concepts.[6]

Collaborative supervision works best with teachers who are enthusiastic workers but need help in focusing and thinking through problems, and with teachers who have ideas about solving problems but do not seem able to translate them into action.

"Reading" or assessing teachers for these two developmental character-istics is useful in planning supervisory interventions. Figure 4.2 shows how a supervisor might use a range of behaviors, from directive to non-directive, each legitimate and appropriate, in response to teacher characteristics. A major goal is to assist teachers in increasing the control, authority, and responsibility they have for their own professional development.

Developmental Stage Theories

Glickman's thesis is based, in part, upon the work of researchers in adult development and those who are examining the relationship between cogni-tive, conceptual, and personality development and teacher development and effectiveness. This research indicates that teachers who are at advanced stages of cognitive, moral, and ego development function more effectively in the classroom in a number of ways. They appear to be able to think more abstractly about a problem and to generate more solutions to it than teachers at lower levels. They are also better able to see differences in the children they teach. As a consequence, they utilize the learner's frame of reference and adjust their teaching styles and methods to meet the needs of individual children as they learn.[7]

Researchers are also beginning to examine the implications of this cog-nitive-developmental perspective for pairing supervisors with supervisees. If teachers at higher conceptual stages of development are more flexible and make their teaching more relevant to the learner, then should not supervisors be highly conceptual as well so that they too can use a range of behaviors best suited to their supervisees? Another question is whether supervisors should be at higher stages of conceptual development than their staff so that the conceptual functioning of supervisees will be raised through interacting with their supervisors.

Peter Grimmett has studied the conceptual functioning and communica-tion behavior of four supervisors and their supervisees during conferences. He reports that supervisors with more abstract functioning showed "flex" in their communication behavior. They were able to "read" their supervisee's needs and the situational constraints. Supervisors who functioned more con-cretely seemed unable to do this.[8] The term *flex* suggests the supervisor's ability to vary or adapt "teaching" from a range of alternative behaviors. During a conference, for example, a supervisor might change roles from counselor to facilitator to evaluator to meet the personal, professional, or situational needs of a supervisee.

Grimmett also noted an increase in the conceptual functioning of teachers who worked with supervisors who were more abstract and conceptual, and a reduction in the conceptual levels of those teachers who were working with

FIGURE 4.2 *Developmental Directionality of the Supervisory Behavior Continuum*

	reinforcing	standardizing	demonstrating	negotiating	problem solving	presenting	encouraging	clarifying	listening
Control	teacher low / supervisor high								supervisor low / teacher high
Directionality	Directive		Collaborative				Nondirective		
Teacher Type	Teacher Dropout		Analytical Observer		Unfocused Worker		Professional		
Teacher Level	Low Abstraction Low Commitment		High Abstraction Low Commitment		Low Abstraction High Commitment		High Abstraction High Commitment		

supervisors who functioned at more concrete levels.[9] A study of student teachers and their supervisors by Lois Thies-Sprinthall had similar findings.[10]

This type of research raises questions about the selection of supervisors and the nature of supervisory training programs. For example, should the goals of such programs be to raise the developmental levels of supervisors and to build their competence in direct, collaborative, and indirect modes of supervising? Should such techniques as role-playing, dilemma discussions, active listening, videotaping, individual conferences, and empathic responding exercises be incorporated to a greater extent into training programs to increase supervisors' conceptual funtioning? Sharon Oja and Sally Glassberg have successfully used these methods with in-service teachers working with student teachers.[11]

Knowledge of developmental stage theories can help supervisors determine strategies for working with teachers. For further information about these theories, refer to the works listed in the Bibliography by O. J. Harvey and associates; Lawrence Kohlberg and Elliot Turiel; and Jane Loevinger. We believe knowledge about adult development and learning and about the professional development of supervisors and teachers can also furnish supervisors with significant and useful information in planning for supervision and in understanding themselves.

Professional Development

Frances Fuller, a pioneer in examining teacher concerns across time, studied the pre-service teaching experience. She and Oliver Bown described the stages of learning to teach in terms of the individual's concerns rather than the content that is being taught.[12]

Fuller and Bown found that as an individual becomes a teacher, concerns shift from self to pupils. Student teachers, still identifying with pupils and not having yet experienced the teaching role, are at first concerned about themselves. They are preoccupied with survival and with feelings of inadequacy. Once they have contact with pupils, they are concerned about their ability to control a class, being liked by pupils, and what supervisory opinions and evaluations of them might be. Later, the student teacher's concerns shift to the teaching situation, particularly teaching methods and materials. Finally, the student teacher becomes concerned about individual pupils, their learning, and their social and emotional needs. Fuller makes an important point about teacher education, which is still relevant for pre- and in-service training today: "It seems pretty safe to assume that most programs meet the needs of teachers in a sequence different from the sequence in which teachers feel the needs."[13]

Lillian Katz identified four stages of development and training needs for preschool teachers already in service. Stage 1, Survival, usually lasts throughout the first year of teaching, when the individual experiences self-doubt and feelings of insecurity. Katz recommends that teachers in this stage receive direct on-site support and technical assistance.[14]

During stage 2, Consolidation, a teacher consolidates those gains made during the first stage and begins to focus on specific tasks and skills. Providing on-site assistance, access to specialists, and advice from colleagues and consultants are ways supervisors can support training needs during the first several years of teaching.[15]

By the third or fourth year, the preschool teacher begins to tire and to feel a need for Renewal, stage 3. By attending conferences, joining professional associations, and analyzing their teaching, teachers can meet their needs at this stage. Finally, stage 4, Maturity, which extends beyond the fifth year, is the time when the teacher benefits most from attending conferences, participating in institutes and degree programs, and writing for journals.[16]

An assumption behind these theories of teacher growth is, of course, that pre- and in-service teacher education and supervisory support should change as the needs and concerns of teachers change throughout their careers.

We apply Fuller's notions to the professional development of supervisors in chapter 6 and to caregiver development in chapter 7. Research studies are needed to examine the phases of professional development in supervisor-supervisee pairs and the effects that matches during various phases have on each individual and on supervisory effectiveness.

Adult Development

Patterns of adult development and learning are common to all human beings, including early childhood staff members. Adults in their late teens are different from adults in their forties or from those in their sixties. Their goals in life, psychological needs, and physical stamina change throughout the life cycle. Priorities in the relationship of career to personal and family life change as well.

Supervisors are adult learners, too, and pass through life stages that affect their work with staff. In chapter 5, we discuss in detail how adult development affects the supervision of adult learners.

In thinking about their staff members and strategies to use with them, supervisors may find that, in some cases, one of the developmental domains noted above may offer more information and greater relevance than the others. With certain supervisees all three domains—developmental stage theories, professional development, and adult development and learning—

may provide the supervisor with significant cues for planning intervention strategies.

THE CONTEXT

Not only is information derived from the various developmental domains important in determining supervisory strategies, but equally significant is the relationship established between the supervisor and the teacher, the particular issue at hand, and the organization of which they are a part. These are salient contextual elements that influence supervisor-supervisee behavior and that can have a bearing on the approach that a supervisor might take with a particular supervisee.

Relationship

The existing relationship between supervisor and the person being supervised affects supervision. Staff members who trust supervisors and believe that supervisors care about them and their professional growth are more likely to be open to a range of supervisory behaviors. If a teacher feels secure with a supervisor, for example, there is less likelihood that he or she will be offended or threatened by criticism or information offered by the supervisor. Of course, relationships that are too close or that have developed into friendships based on race, culture, or class can create division among staff and make it harder for supervisors to take action objectively. A professional/personal balance in the relationship between supervisor and supervisee is most desireable.

The Problem

The nature of the problem with which a supervisor must deal also influences the approach to take. In working with an aide who arrives late and leaves early every day, a worker who talks roughly to children, or a teacher who simply does not have the skills to organize a small group experience with children, a supervisor may need to be direct. On the other hand, if a teacher is involved in an emotionally laden issue with a particular child and cannot gain a clear perspective of the problem, the supervisor may need to reassure and comfort the teacher yet make an executive decision that may be unpopular with that teacher. For example, the supervisor may refer the child to a psychologist for special treatment even though the teacher feels competent to handle the child's problems.

In dealing with interpersonal conflicts among staff members, in planning for children who have special needs, or in exploring ways to improve the effectiveness of a program, collaborative strategies may be most appropriate. A supervisor may use listening, clarifying, encouraging, and other indirect behaviors with the excellent teacher who is disheartened when a thought-to-be exciting lesson falls flat or with a young, inexperienced staff member who is involved in a family crisis that interferes with performance. The specific problem, issue, or concern at hand is always a significant variable in planning for supervision.

Institutional Climate

Organizational variables such as policies and procedures, goals, time, and climate are some of the contextual elements that influence supervision.

In smaller programs, for example, directors teach full-time and often cannot supervise to the extent they might like because of lack of time. In parent-run programs or cooperatives, the supervisor's behavior may be governed by others who have influence over program policy and operation. Lack of adequate space for a program may create problems and pressures, as teaching conditions may be congested and there may not be facilities for private conferences or for staff to relax. A center-based director in a large system may receive pressure from an executive director with different values and assumptions about people and programs. The agency might not allow adequate planning time for supervisor and staff to work together, forcing the supervisor to give up a process approach with staff in favor of issuing orders. Or a program's established system for staff evaluation may prevent a supervisor from evaluating in a way that promotes supervisee growth.

If the climate of an organization is an oppressive one, it can hinder effective supervision. On the other hand, a climate that promotes feelings of respect, trust, and staff involvement in decision making will facilitate the work of supervisors and supervisees.

CONCLUSION

We believe that supervision is a reciprocal process by which the supervisor and the teacher influence each other's behavior. Both individuals function within a context that offers constraints and advantages and has a bearing on each person, the interactions, and supervisory outcomes.

The developmental domains that affect supervisor and supervisee point to the importance of supervisors' knowing themselves, being conscious of their own behavior, and being able to perceive, assess, and accurately "read" supervisees.

In this chapter we have raised questions about the sequence of teacher training experiences, the selection of supervisors and the content of their training, and the "matching" of supervisors and supervisees based on their developmental stages and phases. In the chapters that follow, we will elaborate on some of the ideas presented here.

EXERCISES

1. Think about your family and schooling experiences and your assumptions about your supervisees. Describe how these factors may influence your supervision.
2. Do you have a preferred supervisory style? If so, describe it.
3. Analyze your setting in terms of some of the contextual elements mentioned in this chapter. In what ways do they help or hinder you with your supervision?

5 Supervision as Adult Education

The supervisory role has many dimensions, ranging from being a listener and support person, as in a counseling or helping relationship, to being a manager and evaluator, as in an administrative relationship. It also includes being a facilitator of learning, as in a teaching relationship. It is this perspective, viewing the supervisor as adult educator, that we will consider in this chapter. Two important points serve as a framework for our discussion:

First, the importance of viewing the teacher — or any staff member — as a growing, learning individual cannot be overemphasized. An assumption upon which this book is based is that adults of all ages, in all developmental stages, and at all intelligence levels can learn.

Second, supervisors with previous experience and training in teaching young children have developed perspectives on learning, teaching, and human relationships upon which they can build as they work with adults. But many of these same supervisors have difficulty in changing their perspectives from teaching children to supervising adults. By viewing themselves as teachers of adults and by recognizing the ways adults learn, supervisors can acquire reference points to assist in making the transition to and in defining the new role of helping adults learn.

The emphasis on supervision as an adult-adult relationship is an important one, for learning in this context occurs as a result of the interaction between supervisor and teacher. An understanding of adult learning and development is, therefore, as essential for supervisors as an understanding of children's learning and development is for teachers of young children.

ADULT LEARNING PATTERNS

Although some principles of learning are universal, there are a number of learning characteristics of adults that contrast with those of children. As shown in Table 5.1, Donald Brundage and Dorothy Mackeracher have summarized these differences as an aid to analysis.[1] We will elaborate on several of these distinctive traits and some additional ones to assist the reader

55

TABLE 5.1 *Learning Characteristics of Adults and Children*

ADULTS, IN GENERAL	CHILDREN, IN GENERAL
Adults have extensive pragmatic life experiences which tend to structure and limit new learnings. Learning focuses largely on transforming or extending the meanings, values, skills, and strategies acquired in previous experience.	Children have few pragmatic life experiences. Learning focuses largely on forming basic meanings, values, skills, and strategies.
Major pressures for change come from factors related to social and work roles and expectations, and to personal need for continuing productivity and self-definition.	Major pressures for change come from factors related to physical growth, to demands for socialization, and to preparation for future social and work roles.
Learning needs are related to current life situations.	Learning needs are related to developing organized patterns for understanding future experiences.
Adults are more likely to use generalized, abstract thought.	Children are more likely to use specific, concrete thought.
Adults are likely to express their own needs and describe their own learning processes through verbal activities which allow them to negotiate and collaborate in planning their own learning programs.	Children are likely to express their own needs and learning processes through non-verbal activities, which leads to planning by "expert" observers and interpreters.
Adults have an organized and consistent self-concept and self-esteem which allows them to participate as a self separate from other selves and capable of acting independently of others.	Children have a relatively unorganized and inconsistent self-concept which allows them to perceive themselves as a self separate from, but dependent on others.
Adults are assigned a responsible status in society, and are expected to be productive.	Children are assigned a non-responsible status in society, and are expected to play and learn.

NOTE: Reprinted, with permission of the publisher, from Donald H. Brundage and Dorothy Mackeracher, *Adult Learning Principles and Their Application to Program Planning* (Toronto: Ontario Institute for Studies in Education, 1980), pp. 11–12.

in gaining a better understanding of the implications of teaching adults. The following five elements, in particular, are likely to affect adult learning: (1) self-knowledge and self-concept; (2) life experiences; (3) need for independence, interdependence, and motivation; (4) orientation to learning; and (5) life stage and life transitions.

Self-Knowledge and Self-Concept

"Taking stock" of where one is personally and professionally is a worthwhile exercise and can precipitate major change. As Gordon Klopf notes, it is essential for educators to know themselves:

> It is difficult to separate values, attitudes, and personality from professional performance. The individual is not two or three persons; even though performing different roles, the real self always tends to come through. To change professionally, the educator must understand the real self and analyze how this self is reflected in various role enactments.[2]

Adults who are not self-analytical are less likely to change. Often, they are happy with the status quo and see no need to. These adults do not view themselves as learners and may think that learning is only for children. Supervisors working with them may discover that these staff members are unwilling to take part in learning situations or, if they do participate, may undermine and resist new undertakings.

Unlike children, who are still forming their self-concepts, the adult's self-concept is already formed. This means that staff members may perceive new learning situations as threatening to existing self-concepts unless they can see that the proposed changes will lead to positive results congruent with their idealized self-concepts. The supervisor's role, as an enabler, is to help staff members integrate new understandings into their self-concepts and to build their self-esteem while doing so.[3] When conferring with staff, supervisors have a perfect opportunity to provide them with input about their teaching and to help them become more reflective about their behavior, for it is through feedback from others and from self that adults define themselves.

Life Experiences

A staff member's life and work experiences are rich resources. One of the satisfying aspects of teaching and supervising adults is that even when they have a limited education, have not taken early childhood courses, or are not fluent readers, their knowledge gained through their experience with children and with the world in general can be activated and brought to bear in analyzing their day-to-day work. The other side of this, of course, occurs when a supervisee holds on to personal experience as being the only valid source for teaching behavior. As Robert Peck points out:

> Some people learn to master their experiences, achieve a degree of detached perspective on them, and make use of them as *provisional* guides to the solution of new issues. There are other people who seem to become dominated by their experiences. They take the patterns of events and actions which they happen to have encountered as a set of fixed inflexible rules which almost automatically govern their subsequent behavior.[4]

Through their experience, people develop value systems that create stability in their lives. They tend to rely on meanings they have discovered in the past without questioning them unless challenged by new circumstances that do not match their expectations. When this happens, their need to maintain stability and a sense of adequacy can prevent them from accepting the implications of the new situation. They may deal with this challenge by denying or ignoring the new information; by distorting the facts to fit their existing views; or by confronting the new experience, dealing with its implications, and accepting or rejecting it based on reasonable criteria. Most people tend to use all three of these modes of thinking from time to time.[5]

Adult learning, then, requires a transformation of meanings, values, strategies, and skills derived from past experiences, unless the learning experience is totally new. This modifying and reintegration of meaning and values is a different learning process from the forming and accumulating one characteristic of childhood. It requires greater energy, more time, and an opportunity to test out new behavior in "safe" situations.[6]

Supervisors can help adults learn by taking their experience into account and connecting it to the context in which they are working.[7] Bringing a person's life and work into the supervisory process helps make new experiences meaningful. Arthur Combs, Donald Avila, and William Purkey suggest that this personal discovery of meaning is essential to learning: "Some of our most important learnings actually have nothing to do with new information but everything to do with the deeper and richer discovery of the meanings we already have."[8]

Providing opportunities for staff members to contribute to each other's learning is another way that supervisors can take advantage of their rich and varied backgrounds. This is especially important when there are cultural differences within a staff or between staff members and children. As Combs and associates state:

> The simplest, most obvious facts about the world around us are only true for members of a common culture. So long as we stay in the same culture, a given

fact may never be seriously questioned. When we step outside our own culture, we quickly discover that many facts we consider to be reality have no validity in the new setting.[9]

When staff development activities include mixed groups of teachers, aides, and other personnel, each person can contribute to the group from his or her own experiential perspective. A community aide or minority group member, for example, may be able to furnish significant insights that can inform and deepen the knowledge of other group members. Similarly, the theoretical knowledge of those with early childhood training can contribute to those without formal training. Both learning and motivation result from tapping into this resource in staff meetings, in-service workshops, and supervisory groups.

Independence and Interdependence

Adults want to be independent and self-directing and to be viewed as such by others. They also need to be needed. Thus, they exhibit a range of dependent and independent behaviors as they strive to be part of a group and to have control over their lives. The supervisor's challenge is to recognize and to foster independence, while still providing opportunities for interdependence.

Although it seems contradictory, supervisors who are committed to helping teachers develop independence in children often have difficulty supporting the independence of their staff members. Teachers may be given a good deal of autonomy about the ways in which they work with children, but sometimes this is "benign neglect," resulting from the supervisor's need to juggle time between teaching, administrative duties, and conducting observations, conferences, or staff meetings. When this happens, supervision may become a rescuing, crisis-oriented operation where a direct approach is almost inevitable. Perhaps the major reason may be that supervisors themselves have not had role models who supported the adult need for self-direction and affiliation. They are, therefore, likely to imitate supervisory styles based upon their own experience as students or teachers or their views of what an administrator or supervisor is "supposed" to do.

Even when supervisors feel comfortable encouraging independence, staff members may not have had much experience asserting themselves. Many schools reward convergent thinking rather than problem-solving, and "learning" may be associated with such school experiences for many staff members. Those caregivers who were not very successful in school may be reluctant to risk further failure by voicing ideas they fear may not be "right." Or supervisees may see the supervisor as the one who is supposed to tell them what to do. Thus, supervisors and supervisees may need to learn how to be part of a collaborative, problem-solving process.

A supervisory relationship that respects the adult need to be independent and interdependent can work if the supervisor creates a climate of trust, problem exploration, and "joint inquiry,"[10] a climate in which supervisor and supervisee together explore ways of improving the program for children. Approaching all staff members as adults able to make intelligent decisions when provided with information, assistance, and support is a supervisory assumption basic to this goal. As Jan Diamondstone notes: "If adults truly learn, it is because they themselves have been involved in setting 'objectives' and that they themselves have a hand in selecting or defining what is important or necessary to learn."[11]

We know that some staff members will need highly structured and very directive supervision as a starting point. However, supervisors can gradually bring them into a collaborative process, leading toward the opposite end of the developmental continuum where they function as independent and interdependent professionals, committed to their work.

This collaborative process can begin with the use of self-assessment to identify the needs of both individual staff members and the staff as a whole. (In chapter 7 we provide guidelines and a tool for assessing the individual characteristics of staff.) A logical follow-up to the self-assessment process is for supervisor and supervisee to establish goals as a framework for observations, conferences, and staff development and training experiences. Evaluation, like assessment, can also be a mutual process between supervisee and supervisor since "nothing makes an adult feel more child-like than being judged by another adult."[12]

Staff members can also be involved in program planning. Caregivers can contribute ideas for topics for in-service workshops or other staff development experiences. They can help in selecting leaders, suggesting the format for in-service, and even presenting workshops themselves. Staff input in planning for individual observations and conferences is also appropriate.

Including staff members in decision making and recognizing their expertise increases their status and demonstrates respect for them and their ideas. When people have helped to solve a problem, they have a stake in a project or program, and they become more committed to it.

Orientation to Learning

A fourth major characteristic of adult learning is the adult's desire to apply what has been taught directly to solving problems of immediate concern. In contrast to children, adults are not willing to accept instruction passively on a topic for which they cannot see a purpose.[13] Supervisors may despair at this need for immediacy, for it seems that teachers want workshops only on "what they can do tomorrow."

Yet this desire for useful new techniques and curriculum ideas should not be disparaged or ignored. Supervisors can respond to matters of immediate interest to staff by using a problem-centered approach to learning and involving staff in the process of defining problems and developing solutions. As we have previously noted, not all supervisees are ready for joint inquiry, but they can be supported as they begin to practice these kinds of behaviors in a limited way. Workshops and staff meetings can be planned around issues of mutual concern, and leaders can use teaching or group process techniques that help participants make connections with immediate situations.

A problem-centered approach can also be used in individual staff conferences. This allows staff members to learn to look at teaching as problem-solving and discover that, by working together with their supervisor, they may be able to find the best ways to resolve the issues that confront them. Although for many people, "problem" implies blame, the problem-centered approach, in the long run, actually helps supervisees shift the focus away from themselves and toward the situation, thus removing the sense of blame. Supervisors and teachers thus become able to dialogue with one another, to teach each other, and to make use of their own life and classroom experience — successes, failures, and aspirations.[14]

Although an atmosphere that fosters mutual problem-solving can go a long way toward making needed connections with teachers' day-to-day work, it is not without its difficulties. J. R. Kidd points out that adults know that "solutions have effects."[15] Our assumption usually is that a solution will be salutary, both for the children and for the staff. Many times, however, the effects are unknown. Staff members may be uncertain of their own competence to carry through a new procedure or method, unsure of the attitudes of co-workers toward the contemplated change, or concerned about the possible effects on children's feelings or behavior. Since these fears are not easy to detect, a supervisor may be disappointed and confused when, after a supervisee has agreed to and even seemed excited about a change, little or no action follows.

Combs and associates point out that there is a fine line between being challenged and being threatened by the same situation. When we do not feel adequate to cope with something, we feel threatened. Such feelings make us unsure of ourselves and may cause us to withdraw from the situation. On the other hand, we are challenged by problems we think we can handle and that interest us.[16] Practicing new behaviors in safe situations helps staff members acquire and use them over time. Supervisors can structure and support this practice through role playing of new behaviors, providing more support at team meetings when changes are being shared with co-workers, and being present in the classroom when a new behavior is being tried out. A problem-centered approach implies support at the "firing line" as well as at the earlier stages of discussion and thinking.

Life Stages and Life Transitions

Staff members working in early childhood programs represent all adult age groups. There may be high school and college students, women beginning or returning to work as their children grow up, and senior citizens working part-time to earn extra income or to have something interesting to do. These adults are at varying points in their life cycles. As they develop and change, so do their personal and professional needs and priorities. These changes affect their readiness to learn. By taking into account patterns in adult development, we can plan more effective strategies for working with them.

The important work of life cycle theorists Erik Erikson and Robert Havighurst and life-age theorists Daniel Levinson, Roger Gould, and Gail Sheehy has implications for supervisors.[17] In a handbook on staff development, Judy Arin-Krupp has synthesized much of the research about adults at certain ages and stages and identified implications for staff development. She has taken into account differences in needs between males and females and indicated how these might affect approaches to staff development.[18] Arin-Krupp's work is summarized in Table 5.2.

Associated with many of these stages of development are major transitional periods, which require that adults terminate existing life structures and work toward new ones. As they undergo this process, they reappraise what exists, explore other options, and make choices that will form a basis for a new life structure.[19] During this time of reassessment, their motivation and ability to respond to supervision or to new challenges may be affected.

Marriage, a new baby, divorce, a spouse's change of job, the first (or last) child in school, or the death of a spouse all represent significant events in a person's life, which may cause or be the result of a major life transition. Though they occur outside the work place, these events affect a person's performance on the job. Initially, the staff member may become less involved with work, needing to spend energy on personal or family needs, but crises or marker events often create opportunities for learning as well.

Patricia Cross suggests that adult educators who are sensitive to individual needs can take advantage of these periods by designing experiences that help people make an active transition to a new stage in their lives.[20] After an initial adjustment period, for example, some individuals develop a new commitment to their jobs. They become ready, perhaps for the first time, to work at a more challenging level and willing to take an active part in curriculum or staff development.

SUPERVISING AND SUPPORTING ADULT LEARNERS

Getting to know staff members — discovering what their goals are, how they define success, what their dreams are at a particular stage — is invaluable to supervisors in determining staff needs and helping them learn to change. Talking with staff members about their jobs and about their lives outside of work, joining them at breaks or for lunch, chatting with them during the course of the day, establishing small groups to work on problems, and socializing with them outside of school are all ways to learn more about staff as people and as professionals.

Supervisors need to be good listeners, especially during transitional periods. Advice may be useful occasionally, but by being a good listener, a supervisor can enable teachers to put their dilemmas, thoughts, and feelings into words so that they can more fully understand what is going on. By listening, supervisors can become facilitators who help supervisees launch themselves in new directions once they begin to move toward a new structure.

Supervisors need to be flexible in their demands and standards for those who are experiencing transitional events. Providing physical comfort for grandparents working as aides or being sensitive to the ups and downs that young adults experience as they strive to develop intimate relationships, for example, are special accommodations that may be required.

Recognizing differences in adults' readiness for learning is another means of helping staff members change. This can be demonstrated through the timing of supervisory encounters with staff, through the pacing of supervisory input, and through the ways in which staff are grouped for learning.

One of the most crucial and difficult aspects of timing has to do with our own willingness to allow time for learning, to avoid expecting too much too soon and wanting immediate success. Combs and associates stress that we can too easily forget that it takes time to discover meaning: "The teacher who studies a subject for twenty or thirty years and now believes it can be taught to a student in a few weeks or months has embarked on a frustrating course."[21] It is through slow steps in which experience is increasingly differentiated that meaning is revealed.

Let us also keep in mind that change comes about in many different ways. Sometimes, change occurs in a steady, gradual fashion; at other times, individuals or groups will move back and forth from one level to another with spurts and plateaus. Real change is generally a slow continuous process, with

(*Continued on page 68*)

TABLE 5.2 *Stages of Development and Implications for Staff Development*

STAGE	KEY CONCERNS	CHARACTERISTICS	IMPLICATIONS FOR STAFF DEVELOPMENT
Late teens and early twenties 17-(22-24)	Independence-dependence: Breaking away from parents and family Identity: Fitting into the adult world Searching for a mentor	Physically at peak Explore intimate relationships Time perceived as endless Males concerned with occupational choice Females concerned with family or occupation New teachers concerned about confidence Males ponder viability of teaching Male-female differences abound Active social life	1. Provide these adults with clear definition of what is expected of them 2. Provide an opportunity for independence whenever possible, but recognize a need for dependence as well 3. Try to make a young teacher see the need for change by facilitating growth rather than by directing 4. Facilitate growth by encouraging participation in areas where teacher has background 5. Be sensitive to the ups and downs of intimate relationships 6. Foster exploration of all the ramifications of teaching 7. Do not encourage poor teachers to stay in the program 8. Provide social activities for staff
The 20's 18-28	Identity and Intimacy: Family obligations create stress Marriage and parenting Want to demonstrate competence on the job Males busy working and achieving, no in-depth questioning of occupation Flexibility and stability: maintaining a balance between the two	Unsure of being boy-man or girl-woman Physically in their prime Emotions are modulated Very active socially Time is extensive Idealistic and optimistic	1. Clearly define the parameters of the job 2. Create a climate that permits discussion of life stressors 3. Discuss means of effecting change in areas of defect; teachers will try new techniques if they feel it is the responsible or the supportive thing to do 4. Help young teachers select realistic goals 5. Female teachers may be unsure about their relationships with male administrators; frank discussion of the relationship may help alleviate some initial fear 6. While males avoid self-searching, females want to explore own development

Age/Stage	Developmental Focus	Characteristics	Implications
Age 30	Individuation: Who am I? What is my place in the world? Males are restless and begin to re-evaluate Women investigate iden-tity and role options Marital conflict is common Men establish career goals Women become more independent and career oriented	Physical and mental abilities still in their prime Children replace parents as central concern Decreased interest in social activities Males continue to be assertive Females continue to be nurturing Family life is major stressor	1. Teachers who are self-centered are less able to consider needs of others; may be willing to try new things if those new ideas relate to aspects of self 2. Do everything in your power to make teaching a rewarding, self-fulfilling experience 3. Be prepared for the more assertive, independent, active woman by age 35 4. Provide support to those questioning teaching 5. Find out why teachers have recommitted to teaching and help those individuals explore ways of finding satisfaction 6. Know your staff. Use persons with similar mind sets as support people with one another 7. Be flexible with teachers who have family-career conflicts
The 30's (28-35) – 40	Stability-Advancement: Wants to feel a sense of accomplishment Women become more independent Men move toward career advancement Accommodation and con-stancy sought in marriage and family De-illusionment: Remove unrealistic aspects of the dream and modify it Become one's own person Authority-Mutuality: Interdependence	Past physical prime Family a strong priority for males Time is limited Social life revolves around family Men full of doubts and anxiety, while women are content and have more self-direction	1. Discuss career-family duality 2. Consider long-term staff development 3. Women working for the first time need support 4. By end of this period, male teachers need support, they tend to be more open 5. Women returning to the field need mentors

(continued)

TABLE 5.2 (Continued)

STAGE	KEY CONCERNS	CHARACTERISTICS	IMPLICATIONS FOR STAFF DEVELOPMENT
Age 40 Transition 40-(45-47)	De-illusionment Career—to change or not to change Marriage—each partner respects autonomy of the other Changes are greater for males than for females Task—to integrate best of youth and best of old Mortality—immortality Generativity—using self-knowledge to help humanity	Time left to live Strength and endurance have peaked Mental activities still in prime Friends are more important Men emphasize interpersonal experience Women emphasize social-service-oriented values	1. Know teachers—individualize to meet teacher needs 2. Support those who feel they have failed 3. Help teachers set realistic goals to avoid depression 4. Teachers need to be facilitated rather than educated 5. Value the insights of middle-aged staff 6. Respect differences among teachers
Age Middle Adulthood 45-47-(50)	Stability-Satisfaction: To live out life within established structure Mellowness	Signs of aging continue Marital satisfaction is high Males more concerned about sharing their adult careers Talk about retirement begins Socialize to meet self-defined needs Males more affectionate and expressive Women want to "get ahead"	1. Teachers less willing to change—know teacher, build trust and understanding 2. Teachers may be more willing to work after school 3. Need advance warning of changes 4. Encourage teachers to be mentors 5. Encourage older teachers to share
The 50's 50-60	Mellowness Feel creative, productive and self-satisfied Integrity—acceptance of life lived to best of ability Death is accepted	Serious health and physical changes Mental ability is acute Attempt to capture life now Spouse is valued as companion Emphasis is on sharing joy and sorrow Women have more roles than males	1. Provide for comfort in school 2. Include teachers in decision-making 3. Let complaints be aired 4. Discuss problems 5. Continue to listen to be supportive 6. Listen to what staff has to say and act on it

60 plus	Integrity—they demonstrate wisdom Accept selves as part of the elder generation	Lessening in general well-being Mental ability is slow but effective Task—to create new roles in retirement Time is finite Enjoy leisure pursuits	1. Find and capitalize on the unique contribution that these teachers can make 2. Prepare teachers for retirement 3. Counsel those who are ineffective 4. Provide single or small group staff development
60-retirement			

SOURCE: Judy Arin-Krupp, *Adult Development: Implications for Staff Development* (Manchester, CT: Adult Development and Learning, 1981).

periods of high activity and static periods when individuals assimilate new understandings. Sometimes growth occurs after we have despaired that our efforts have had any effect at all! A Head Start supervisor relates such an experience:

> When I first came in, I was really frustrated because people didn't want to listen, and yet I'm seeing some of those same people, after a summer, come back and do the things I had wanted them to do. They couldn't do it immediately. They had to get used to it.

Supervisors can use knowledge of an adult's level of personal and professional readiness as a guide in determining when to offer correction, when to suggest new ideas, and when to support and encourage. Jerome Bruner suggests, for example, that feedback on how well a person is doing should optimally come at the time that the person is evaluating his or her own performance. Reinforcement that comes too soon, he states, will be confusing and will discourage further exploration. If it is too late, it is beyond the point at which it would have been helpful.[22]

Katz notes that if we are to err in the pacing and timing of input, it is probably better to do so on the side of more time: "Greater latency, which allows more of the learner's behavior to unfold, increases the quantity of information upon which the teacher can formulate a response. . . . Hypothetically, there are likely to be optimal latencies for every teaching-learning experience."[23]

The concept of developmental differences also provides us with a way of thinking about how to work with staff in groups. Sometimes supervisors may want to group staff by role or experience level to address a common training need or concern. At other times they may prefer to form completely mixed groups, depending on the kinds of learnings that are expected to take place. In chapter 14 we will describe staff development and training experiences for groups of staff with similar and different kinds of needs.

CONCLUSION

Learning is not automatic for adults. Adult learning characteristics suggest that supervisors can support growth most effectively by

- Being patient
- Acknowledging that staff need time to assimilate new ideas
- Recognizing that making mistakes and even failing are part of the learning process

- Appropriately pacing the introduction of new knowledge and skills
- Being specific
- Offering examples of and options for new behaviors that can replace the old
- Helping staff step back and look at themselves
- Recognizing that the thoughts and feelings of staff are important

Through these behaviors, supervisors can help staff members to learn, to change, and to gain greater satisfaction from their work.

EXERCISES

1. Describe specific examples from your own experience that illustrate some of the major points raised in this chapter.
2. As you think about the concepts of adult education, learning, and development described in this chapter, what are some implications for supervision that have not been mentioned?
3. Study Table 5.2. Think of each staff member with whom you work in terms of the stages described. As a result of this analysis, what are some supervisory strategies that you plan to use with them?

6 Supervisor Development

As supervisors gain experience in their roles, they undergo a series of changes about how they view themselves and their jobs. Their feelings and concerns about supervision change over time.

We have identified three general phases that supervisors experience as they grow in their roles: beginning, extending, and maturing. Characteristic patterns of thinking and behaving tend to emerge during each of these phases as supervisors acquire new realizations concerning the supervisory role and the people with whom they are working. The significant characteristics of each phase are summarized in Table 6.1.

We acknowledge that this conceptualization may need further validation. We invite others to refine our initial attempts.

PHASE 1: BEGINNING

Beginning supervisors, like most novices, tend to have personal concerns: Will I be able to carry out the responsibilities of my position? What is my role? What is going to happen to me? Will I be able to meet the expectations that others have of me? These are some of the questions they ask of themselves.

Beginners develop a number of coping strategies to survive the early months on the job. One such strategy is to play the role of supervisor by imitating such role models as parents, teachers, managers, directors, grandmothers, nuns, or deans. These role models have left indelible imprints as to how individuals in authority positions should behave, and it is only natural to imitate these familiar behaviors. Yet there is risk to coping by imitation, since learned authority behavior may be inappropriate for early childhood programs, although it does give supervisors the feeling that they have "taken charge" and are "in control." This increases a supervisor's confidence, but only until problems develop. Solving problems requires meaningful deliberation and interaction with staff or board members based on an in-depth exploration of issues. Playing supervisor does little to resolve problems.

A second survival strategy novices use is to avoid the responsibilities of the role by appearing not to have adequate time to devote to supervision

70

TABLE 6.1 *Supervisory Development*

PHASE 1: BEGINNING	PHASE 2: EXTENDING	PHASE 3: MATURING
Concerned with self	"If only I...."	Knows self and can evaluate self openly
Anxious Critical of self Seeks support from many sources Rewards are self-centered	Accepts leadership with ambivalence	Sense of being in charge
	Can discuss problems and concerns more objectively	Greater sensitivity toward and understanding of supervisees
Copes in several ways	Concerns are centered on others	Recognizes expertise of supervisees
Plays the role of supervisor Avoids responsibility Orients self to role Uses trial and error	Better understanding of others and of program	More realistic about job and what can be done
In process of conceptualizing the role	More comfortable with authority	Concerned with ideas/issues
Uncomfortable with authority	High expectations for self	Has well-defined philosophical frame of reference
Develops new realizations about self	More confident, more relaxed	Stimulated by outside contacts; gets rewards from solving problems
		Continues to be critical, but sees self as learner

because they are preoccupied with other urgent administrative issues. These supervisors continually find themselves preoccupied with other business and somehow never take on their supervisory responsibilities. Some may believe that supervision is not their forte, a rationale for devoting all their time and energy to administrative duties where they do have competence. Avoidance behaviors enable supervisors to pretend they are doing a good job and their programs are running smoothly. In the meantime, problems snowball.

A third way beginners cope is to reserve a period of time to assess and orient themselves to their new setting if circumstances allow. They do this by observing and gradually getting to know people, programs, and routines. A new director explains how she is going about this task:

> Right now I am sort of filling the role of somebody that had been with the center for, I guess, six years who is very well loved and, in some ways, a mother figure for a lot of the staff. I have been listening to a lot of the kinds of interactions that went on with this person in terms of staff meetings and that kind of thing. I have been sorting out for myself what I would like to do without rocking the boat too soon. So, I'm following a lot of the things that were set up by that person.

Information gathered during this initial period can be valuable in making important decisions later.

New supervisors also learn through trial and error, even more so when they do not have an experienced teacher or other support system to point them in the right direction. They often try different approaches to solving problems in search of one that works.

Learning to Handle Authority and Confrontation

It is not at all uncommon for new supervisors to feel uncomfortable about directly confronting a staff member about a particular problem. Beginners are often concerned about being too bossy or offensive. They are not sure they can deal with problems in a sensitive and constructive manner. These feelings are understandable, as early childhood supervisors have frequently moved into their new roles from teaching and are still learning to shift from nurturing children to working with adults.

Although supervisors may have worked out their authority relationships with children in their previous roles as teachers or parents, working with adults is quite different. The diversity of caregivers in terms of cultural background, experience, age, and maturity levels can present serious challenges to the authority of an unsure supervisor. Coming to terms with authority is part of the process of defining and formulating a conception of the supervisory role. It is often painful and worrisome as this director describes:

> I think basically confronting and being able to say I am not happy with this or I don't like it is very hard, even though that is not exactly the way I would say it. I am trying to sort through in my own mind how to confront some situations and I haven't done particularly well. . . .

The new supervisor is faced with authority dilemmas daily in dealing with staff, parents, and curricular issues.

Conceptualizing the Role of Supervisor

Sifting, sorting, assessing, and testing are typical behaviors beginners use as they learn what a supervisor is and what a supervisor does. A conceptualization of the supervisory role emerges slowly: first, in a narrow and ambiguous sense, and later with greater clarity and scope. Inexperienced supervisors, for example, tend to view their supervisees in general terms rather than as complicated individuals with special needs. They describe staff in terms of numbers and categories — "I have one head teacher and three aides" — rather than in terms of personal characteristics, strengths, and weaknesses, as experienced supervisors do. They simply don't know their staff members well enough to differentiate among them or to make discrete assessments of them.

New supervisors must also develop a total picture of the programs in which they are working. During the first months on the job, they need to learn about personal relationships among staff members, the political implications of decisions they may make, the special needs and problems of the community being served, the expectations of outside funding agencies or institutions that supply temporary staff, and other factors that will affect their success on the job.

Seeking Professional and Emotional Support

Beginning supervisors function in their own world, concerned and preoccupied with self. Most are aware of their own weaknesses and are interested in becoming more skilled. Self-critical beginners willingly identify deficiencies and are open to experimentation. They want to improve their supervisory behavior.

First-year supervisors need and seek professional and emotional support from many sources, including administrators, parents, board members, and staff members, as well as from friends and relatives. As one supervisor put it:

I guess I need support. I need support from the staff. I need feedback from people in terms of what's happening from my end of things and how it is coming across to other people. I need open communication. I guess that is why I keep trying to work at building relationships because I feel it is really important that teachers be fairly open with me. And I need to learn a lot. I feel a little overscheduled sometimes about the role that I do play and I guess I need to develop my own skills.

A number of supervisors we interviewed gained assistance from other directors who were part of a local group that met on a monthly basis. Such nourishment from others helps beginners acquire the confidence they need.

Rewards for novices tend to center around self, since they are less other-person oriented than more experienced supervisors. Compliments from parents or from people in superior positions, such as chief administrators or board members, are especially appreciated. Solving difficult problems or accomplishing important tasks bring feelings of satisfaction to beginners.

Supervisors in this phase, and in the ones to follow, are continually learning about themselves. They are forced to reflect on their personal style, philosophy, and goals as they confront such challenges as implementing change; supporting, training, and evaluating other people; coordinating many activities within one program; raising funds; and conveying a center's philosophy and activities to the outside world. After four months on the job, a new supervisor talks about what she has learned about herself:

I guess what I think about is that there are a lot of things that I can handle simply by jumping in and doing them. I don't panic. I'm not afraid to do things although I still have my nervous moments. I know what I feel like when I am nervous, but I still follow through. I can try new things and accomplish them. In terms of myself, I guess that I have learned that I am somewhat approachable and that is nice. I have relearned that I am a real workaholic in some ways. I have a hard time cutting down my hours. I guess that my feelings about being able to confront others is something I have wanted to develop.

PHASE 2: EXTENDING

Supervisors in this phase are no longer novices, yet they have not yet reached professional maturity. They are consolidating gains made as beginners, extending their knowledge and competence, strengthening their leadership, raising their expectations, and reaching out to staff:

If only I had more time! If only we had more money! Wouldn't it be wonderful if I could send some of my staff to NAEYC? I wish we had greater racial and economic diversity represented in our enrollment.

> I wish I had somebody who was observing me and telling me what I'm doing wrong and what I'm doing right. . . . And I'm not at all satisfied with my performance or my role or anything. I think that I wish I had some magic . . . some magic potion.

Wishing for a magic potion or a wand that could make every part of a program perfect is the quintessential fantasy of supervisors in this second phase. Having survived the first year and gained greater confidence and assurance in coping with daily crises, supervisors in this phase are concerned with perfection. Now able to look beyond personal wants, the supervisor thinks about the needs of others, the prevailing conditions under which the staff operates, and the positive and negative aspects of the learning environment created for the children.

Reflecting an innocence and naivete, supervisors in this phase tend to believe that if they work hard and do their best, all of a program's problems and weaknesses will be corrected. Transitional supervisors set lofty goals, determined to make their programs exemplary ones, with visions of walking off stage with the "Early Childhood Emmy" flashing through their minds.

In contrast to beginners, who do not feel like supervisors and may even reject the notion of being boss, transitional supervisors accept the leadership role but are still ambivalent about it. As one day care director explained:

> I feel strongly that supervision is a big job and there are a lot of people to supervise. I do feel like a supervisor in the sense that I know people are looking for supervision and I try to do it. In the sense of feeling that I am really supervising every single person as it should be done, absolutely not. I know that there is no time. I don't have enough time to spend in classrooms really looking at what everybody is doing.

Another phase 2 supervisor was still unsure as to how to enact authority appropriately:

> My problem is how do you get somebody to see that she needs improvement in a particular area? Just because it is my problem doesn't mean it is going to be theirs. How do you get them to be motivated to change? How do you get them to ask, "How do you do that?" How do you tell them that you are not 100 percent satisfied with their work without sounding like you're extremely unsatisfied?

Unable to meet their own expectations of perfection, supervisors in this phase are often faced with frustration. They constantly fall short of mastering the art of supervision, yet continue to try to do better. One director commented, "There is this story that no matter how much you do, it is always less than what you want to be doing. . . . " In some respects, these feelings are prerequisite to realizing that all of one's goals cannot be achieved. They are part of a process of acquiring a truer picture of what a supervisor can accomplish and what is beyond his or her control. Reassessment and reconceptualization of the role of supervisor occur over time as supervisors engage in trial and error and meet with success and failure.

Phase 2 supervisors who are extending their leadership can begin to discuss problems and conflicts more objectively. They are better able to separate themselves from their roles, to stand back and look at problems analytically, rather than ignore them or feel overwhelmed as beginning supervisors do.

Concerns, then, move away from self and are centered to a far greater extent around other individuals and specific issues. Supervisors in this extending phase are more conscious of the need to provide reinforcement and support to staff members. They begin to see themselves as mentors who can guide staff members toward new realizations and self-improvement. They strive to provide an atmosphere of trust and openness to enable staff to identify and engage in group problem-solving experiences. They recognize the need to develop good group facilitation skills in order to foster positive interpersonal relationships among staff members.

With more experience, Phase 2 supervisors begin to make distinctions among staff members, to see them as unique individuals with special needs and concerns. They begin to realize that some supervisees need specific direction while others respond well to casual suggestions or praise. They provide different kinds of training for volunteers, part-time staff, and experienced full-time staff. This ability to vary one's approach to working with others, to individualize supervision, is more characteristic of supervisors toward the latter part of this second phase.

Gaining a greater understanding of a program, its people, and its parts is also characteristic of Phase 2 supervisors. This new awareness of a program's complexity is linked to the development of a less idealistic and more realistic sense of what a supervisor can and cannot do or change.

Supervisors in this phase often feel isolated. They discover that there really isn't anyone on the job at their level in whom to confide. They look for sources of support among associates in similar fields and other supervisors in similar positions. Reliance on new professional contacts for support lessens the burden on family and friends on whom beginning supervisors usually depend for nuturance.

Although there continues to be some self-centeredness in what Phase 2 supervisors find rewarding, they derive great satisfaction when they receive praise from individuals they supervise rather than from those who supervise them, and when they see others making progress. As one supervisor stated: "I love it when people get excited about teaching children, when people can learn to relax and enjoy teaching." Seeing the center run smoothly, observing supervisees improve their ability to work with children, or motivating a caregiver can be especially rewarding.

Supervisors who are extending their leadership also feel more relaxed, less panicky, less overwhelmed, and in greater control. It is at this time that they make enormous gains in professional development. They move from being anxious, self-centered beginners to individuals who grapple with issues, strive to support others, and feel a sense of accomplishment. Although still occasionally subject to feelings of ambivalence, guilt, or frustration, supervisors in this phase develop greater confidence and the security that comes from success and familiarity with the job, the program, and its people.

The experiences supervisors have during this middle phase affect whether or not they remain in a particular setting or even in the profession. It is during this transitional period that many supervisors make a commitment to the field or decide to look elsewhere to fulfill their career aspirations.

PHASE 3: MATURING

Phase 3 supervisors possess the characteristics of mature professionals: self-knowledge, self-confidence, in-depth understanding of the problems and issues associated with their work, and the skills necessary to do an effective job. Maturing supervisors bring rich and disparate life experiences to their roles and can look back and understand how those experiences have made them who they are and how they contribute to present-day success.

Seasoned supervisors know and evaluate themselves. They discuss strengths and weaknesses openly:

> I keep reminding myself that I need to listen to people very carefully. I think that this is essential. It has been an improvement in my supervisory style to be a better listener; it is a positive development in my personality.
> I have become conscious of the way I must come across to people, and I am cautious because these are young people. I think a supervisee is in a very vulnerable position very often, so I have to be sensitive to that and cautious about being too overwhelming or too opinionated or coming on too strong. . . . I think that I see my work all the time as a process of growth for me.

The supervisor who made the above statement shares some of her anxieties about being too overwhelming or too directive with caregivers, a common concern of her colleagues who are in earlier stages. A difference, however, between individuals in this mature stage and those who are less experienced is the ability to make accurate assessments of behavior: to ac-

knowledge their weaknesses and to be conscious of them as they strive to
change, to compensate, or to live with them. Maturing supervisors have a
sense of being in charge of their lives, of making conscious decisions, and
of being accountable for their actions.

One of the most striking characteristics of experienced supervisors is their
sensitivity to supervisees as unique individuals and their ability to individualize supervisory strategies. Mature supervisors view being able to assess
each supervisee and plan appropriate interventions as a special challenge,
as exemplified by this supervisor who talks about the teachers in her program:

> In terms of personality they are all different and I enjoy the differences. I think
> that because of their differences, they bring various agendas to supervision
> sessions. I do feel that supervisors can fall into all kinds of traps with super-
> visees — among them being overnurturing or undernurturing, being too critical,
> being too demanding. A supervisor has to be careful not to fall into that kind
> of trap. I think that we need to look at people's personalities. I think that our
> supervisees have different needs which evoke different kinds of responses.

In the following comments an experienced supervisor shows great insight
and understanding of her staff members, and values and appreciates the
special qualities each of them has:

> The three head teachers in this school are three different kinds of personalities
> and lead very different kinds of classrooms. For example, the head teacher
> upstairs works with the younger crew. I think that she is one of the most suc-
> cessful non-directive teachers I have ever come across. She is a rather young
> woman. This was her first job. She was trained here; she did a year's intern-
> ship here and she became a head teacher after that. She has a very unique
> way of communicating with children. One never hears her voice in the class-
> room. And yet, she is always talking with them or is at their side listening and
> communicating in other ways. Her presence is very much felt. The children
> are very busy doing their own thing. It is wonderful to see. That is a very
> special kind of personality and a very special set of characteristics.
> Downstairs we have a teacher who has had a lot of experience in a lot of
> settings with special needs children and so on. She is mature, experienced, and
> a very directive person. She understands children and her values are right,
> and I trust her explicitly. There is a vast difference in her approach. She does
> the right things for children. She is very good.
> In the afternoon, we have another teacher who has . . . who is a very chat-
> ty, very warm, very connected with everybody. She is very interested in do-
> ing special projects with children. She has a special kind of energy that is just
> perfect for children who are tired in the afternoon. She works from 11:00 A.M.
> to 5:00 P.M., yet she doesn't get tired. . . .

Supervisors who are professionally mature recognize and respect the strengths of their staff members. They are willing to share their authority, demonstrating a trust in their supervisees. They encourage their staff members to share their knowledge and skill with each other, recognizing that their diverse strengths provide mutual support for all and bring a richness to the program. Sharing authority is not intimidating to the mature supervisor.

Unlike beginning supervisors, who may not be aware of the problems around them, or moderately experienced supervisors, who acknowledge problems but are unsure of how to deal with them, experienced supervisors recognize and comprehend the depth and range of existing problems. They understand how much needs to be done and see problem solving as an ongoing task. Supervisors in this phase are less frustrated because they understand that, even if certain goals cannot be achieved, at least they can be addressed.

Seasoned supervisors tend to be less emotionally burdened by the problems they encounter. They have gained greater perspective and have acquired skill in managing time, coordinating and keeping track of tasks, motivating staff members to change, and building morale within a program. They are still concerned with resolving interpersonal issues among staff members, and they still need the emotional support of others, but they are no longer as overwhelmed by the overload of demands placed upon them. They don't feel as helpless or as powerless as colleagues who are in the earlier phases.

Maturing supervisors tend to be more concerned with ideas, with groups, with relationships, and with broad issues. They possess a well-defined philosophical frame of reference and a commitment to standards of education for children. They are perceptive, sensitive, discreet, and tuned in to staff members. They seize opportunities for leadership:

> What I do is observe a lot, see a lot, and then confront a lot. From time to time, I remember calling a meeting of last year's staff to redefine our ideas for curriculum before we started again this year.
>
> I thought that was the best way of saying, "Look, gang! This is the way I would like it to be here," without telling any one person that . . . and they had a lot of opportunity to discuss this. I don't really have to have it my way. There is room enough for other people's ideas. Every once in a while, I feel as though I have to pull things in and pull things together. I think this school has style. I like us all to be sure we know what it is that we are doing and why we are doing it. These are very important times when we talk about children and our ideas about curriculum.

Like their less experienced colleagues, seasoned supervisors enjoy a "pat on the back for a job well done." The rewards they receive from the job now tend to be other-person, program, and professionally oriented rather than centered around self. They receive stimulation from work in their own centers and in the educational community at large, interacting with other professionals through local and national professional organizations, boards, and committees. They achieve satisfaction from the gradual resolution of difficult problems, from developing and improving their programs, and from new responsibilities. Supporting staff members as they strive to accomplish their goals provides maturing supervisors with additional satisfaction.

Supervisors at this stage are wise and skilled. They view themselves as individuals who are still growing, still learning, recognizing the need for renewal, reeducation, and challenge. They believe they can play a vital role in making this a better world for children and families.

CONCLUSION

Supervisors undergo a process of growth and development over time. They face similar problems and frustrations in each phase, but their ability to handle problems changes as they move toward maturity (refer to Table 6.1).

Their growth during the beginning, extending, and maturing phases is ongoing but frequently uneven. Supervisors move back and forth from one phase to another during their careers, and even mature, educated, and talented supervisors may demonstrate some characteristics of beginners when they work in new roles, in unfamiliar settings, or with people they don't know. Some supervisors may never move beyond the first or second phase.

EXERCISES

1. Which phase would you place yourself in and why?
2. Describe the ways in which your present phase of supervisory development affects your job effectiveness.
3. What kinds of support do supervisors in each phase need?
4. Keep a journal; record your thoughts about your supervision.

7 Supervisee Development

In interviews about their work, caregivers of different ages, in contrasting roles, and at various stages of development described key areas for professional growth, which resemble in some ways those that supervisors go through as they become more familiar and expert in their jobs. The competencies we describe below do not represent the full range of skills and abilities needed to work effectively in early childhood programs, but they can serve as guides for informal mutual assessment of staff members and as a basis for planning for continued improvement.

LEARNING TO COMMUNICATE EFFECTIVELY

In order to teach and care for young children, staff members learn to communicate with a variety of people for different purposes as part of their daily experience. As team members responsible for a group of children, teachers learn to plan together, to share duties, and to cooperate with each other to support the children they serve. They participate in the supervisory process with head teachers and/or directors. They interact with outside consultants such as doctors, social workers, psychologists, and community workers who provide support to children and their families. Sometimes, caregivers become board members and teacher trainers, roles that require good listening and effective speaking skills. And one of their most important and difficult jobs is working with parents, helping them to increase their understanding of young children.

Being an effective communicator is critically important to forming relationships with colleagues. Working productively with other staff members requires mutual exchange, which can only take place in an atmosphere of openness and respect, where people are honest with each other. The caregivers we interviewed who appeared to be happiest and most successful in their roles were those who had become effective communicators.

BECOMING A SELF-CONFIDENT TEACHER

Some teachers enter the profession with little experience or knowledge of the field of early childhood education. In fact, quite a few of those we interviewed became involved in child care because their own child or younger sibling was enrolled in day care or Head Start. They often began their careers as volunteers, some eventually returning to school to complete requirements for a high school diploma. For those who dropped out of high school to marry and have children, the position of aide or assistant teacher may have been their first job as a professional, although they gradually moved up the ranks to become a teacher or head teacher.

Teaching young children, which requires an understanding of child development and an ability to communicate with other professionals, can be threatening to persons with previously unsuccessful experience in school settings or to those who are holding a regular job for the first time. Beginners require time to become comfortable in the work setting. It is common for them to feel timid when leading children or when talking to strangers, as this caregiver describes:

> When I first came here, I was very shy as far as talking to parents. I was very shy at starting out like leading songs in front of a big group, sitting on floors, and really getting to play with the kids. Now, I don't think anything about going up to a parent and saying, "You know, your kid had a great day!" or "You know, he didn't have such a good day." I don't feel funny about leading songs in a great big group; I don't feel funny about getting down on the floor and pretending to be an animal with the kids . . . where, at first, I was a little shy about it.

As they become more confident, caregivers tend to be less dependent on supervisors. They no longer have to be told what to do and how to do it. In supervisory roles themselves, they make their own judgments about whether to step in if a teacher is having a difficult time with a child. They act without needing a director's assessment and opinion. A teacher shares her thoughts about responsibility:

> When you're a trainee, you have someone who is, more or less, directing you and telling you what to do. You don't have as much responsibility as you do as a teacher. As a trainee, all you have to say is, "Well, I have a problem with this. Will you help me? I'm not sure how to do this!" and someone will say, "Well, do it this way." You have a teacher to kind of fall back on. But when you're the teacher, you are the one who's doing the supervising and who has the responsibility for the children in the classroom. The health and safety of the children is all your responsibility. Everything falls back on you.

Training and staff development can have an exciting effect on the self-confidence of those caregivers who began at different developmental levels. One teacher describes the profound changes that participation in an associate's degree program had in her confidence:

I think, too, that my education had a lot to do with making me feel more confident and being able to relate to people on different levels of a profession. This past year, I had a meeting at Children's Hospital about a child I had in my room who had a special problem. I had to meet with the social service director, the educational director, two doctors, a psychologist, and a dietician. They wanted to hear my opinion. "What!" I thought. Six or seven years ago, I probably would have died, "Oh, my God!" But I knew what I was talking about. I felt comfortable because I knew what I was talking about.

UNDERSTANDING CHILDREN

Working with children on a daily basis over time advances a caregiver's knowledge and understanding of child development. Even though many supervisees are parents before they become early childhood professionals, they often lack such basic information about child growth and development as when most children should be speaking or walking or using alternative feet to climb stairs. As a result of their experience in early childhood programs, two workers help us to realize the metamorphosis that some caregivers undergo:

> I now look at children differently. I looked at them before as more of a parent than as a teacher because I am a parent. I would be saying, "Oh, you don't want to do that because you're going to get yourself all dirty." Whereas now, I let them go ahead and do it. We can always take their clothes off and wash them. I was looking at children from a parent's eye rather than with a teacher's eye.

> All I can think of is there was a time in my life when I know I didn't know that a baby doesn't go to sleep when they're tired. You know, my conception was that they just fell asleep. The fact that you have to put them to bed was pretty obvious, I guess, but I didn't have basic knowledge of how infants should be treated.

Caregivers report that their understanding of young children deepens as they learn to observe children and be more in tune with their needs. As beginners they might have overlooked the clumsy, withdrawn, or abused child, but as experienced teachers with new understanding, they are more sensitive and can note and address important problems. Caring for children who may be unloved, undernourished, culturally different, bilingual, or delayed in their language development increases a child care worker's ability to look at the whole child and to recognize the interconnectedness of a child's emotional, social, cognitive, and physical development.

UNDERSTANDING ONESELF

The very nature of work with young children — observing children, interacting with parents and other professionals, teaching adults and children, and participating in in-service education activities — challenges staff members to change their own attitudes and behaviors and to reflect about their own growth and development. As one infant caregiver puts it:

> I look at infants and I am constantly learning about myself; just how people become and how they are. It all starts when you're born and then, I think about how I was treated in a certain way . . . and how I turned out the way I did. You see how infants are so honest and uninhibited and unable to cover up anything about themselves. I mean, it's all written on their faces. You know, the older you get, the more and more you learn how to protect yourself, to cover up. . . .

Some supervisees completely change their own attitudes toward learning. They come to view themselves as learners, embracing and valuing education. This new perception of self can represent a transformation from an earlier time characterized by school failure or drop-out. A caregiver's motivation to enroll in workshops and courses, some leading to a GED (General Educational Development) certificate and even a college degree, is an indication of this new outlook. Involvement in such activities, at a stage in life when one has obligations as spouse and parent, can create family disruptions, stress, and conflict. But staff members often see these opportunities to achieve new meaning in life, to enhance their self-concept and self-respect, as outweighing the inconveniences and sacrifices they might endure.

Strength derived from supervisory support can help supervisees to understand themselves better as they cope with crises confronting the children with whom they work. An assistant teacher talks about contending with child abuse:

> When I first came here, I just did not want to talk about or even think about child abuse. I mean I could not accept it. I didn't want to deal with it. I felt that there was just no way that I could deal with it myself. . . . As time went on, we had a lot of workshops, a protective service course, and I really got to understand where child abuse might begin, things to look for, and ways of working with children and families. I had a lot of support.

As they gain more experience on the job, supervisees are better able to deal with the developmental tasks that are part of the life cycle. Supervising others, as well as having support from a supervisor, provides caregivers with experience and nurturance that, as one worker describes it, stimulates them to "think about how I would like to be, where I am, and what I need to do to improve. It also makes me think about what's going on with me that I'm not performing the way I'd like to. . . . "

RESPECTING OTHERS

Developing a deeper understanding of oneself also promotes greater understanding and respect for others. Working with children, families, and professionals enables caregivers to meet people they might ordinarily not have had the opportunity to know.

For those who come from backgrounds where relations outside the immediate neighborhood or community are limited or who have associated mainly with white, middle-class individuals, exposure to people from other cultures and who speak other languages can be especially meaningful, as this co-teacher points out:

> I've learned to respect other people's ways. We have a lot of Hispanic people here. I was brought up in another part of town where there were not many Hispanics, so I did not understand the culture. By working here, I understand. I have really broadened my thinking about other people's cultures: they might be different, but they're not strange, they are okay. I've learned about all different types of holidays because we are a multicultural school. We celebrate many holidays, including Three Kings Day, a black holiday which I had never heard of. I've learned a lot of things about other people's cultures. You can respect them.

Supervisees learning to appreciate the cultural and ethnic differences of others will often need help and training. Staff development experiences that provide information and allow discussion of stereotypes and feelings can be of great value in helping staff gain this understanding.

Staff members show that they value other human beings in their daily work by the empathic and understanding ways that they communicate with parents, by the approaches they take to resolve differences with colleagues or supervisors, and by helping peers in times of need.

DERIVING SATISFACTION AND STIMULATION FROM PROFESSIONAL GROWTH

Like supervisors, staff members with less experience and limited expectations about their roles tend to be satisfied with rewards that are personal and immediate. Foster grandparents or high school volunteers, for example, are likely to receive adequate gratification from a child's spontaneous hug or kiss. They derive satisfaction from loving and taking care of children and from getting to know their families. Displays of affection brighten any caregiver's day of course, but as an individual grows and develops professionally, other rewards come into play.

More experienced caregivers, for example, gain satisfaction from observing children for diagnosis of problems or to obtain greater understanding of their lives. More abstract rewards for experienced caregivers are the challenges of the job; the planning, development, and implementation of new programs; working as a team with colleagues; and participating in professional groups and associations.

One of the most remarkable aspects of the growth process of teachers is the way in which their roles change over time when they are fortunate enough to work in nurturing environments. Centers that lack organization and flexibility, where supervisors ignore staff development in favor of administrative duties, are environments that foster burnout, rather than excitement, creativity, and growth. In programs where individuals are valued, it is not uncommon for supervisees to begin their careers as volunteer workers or floating substitutes and take on new roles with major obligations as they gain experience. They may broaden their roles by training and supervising other adults, by greater involvement with families and communities, and by assuming such administrative duties as recruiting aides, helping with supplies, formulating agendas for team meetings, planning menus and preparing food, organizing social functions, and doing general paperwork. In centers where caregiver interests are considered, staff members create new roles and responsibilities for themselves based on their personal interests, which may vary from playground or classroom design to child advocacy work.

Children, of course, always come first, but professional growth opportunities for staff increase their competence and enable and motivate them to explore new dimensions of their jobs. Supervisees who feel challenged, stimulated, and enriched by their daily work may be willing to remain in their jobs over longer periods of time, despite the low pay and occasional frustration.

FORMULATING A PHILOSOPHY OF LEARNING

With experience, teachers tend to develop strong points of view about how children learn best. Early years in the education profession are usually characterized by tentativeness and ambivalence regarding teaching the right or the best way. Over time, these feelings of uncertainty are usually replaced with well-developed views of what comprises good education and child care.

As beginners, staff members are concerned with survival: learning new routines, meeting supervisor's expectations, and coping with hard to manage children. Everyday challenges prevent the neophyte from thinking about deeper issues pertaining to educational philosophy. Lack of experience and education, combined in some cases with little knowledge or expectation about their roles, can also slow the pace of development of a set of values and beliefs about what is best for young children. With experience and training, however, supervisees begin to formulate their views of how things should be done. Disagreements with supervisors or conflicting opinions with colleagues about how certain children should be handled or how a play area should be designed can be viewed as a positive signal of professional maturation. This comment made by a day care provider reflects the type of growth we are describing:

> Three years ago, I had much less confidence in how I felt about my work. You know, I was the one who would watch everybody else and often I worked with teachers whom I disagreed with. I wasn't sure if I was right. I knew that I didn't agree with them, but I had no idea if my ideas were better. I just knew they were mine. Now, I can definitely walk into a situation and observe and see if the program is good or not.

VALUING GOOD SUPERVISION

Staff members also grow and change in their expectations about the type of supervision they want to receive. Expectations differ depending upon supervisees' age and experience, the positions they hold, whether they are full or part-time, and whether they are volunteers or part of the regular staff. The standards that supervisors set for them also affect their views of the supervisory process.

Part-time volunteers, for example, who help out several mornings a week with routine tasks and who provide various children with individual attention, expect little from a supervisor. They do not expect to be trained, observed, or evaluated. They often view themselves as ancillary help who are not an important part of the program. They may not anticipate that their roles will expand or change in any way. Supervisors who do not perceive volunteers to be an integral part of a center's operation may provide them with some initial direction and then leave them alone unless they create problems. This is hardly a desirable state of affairs.

The picture is quite different for regular, full-time, paid staff, particularly those who are experienced and who have gained confidence as professionals in the field. They have high expectations for supervisors and can be critical when adequate supervision is not provided. Our interviews with caregivers reveal that they hold definite opinions about the qualities they want their supervisors to have.

Honesty is one quality that was mentioned repeatedly. A caregiver who works with infants and toddlers sums up her feelings about supervisors this way:

> First of all, a supervisor should be someone who can be honest. Someone who can tell you what they think. Someone who can criticize you and praise you productively in ways that you can learn and understand and get whatever reinforcement you're supposed to get from them. Somebody who is sensitive to your needs and to the job. Somebody who believes in what you're doing, not somebody who thinks that babies would be better left at home with their parents. Somebody who knows what they're doing and knows the field. . . .

Many supervisees emphasized the value of a supervisor willing to spend time with them, to listen to their thoughts, feelings, and concerns. They also wanted to be supervised by someone knowledgeable in the field. As one teacher noted:

> Somebody who can really talk about things, you know, very personal things about families, kids, and yourself. Somebody who can really, really see before a problem hits and be able to talk about it. Someone who can say, "Is something wrong?" To be able to come out and ask you this. Somebody who really has a lot of training; who can really understand because we are dealing with a lot of people who have very little in common. Supervisors need to understand how to help out families and how to help us out.

Supervisees appreciate receiving criticism that is direct and constructive. As one caregiver put it, "To give constructive criticism that would help you, not make you kind of back down. Also, to let you be creative. To make you feel that your creative ideas flow a little, too! And to be there when you need help." She also commented on the importance of feedback: "Giving feedback and following through on actual goals and work responsibilities rather than being palsy walsy; being practical and to the point."

Staff members believe, too, that they should be able to give their supervisors constructive criticism. As one caregiver stated: "Just because their title is supervisor doesn't mean they're perfect. They shouldn't act defensive when they are criticized when it's good criticism."

Supervisees want supervisors who seek their input when making important decisions, who engage them in group problem-solving activities, and who are good role models. Such ideal supervisory qualities are not easily found in one person. A major point, however, is that staff members, especially those in advanced stages of their professional development, have high expectations for supervisors.

SEEING THE BIG PICTURE

Supervisees often begin their careers with a limited understanding of themselves, of the children and adults with whom they come in daily contact, and of the programs in which they are employed. Like supervisors, they progress through stages of concern from self, to task and others, to impact. Experience and maturity enable supervisees to see themselves and their work not only within the context of their programs and communities but within society at large.

With maturity, they gain understanding of the complexity of the problems facing children and families; of their social, political, and economic contexts; and of the relatedness of people and programs and the dynamic forces affecting them. This new awareness enables caregivers to be more realistic about their work and to set priorities for the future. By knowing who they are and what they want to do, they gain a sense of comfort and power.

CONCLUSION

We hope the growth shown by caregivers in our interviews offers encouragement to supervisors. Staff progress points to the value of education and supervisory support. Professional maturation does not come about automatically, quickly, or in a natural progression, but all staff members have the capacity to improve. In parts III and IV, we will describe the specific strategies supervisors can use to help staff reach their potential.

EXERCISE

Use the instrument in Figure 7.1 for an informal assessment of staff members in your program who are at different points in their development.

FIGURE 7.1   *Growth Areas of Staff*

Directions: For each area of development, consider the criteria listed, and circle the number on the continuum that best describes the staff member at this time. Have your staff member complete this inventory as well. Get together to share perceptions.

Name of Staff Member _____ Age _____

Number of years in program/school _____ Sex _____

Number of years in the profession _____

Education/Training _____

(continued)

FIGURE 7.1   *(Continued)*

A. _____ LEARNING TO COMMUNICATE EFFECTIVELY _____
1   2   3   4   5
Ineffective   Effective

   1. Communicates effectively with colleagues
   2. Communicates effectively with professionals outside the program
       who interface with it (doctors, social workers, consultants, and
       so forth)
   3. Communicates effectively with parents
   4. Communicates effectively with children
   5. Communicates effectively with supervisors

B. _____ BECOMING A SELF-CONFIDENT TEACHER _____
1   2   3   4   5
Insecure   Secure

   1. Feels comfortable when working with children
   2. Talks to parents readily
   3. Believes in own ability to care for children
   4. Participates in staff-meeting discussions
   5. Is willing to deal with conflict
   6. Easily interacts with other professionals
   7. Displays independence/takes initiative
   8. Uses own judgment
   9. Can cope with change

C. _____ UNDERSTANDING CHILDREN _____
1   2   3   4   5
Limited   Extensive

   1. Has realistic expectations for children
   2. Recognizes children's various stages of development
   3. Is sensitive to children's individual needs
   4. Has good observation skills
   5. Recognizes the interconnectedness of social, cognitive,
       emotional, and physical development
   6. Understands that many factors affect a child's growth and
       development

D. _____ UNDERSTANDING ONESELF _____
1   2   3   4   5
Limited   Extensive

   1. Is reflective and analytical of self
   2. Views oneself as a learner
   3. Can confront self and grapple with personal issues
   4. Can cope with children's crises
   5. Has self-respect and sees self as important part of program

E. _____ RESPECTING OTHERS _____
1   2   3   4   5
Low level   High level

   1. Respects individuals (children, parents, colleagues) who are
       culturally and linguistically different
   2. Supports colleagues when needed
   3. Respects opinions and feelings of others

FIGURE 7.1 *(Continued)*

F. DERIVING SATISFACTION AND STIMULATION FROM PROFESSIONAL GROWTH

1	2	3	4	5
Low level				High level

1. Finds challenge of job rewarding
2. Participates in professional groups and associations
3. Enjoys team work with colleagues
4. Likes to plan and implement new programs
5. Likes to take on new and different roles and responsibilities
6. Is more extensively involved with families and community

G. FORMULATING A PHILOSOPHY OF LEARNING

1	2	3	4	5
Undefined				Well-developed

1. Can disagree with supervisor and colleagues
2. Has strongly held and well-developed educational views

H. VALUING GOOD SUPERVISION

1	2	3	4	5
Low				High

1. Can be critical of supervision if adequate supervision is not provided
2. Has firm opinions about qualities a supervisor should have
3. Has high expectations about supervision and program

I. SEEING THE BIG PICTURE

1	2	3	4	5
Limited				Broad

1. Sees self and work in context of program and community
2. Is realistic about work, sets priorities
3. Sees children, families, community, and programs as interdependent and interrelated

8 The Developmental Dynamic at Work: A Case Study in Supervision

BACKGROUND

The Supervisor

Florence is a graduate of a liberal arts college where she majored in politics and government. After graduation, she spent a year as a trainee in a large department store chain but left since she did not like the work. She is single, twenty-nine years old, and lives on the outskirts of a major city on the East Coast. Florence received her master's degree in Early Childhood Education after teaching in a Head Start program for three years. For the past three years, she has been the director of a medium-sized day care center.

As a third-year supervisor, Florence feels pretty comfortable in her role. She has a strong theoretical base in child development. The experience she had working in Head Start has been enormously helpful to her. Florence is reasonably confident in her ability as director of this program but occasionally gets thrown off guard when conflicts arise.

The Supervisee

Mrs. Warren is a sixty-six-year-old widow who lives with her daughter and two grandchildren. She belongs to a senior citizen's organization which has provided her with part-time employment in this children's center. The job enables Mrs. Warren to earn spending money and to feel that she is doing constructive activity in retirement. She has been on the job for three months. She is in excellent health, dependable, and always at work early.

92

Mrs. Warren enjoys her work, especially the unqualified love and affection she receives from most of the children.

The Context

Located in a small city, the East Side Child Development Center is a nonprofit center funded through the state department of social services. Most of the children are from low-income families, and about 15 percent are "protective" children, placed in the center because of abuse or neglect. The center has two groups of three-year-olds, two of fours, and a kindergarten. Each classroom has a teacher and an aide, and at least one senior citizen aide from a state-funded program. There are also several practicum students from the local community college. Florence has the help of a Head Teacher who is released half time to work on curriculum and staff development.

Florence has strived to establish a collaborative atmosphere in her program where people work together. She places great trust and confidence in her staff members, but she does find it difficult to confront them about problems, as she does not want to be disrespectful toward them or tarnish the humanistic climate she has worked so hard to establish.

The Problem

Mrs. Warren is great with kids, except in areas of discipline. When she does take disciplinary action, she often shouts and sometimes overdoes the punishment. For example, when a little boy was flipping a plant around on a wire hanger, she went across the room and shouted loudly at him to stop and made him sit in a corner. After ten minutes, the Head Teacher told the child to return to his play. Mrs. Warren felt that her authority had been undermined. The one time that Florence raised the issue of disciplining children with Mrs. Warren, Florence was flabbergasted when Mrs. Warren admonished her for letting the children get away with certain things.

ASSESSING THE SUPERVISEE

At this point in her life, Mrs. Warren has developed strongly held views of child rearing. Whether she is open to learning and to modifying her ideas and values is a question Florence plans to explore. Having only been in this position for three months, however, there is much that Mrs. Warren could learn about group care for young children.

Mrs. Warren does not see herself as an important part of the center. She keeps pretty much to herself. She carries out assigned duties, as a beginner, but she does not have a total picture of the operation and mission of the program.

Florence has noted Mrs. Warren's enjoyment of her work and that she is effective most of the time; on the other hand, her apparent lack of flexibility is an area of concern to Florence.

Based on observations over time, Florence views Mrs. Warren as being at the lower end of the continuum in terms of level of abstract thinking and in the middle to upper range in terms of commitment to her job, suggesting that a collaborative approach would be the most productive one to take with her. Taking this information into account with what she knows about Mrs. Warren's status as a beginner in the program, and what she has summarized about her strengths and her needs and goals during retirement, Florence has determined that her initial supervisory approach will be both directive and collaborative.

ASSESSING THE SUPERVISOR

Two years ago, Florence probably would have ignored this problem. Although she is anxious about her upcoming conference with Mrs. Warren, she is determined to go through with it, since she knows she cannot permit staff members to use such punitive measures with children.

Although she is certain she will feel uncomfortable in being directive with a proud woman who is old enough to be her mother, Florence has been gaining confidence in herself as a supervisor. She knows which behaviors are developmentally appropriate for children, and she has very clear ideas about the nature of the environment she wants to create for them. Because of her graduate work and previous teaching experience, Florence is aware of resources she can use to train her staff, and she has definite ideas as to what the content of the training sessions should be and how to conduct them. Florence is determined to make her program a model one and she devotes a great deal of time and energy to her work.

THE SUPERVISORY PLAN

1. Florence has decided to go out of her way to make Mrs. Warren feel like a special person and to recognize the good work she has been doing.
2. Florence has worked out a structured daily schedule for Mrs. Warren that emphasizes routines and clarifies her role in working with five-year-olds.
3. Florence plans an immediate conference with Mrs. Warren to deal with

the issue of shouting at children. She expects to be very directive in dealing with this issue.

4. Florence plans to take time to observe Mrs. Warren in the classroom.
5. Florence plans to hold individual conferences with Mrs. Warren on a
   regular basis. Recognizing that Mrs. Warren is a mature adult who has a
   high degree of self-respect and self-esteem, Florence believes that through
   these conferences, Mrs. Warren will feel respected, even though she and
   Florence may disagree on when and how children should be reprimanded.

   During these conferences, Florence hopes to learn more about Mrs.
   Warren's previous work and family experiences. She also plans to discuss
   the issue of disciplining children by eliciting from Mrs. Warren descriptions of her past experiences in raising children and connecting those to
   the conditions, needs, and behaviors of children in the program.

   By providing feedback to her from observations and by raising questions to clarify situations, Florence expects Mrs. Warren to begin to reflect
   on her behavior in disciplining children.

6. Florence plans to provide monthly training sessions for Mrs. Warren and
   the other two senior assistants to deal with child care techniques and to
   provide them with opportunities to share their thoughts with each other
   and with Florence. These sessions will include demonstrating and role-
   playing behaviors, which will illustrate how to respond to children when
   they misbehave. Child growth and development issues will be discussed.
   In this way, Mrs. Warren will be able to test new behavior in safe situations and test her thinking with peers.

7. Florence plans to invite Mrs. Warren to staff meetings with the full-time
   staff so that she will feel part of the program and learn from other staff.

CONCLUSION

In formulating her supervisory strategy, Florence has considered Mrs. Warren's stage of professional and personal development and the specific issue
at hand—how and when to discipline children in light of their own growth
and development. Florence has also made some judgments about Mrs. Warren's commitment to the job and her ability to analyze problems and generate solutions to them.

Florence and Mrs. Warren are at different points in their lives and careers.
The knowledge, experience, competencies, and goals that each has will, of
course, affect the outcome of this case. By taking into consideration personal,
professional, and contextual factors relating to Mrs. Warren and to this particular problem, Florence has been able to develop a plan that is both
realistic and growth-oriented. She has mapped out a variety of avenues for

supervision, so that she can confront the problem while also providing support. She will then be able to use a collaborative style, perhaps move eventually toward an indirect mode, while maintaining the humanistic climate that she values.

EXERCISES

1. What aspects of the "developmental dynamic" described in chapter 4 are illustrated in this situation?
2. Develop your own case study based on a problem that you have encountered with a staff member. Use the information from the chapters in this section to make a plan for assisting your supervisee.

Part III

A FRAMEWORK
FOR SUPERVISION

9 The Five Stages of Clinical Supervision

Developed in the 1960s at Harvard University by Morris Cogan, clinical supervision focuses on the improvement of teachers' performance through direct interaction of supervisors and teachers in natural settings. We think of clinical supervision as a means of improving the performance of staff members who provide care and education to young children.

Clinical supervision is carried out through a series of stages that are repeated to form an ongoing cycle. The five stages are pre-observation conference, observation, analysis and strategy, supervision conference, and post-conference analysis.[1] The behavioral content of these stages varies depending on the purpose that the supervisor and/or supervisee have established.

Stage 1: Pre-Observation Conference

During pre-observation conferences, supervisors have an opportunity to begin to establish positive working relationships with supervisees. Mutual trust and respect will continue to develop throughout each stage of the supervisory cycle.

The initial conference with a staff member is a good time to diffuse anxiety and to explain the cycle of clinical supervision and the supervisee's role in this new relationship. Pre-observation conferences, in general, offer opportunities to discuss serious concerns, to review the purposes and procedures of an upcoming lesson with children, to make plans for an observation, to agree on its focus, and to establish a time for the post-observation conference.

Stage 2: Observation

Supervisors may observe teachers and/or children at work during formal lessons or informal periods. The specific purpose of the observation is usually agreed upon during the pre-observation conference; it shapes the type of observation and the tools for observing that the supervisor uses. The observation is the link between the plans made during Stage 1 and actual practice. It affords supervisors an opportunity to see the situation where the supervisee's questions and concerns originated and to determine whether or not answers can be found.[2]

Stage 3: Analysis and Strategy

Although it is tempting to provide immediate feedback at the conclusion of an observation, and although many eager teachers prefer to talk with their supervisors right away, taking the time to analyze an observation and to think about the conference that is to follow increases the success and power of the clinical supervisory cycle. During the analysis and planning stage, supervisors "reconstruct" observed events, note the context in which they occurred, identify patterns of behavior and critical incidents that developed. Observed events are analyzed in terms of the concerns raised during the pre-observation conference, and supervisors plan strategies to be used during the post-observation conference.

Stage 4: Supervision Conference

Cogan states that "the conference is a shared exploration: a search for the meaning of instruction, for choices among alternative diagnoses, and alternative strategies for improvement."[3] The conference is a time for the supervisor to provide feedback to the teacher about the observation; for supervisor and supervisee to formulate strategies jointly for dealing with problems; to raise issues of concern; to offer specific help if appropriate; to explore the rewarding and satisfying aspects of a staff member's performance; and to plan for the next observation. Each conference varies in purpose, content, and in the nature of supervisor-supervisee interaction, depending upon the individuals and circumstances involved.

Stage 5: Post-Conference Analysis

The post-conference analysis is a means of self-improvement for the supervisor. It is the time when the supervisor assesses the nature of communication during the conference, the effectiveness of the strategies used, the role of the teacher during the conference, and the extent to which progress was made on the issues that were discussed.

CONCLUSION

Clinical supervision offers early childhood supervisors a structure for working with their staff members by conferring, observing, and evaluating. It is a planned and systematic procedure for fostering the development of caregivers. The clinical framework allows supervisors to plan various ways to support individuals who are undertaking different personal and professional tasks. For a more detailed description of clinical supervision, we suggest that you read the texts cited in the notes for this chapter.

In the three chapters that follow we will discuss specific aspects of clinical supervision in more detail. In chapter 10 we describe the purposes of the supervisory conference, communication skills that supervisors need in order to conduct successful conferences, and the key ingredients to any supervisory conference. The material in this chapter is directly connected to Stages 1 and 3 of clinical supervision. In chapter 11, we describe approaches to observing staff and give specific suggestions for constructing observation instruments. And finally, we discuss issues, methods, and instruments associated with evaluating staff in chapter 12. We view evaluation as part of supervision. As diagnosis, evaluation takes place throughout the cycle of clinical supervision, but it occurs at the end of defined periods as well.

10 The Supervisory Conference

The conference is the heart of clinical supervision. It enables supervisors and supervisees to come together to jointly solve the significant problems of caregiving and teaching. Teacher and supervisor have not always shown enthusiasm for the supervisory conference, however. Some have viewed it as an arena where "strategic gamesmanship" is carried out and where both parties, with strong defenses, try to leave unharmed.[1] Noreen Garman has likened the conference to a religious confessional where

> Supervisor officiates
> Teacher confesses his/her transgressions
> Supervisor suggests ways to recant
> Supervisor assists in penance
> Teacher makes act of contrition
> Supervisor gives absolution
> Both go away feeling better.[2]

The supervisory conference need not be a superficial ritual or a ceremonial play without meaning. It should be a time for dynamic interchange and sharing authentic thoughts, ideas, and reflections about behavioral change.

WHY CONFERENCE?

In addition to ensuring ongoing and systematic communication between supervisor and supervisee, there are many reasons for holding supervisory conferences:

1. To discuss, interpret, and evaluate issues pertaining to teaching/caregiving, curriculum, and learning environments
2. To develop long- and short-range plans with staff members
3. To discuss specific children and/or families

4. To enable supervisors and supervisees to raise concerns and to resolve problems
5. To transmit basic information about program policies and procedures
6. To teach staff members specific skills
7. To show interest in teachers' work
8. To discipline staff members
9. To evaluate staff members formally
10. To enable the supervisor to obtain advice and information

Regardless of the reason for meeting with teachers, a goal of the conference is to help staff members think about, think through, analyze, and make decisions about their work with young children. Through the conference dialogue, which includes asking questions and offering information, supervisors can assist teachers in the decision-making processes involved in planning for teaching, evaluating, and applying what they learned to future situations.[3]

Although a supervisor may have informal conversations with a supervisee during the course of a day, these meetings are not good substitutes for scheduled conferences where issues can be explored in depth and in thoughtful ways. When supervisors make a commitment to confer with staff members on a regular basis, caregivers believe that supervisors value them and their work.

THE CONTEXT

The success of the supervisory conference is largely determined by the nature of the existing relationship between supervisor and supervisee and by the ethos in which they are working. The climate, context, and mood of a conference are affected by previous contacts that the two individuals have had with each other, and by the assumptions, beliefs, expectations, and perceptions that they have about themselves, each other, and each other's roles. The conference is not an egalitarian situation, for one of the individuals has more power, influence, authority, or wisdom.[4]

Power and Control

Arthur Blumberg believes that the supervisor sets the tone for the interaction that takes place during the conference: "Because the supervisor is in control, represents the larger system, and may have an evaluative role, his behavior sends off social and emotional messages that set the climate and to which the teacher pays attention."[5] Pickhardt suggests that supervisors think about helping as a power. What kind of powers do early childhood supervisors have?[6]

They possess knowledge and expertise about young children and strategies for facilitating their cognitive, social, and emotional development. These can be shared to strengthen a caregiver's capacity to cope with problems of teaching and caring. They have access to material resources and a network of human resources that can make the role of caregiver an easier one to carry out. They have control of the ways in which a caregiver spends time within a program, which permits them to limit the demands placed on a staff member. They can directly influence how peers and those in higher positions think about particular staff members. Most importantly, they can use their power to encourage supervisees to become more independent.

Supervisees also have power. They have expertise — in some cases more than their supervisors. They have contractual agreements, especially in public school settings, that guarantee them certain rights and privileges and that protect them from abuse. They can influence the opinions and attitudes of their peers. And they have the power to refuse help.

> Helping, in fact, is usually a negotiated settlement between help giver and help receiver, each side applying conditions and agreeing to compromise as they build a contract both can accept. In the helping relationship, supervisors are not the only party with power. The teacher has power — when the teacher refuses to cooperate, the supervisor is helpless to help.[7]

The conference is the structure that enables supervisor and supervisee to explore, to plan, and to negotiate around the full range of lower- and higher-order needs and concerns so that a caregiver's full potential can be realized. The intimacy of child care offers educators opportunities that are emotionally and socially satisfying, but helping staff members to develop their higher-order needs — their talents, ideas, and interests[8] — is a supervisory aim that can be deliberately addressed in the conference.

Either party can control the conference. The person doing most of the talking may be dominating and controlling the conference if he or she allows the listener few opportunities to ask questions or to make a point. On the other hand, supervisors who *consciously* refrain from talk to permit supervisees to express their thoughts and feelings are in control and are helping without dominating.

Establishing the conference agenda is another form of power. If all or most of the issues discussed are supervisor-initiated, then the supervisee may not have had an opportunity to set priorities and may not have thought about those issues previous to the meeting. Such "ceremonial" conferences lead to supervisees' feeling cut off from expressing immediate concerns and choosing instead to end the ritual as soon as possible.

The pace and timing of conference dialogue are other indicators of who is controlling the conference. One party or the other may rush through or abort discussion of a certain issue. Refusal by the supervisee, or the supervisor for that matter, to elaborate on a problem and to express true thoughts about it is a way of exercising power.

Developmental Levels

The stage of professional development of the staff member is another factor for the supervisor to consider in determining the nature of help to provide during a conference. Staff members who have difficulty analyzing problems and thinking of solutions may be assisted by supervisors who probe and ask clarifying questions that focus and gradually lead supervisees toward solutions. In other cases, supervisors can be enablers by holding back, listening to a teacher think through a problem, without raising questions or offering information. By informally assessing the developmental levels of staff members, supervisors can make better decisions about which strategies to use with which individuals.

Communication Skills

So much of the success of a conference depends upon the clarity of communication that takes place between supervisor and supervisee. Carl Rogers's characteristics of helpers who facilitate the growth of others have special relevance in terms of viewing communication within the context of helping. According to Rogers:

> The helping person is more likely to make the relationship a growth promoting one when he communicates a desire to understand the other person's meanings and feelings. This attitude of wanting to understand is expressed in a variety of ways. When he talks, the helping person is less inclined to give instruction and advice, thus creating a climate which fosters independence. He avoids criticism and withholds evaluative judgments of the other person's ideas, thoughts, feelings, and behavior. He listens more often than he talks and when he speaks he strives to understand what the other person is communicating in thoughts and feeling. The comments of the helping person are aimed at assisting the other individual to clarify his own meanings and attitudes. Such behavior on the part of the helping person communicates the all important desire to understand, which in turn breeds the trust and confidence which are so essential to growth and development.[9]

By conscious use of specific communication skills, supervisors can increase the possibility that they will attain shared meanings and understandings with supervisees. Listening, questioning, and offering information are three of these communication behaviors. Paying attention to non-verbal messages is also a consideration when conferring with staff.

NON-VERBAL COMMUNICATION

Charles Galloway has developed a set of well-known categories of non-verbal communication for use in analyzing teacher-pupil interaction.[10] These categories can also be useful in analyzing supervisor-teacher conferences. According to Galloway, non-verbal expressions of enthusiastic support, helping, and receptivity encourage communication, while non-verbal expressions of inattentiveness, unresponsiveness, and disapproval discourage communication.

Facial expressions that imply understanding and approval and those that exhibit patience, interest, and attention to a partner's talk encourage communication. So do actions that portray acceptance, attentiveness, greetings, and praise. Voice intonation or inflections that indicate pleasure, acceptance, and approval also facilitate communication. Much of what Galloway describes as behavior that encourages good communication is also behavior that is an expression of active listening.

ACTIVE LISTENING

Active, attentive listening is one of the most critical supervisory conference skills to facilitate open and effective communication without dominating.

Like teachers, supervisors often believe that they are not helping another unless they are telling, advising, and offering suggestions. In fact, in the fifty conferences Blumberg studied, supervisors spent almost half of the conference period talking and most of their talk was directive. They were four times more likely to tell than to ask questions.[11] The tendency of supervisors to talk a great deal during conferences can have the effect of making them feel good about themselves but can also cut off serious communication and, despite good intentions, can prevent helping.

Listening is a difficult skill and a complex act. It involves showing respect for the individual, being sensitive enough to discern various levels of meaning expressed by the individual, and being aware of assumptions that underlie the words being spoken.[12] The good listener works on several levels to understand both the person and the message.

SILENCE

Supervisors striving to be good listeners need not fear moments of silence. As Robert G. Johnson has written, in certain situations, silence is golden:

> *Silence almost never offends.* While almost anything someone says can be seen as offensive under some circumstances, silence is gloriously neutral. It calls for no rebuttals, defenses, or new evidence.

Silence is a verbal cathartic. Most people are unable to tolerate silence for long. If two people are in a room together and one is silent, the other will feel a compulsion to say something, if only to fill the silence. If you want someone to speak, keep quiet, and before many seconds have elapsed he will.

Silence is nonjudgmental. Most people are careful of what they say because they expect to be judged. When a subordinate tells you he hates his job and would rather be on welfare than work another day, and you respond with silence, he will be greatly relieved at your failure to make a judgment. If you aren't more careful with your silence, he may even wind up thinking you're a nice guy.[13]

ASKING QUESTIONS

Questioning is critical to accomplishing conference goals and in training supervisees to think through and analyze their behavior. Supervisors ask questions for different reasons, so the form of questions should change based on their purpose. For example, soliciting information from a supervisee usually requires *simple questions* to bring out facts or to clarify a problem so that both supervisor and supervisee have a common basis to build on for discussion:

- Can you tell me something about how you and your aide plan together?
- Why don't you describe your daily schedule so I have a clearer picture of how free play fits into the whole program?

Supervisors also ask questions to help teachers understand children's behavior, the causes of behavior, and the relationship of observed behaviors to previous behaviors. *Probing questions* invite the caregiver to think about the teaching act and to articulate reasons for behavior:

- Mario was throwing paper and hitting other children during cleanup. I've noticed that he has done this before. Do you have any thoughts as to why he tends to act out during these times?
- Tell me your strategy for working with Yolanda. She has improved so much. Why do you think she is responding?
- What would you like the children to gain from the lesson you plan to do on the calendar?

Questions that solicit consideration of *alternative decisions*, and *predictions* of what might happen with each alternative, help the caregiver make plans for future teaching:

- Can you think of some ways to change the arrangement of the dramatic play area that would encourage the children to put the clothes away when they are through?

- What do you think they're likely to do if there are cartons for the clothes versus having them on hangers?

Questions that *ask for opinions*, whereby supervisees evaluate something that has taken place; questions that encourage supervisees to *express their feelings* about a particular situation; and questions that ask supervisees to *clarify* by repeating a statement or by providing an example or illustration also contribute to clear communication:

- That was the first time that you used the "Wiggly Fingers" song with the children. In your opinion, was it effective? Why? Why not?
- The children really got into finger painting. You seemed a little overwhelmed. Did the mess bother you?
- When you say, "It's always so wild," are you saying that they are too excited about going out or that they aren't sure what they're supposed to do?

OFFERING PRAISE

Regular conferences, whether to discuss particular problems or not, are a perfect opportunity for the supervisor to offer praise. Praise needs to be authentic, however, before its true value as a positive reinforcer and climate builder can be realized. Most teachers understand themselves well enough to know when praise is deserved. They can easily distinguish between superficial "stroking" and sincere encouragement, appreciation, and praise.

Praise is more effective when it is specific, as that enables supervisees to know which behaviors supervisors are pleased about. Reinforcing staff with praise when they demonstrate desired behaviors encourages them as they struggle to develop skills or to overcome problems. Pointing out these behaviors and avoiding the use of "good" is a more effective way of praising:

- When the children were pushing each other and you quietly walked over and gently placed them in line, they quieted right down.

Supervisors are often preoccupied with staff members who have problems and sometimes overlook and take for granted those caregivers who meet their expectations. These individuals need support as much as the others. Offering special encouragement or recognition when a staff member believes that he or she has just overcome a hurdle or made a significant accomplishment can also have lasting benefits.

OFFERING INFORMATION

Supervisors frequently offer information to supervisees during conferences. As leaders with knowledge and experience, supervisors are expected to share their expertise with staff members at appropriate times.

One of the most difficult supervisory habits to overcome, however, is offering too much information too often. This tendency probably arises out of a supervisory perception of "information giving" as helping, coupled with a need and desire to help.

A different conception of helping is to hold back information in favor of listening or questioning. This is a valid means of providing the supervisee with "thinking space" to arrive at his or her own solutions to problems. The trick, of course, is to make the right decision about when to offer information and when not to, keeping in mind the goal of enabling staff to be effective in their work and to assume responsibility for their own improvement.

There are many instances when giving supervisees specific information is appropriate. Staff members may need new ideas and specific suggestions. They may want to be connected to human and material resources to provide for an enriched program. They might benefit from specific illustrations of individual or group behaviors as a way of understanding themselves or the children with whom they are working. But this information is best brought forth after they have had time to try to discover it for themselves and when they are ready to hear it.

Another consideration in offering information is how to disclose data. Supervisors often confer with supervisees after a classroom observation, during which they collected data about teacher and child behavior and/or the learning environment. Showing this information to the staff members in a non-evaluative manner can become a basis for mutual discussion. Supervisees then have an opportunity to select which issues to explore and to determine whether or not their behavior is congruent with their values and goals.

Listening, questioning, praising, and offering information are communication behaviors that need practice to become natural parts of the supervisory dialogue.

STRUCTURING THE CONFERENCE

Each type of conference has a different focus and purpose, which can alter its structure. A supervisor and supervisee might confer to resolve a particular problem, to plan an upcoming observation, to discuss one already completed, or simply to maintain good communication. A conference requested by a staff member to discuss serious concerns might be open-ended in nature, while a post-observation meeting might be formal and highly structured. There are, however, common elements to all conferences, regardless of the topic being discussed: preparing, climate building, purpose setting, guiding, closing, and analyzing.

Preparing for the Conference

Careful thought about an upcoming conference offers greater assurance that it will be productive and successful. The extent of preparation necessary varies depending on the purpose of the conference and the sensitivity and seriousness of topics being discussed.

Location is an important consideration. Finding a suitable and private place to talk is most desirable. This can be a problem for supervisors who work in more than one site or in a small or crowded center.

Arranging for a block of uninterrupted time, free from telephone calls and other disruptions that disturb the flow of communication, can also help both parties relax and think more clearly. Having adequate time and setting a time limit furnish individuals with guidelines for their talk and for bringing the meeting to a close.

In preparing for a conference, a supervisor can ask the following questions:

- What do I want to accomplish as a result of this meeting?
- Are there specific understandings to develop with the caregiver?
- If the conference is one of a series that has focused on a staff member's behavior in certain situations, what do I want that individual to know or to learn about his or her behavior?

Supervisors may also want to plan conference questions or statements ahead of time to use as needed, especially when anticipating difficult conferences concerning interpersonal or evaluative issues. If it is a post-observation conference, it is helpful to study the data collected at the time of the observation to refresh one's memory. If it is an evaluation conference, it may be useful to review notes kept over time and to examine the materials in the staff member's portfolio. Re-reading the program's evaluation policy statement, having at hand pertinent materials such as evaluation forms or the center's handbook, and thinking about how they might be used during the conference are also steps that can be taken to increase supervisory confidence, to add depth to, and to facilitate the meeting.

Supervisors often find it helpful to identify a conference agenda beforehand and to prioritize issues that should be discussed. Flexibility is important, however, since an agenda may have to be abandoned to deal with a supervisee's immediate concerns, or it may have to be limited to covering one or two main issues in depth, instead of superficially covering a range of issues, which can serve to raise the anxiety level of a supervisee.

Creating a Climate

The supervisor who is competent, helpful, and in control of the situation creates a positive conference climate. Actions that convey honesty and professionalism and that focus on performance contribute to the image of supervisor as a qualified and supportive individual.

Conferences can be threatening to staff members, since topics that are discussed often have to do with a supervisee's performance. If a delicate issue is to be raised, the supervisor might also be anxious about the meeting. Anxieties are lessened when the supervisor, as leader, takes the initiative to set a working tone for the meeting.

The physical arrangement of the conference space—the placement of furniture, noise level, ventilation, and so forth—adds to or takes away from the tone the supervisor wishes to achieve. A supervisor who sits behind a desk establishes a formal atmosphere, one in which the supervisee is clearly in a subordinate role to an authority figure. There may be times when a supervisor will need to reinforce and execute his or her authority through a formal setting, but in most cases supervisors are likely to prefer environments that help staff members feel at ease, raise concerns, and ask for suggestions and advice. An informal arrangement, which puts supervisor and supervisee face to face on the same level without artificial physical barriers, is much more conducive to these goals.

Friendly comments, a cup of coffee, or a humorous story can break the ice, diffuse anxiety in either individual, and lay the foundation for a productive meeting. On the other hand, if both parties are braced for a tense encounter, it may be best to get to the issue directly. The decision of when to address the key concern often has to be made on the spot.

Setting the Purpose

When the purpose of a conference is clear and agreed upon, there is no need for supervisor and supervisee to guess the reason for meeting. They can focus on the agenda much more quickly. Supervisors might wish to set aside a few minutes at the beginning of the session to clarify its purpose and to enable caregivers to suggest issues to be explored. Once an agenda is mutually agreed upon, items can be prioritized.

For example, the following issues might be discussed in a post-observation conference after a single classroom visit:

- Making clean-up go smoothly
- Settling the children into nap time
- Handling a disruptive child
- Extending children's thinking during free play

Although the overall conference purpose would be to analyze the afternoon period, each specific issue could become the central theme of one or several conferences. The caregiver may raise issues independently and decide that getting help in working with the disruptive child is most critical at this time. Concurring, the supervisor will encourage the staff member to share that concern. If the teacher failed to raise this important matter, the supervisor would need to do so.

Unexpected issues, which cannot be planned for, also arise during conferences. Artful supervisors learn when to pick up on a thought, when to screen it out, and when to pull back from and/or push ahead to another issue.

Guiding the Conference

The body of the conference is when the issues selected are elaborated upon, explored, and discussed. During this phase, the conferees describe the behavior of teacher and children, share and analyze data from an observation, raise problems, note progress, and exchange basic information. The supervisor has an opportunity to reinforce a staff member and to put into practice the skills of asking good questions, listening attentively, and offering appropriate information. During this phase,

> The astute and sensitive supervisor will make comments that mirror the teacher's behavior, essentially distilling and clarifying that behavior so the teacher can focus on and examine it. . . .
> Teachers benefit most from being guided to think critically about their own performance and encouraged to engage in problem solving as a part of their approach to teaching. Therefore, the supervisor should describe rather than evaluate, as much as possible.[14]

Describing means to provide the supervisee with an account, a portrait of what was observed, without making judgments about it. For example, here is a non-judgmental description by a supervisor:

> I noticed that Mark was poking Sharon and Gail during circle time. When it was over, he went into the block area and knocked over Josh's tower and

kicked the blocks with his feet. He then took the cards that Josh was using to label his buildings and ran to the far corner of the room with them. You were getting ready for the cooking lesson when Mark was disturbing Josh in the block building area.

Once the behavior has been described, the supervisor can begin to assist the supervisee in interpreting and evaluating it by questioning and listening:

Why do you think Mark was so disruptive today? He started to misbehave during circle time. How did you respond to him then? How else might you have handled the situation? What could you do to be more aware of what is taking place in various parts of the room?

When the conversation goes off on a tangent, supervisors will find it necessary to bring it back into focus. A way to signal the end of one discussion and the start of another is to summarize what has been said and change the subject by moving to another that needs to be talked about.

Planning the Next Steps

In planning next steps, supervisor and supervisee identify and develop problem-solving strategies, which usually involve changes in teaching behavior. Once new behaviors or possible strategies have been explored, supervisor and supervisee agree on which of these should be implemented, when, and how. The supervisee may say:

Before I start circle time activities tomorrow, I plan to describe to the children how I expect them to behave. If Mark continues to misbehave, I will tell him in a very firm voice to stop, instead of ignoring him as I did today. I also will make certain that I am sitting next to him before we begin. . . . I'm also going to set up the cooking area before school so I can move about the room during the transition from circle time to activity period.

The supervisor may respond:

Those are excellent ideas. As you suggested, I'll come in tomorrow at the beginning of circle time. I'll especially watch Mark and I'll pay special attention to the transition from circle time to activity period. Let's get together tomorrow afternoon to talk about the effects of these changes and share more ideas.

An agreed upon and limited set of steps that both the supervisee and supervisor will take before the next conference gives both individuals a sense of accomplishment and direction.

Closing the Conference

During the closing, the supervisor summarizes what has taken place during the conference period, reviews initial goals in terms of conference outcomes, and restates agreed-upon future plans. If progress has been made, both parties sense achievement. The closing is also a good time to ask caregivers to offer feedback about the conference itself. This is not a time for a supervisor to be defensive, but rather to be a good listener. Asking the supervisee to share thoughts and feelings about the conference builds trust and open communication.

After an evaluation conference, supervisors often find it beneficial to write a brief summary of what has taken place. A signed copy of the summary can be forwarded to the supervisee for his or her signature. If the supervisee disagrees with the summary and both parties cannot agree on revisions, then the supervisee can have the option of submitting a written summary of his or her own.

Preparing, building the climate, setting the purpose, guiding, planning next steps, and closing are six phases that give a conference structure and flexibility, regardless of its purpose and the number of individuals participating. A final, post-conference stage is analyzing the conference.

ANALYZING THE CONFERENCE

One way for supervisors to improve their performance is by consciously and systematically thinking about and questioning their own supervisory behaviors. This is an aspect of the conference that is often overlooked. Such self-analysis takes time, but the result makes it worthwhile.

We recommend that supervisors make audiotapes of at least a few conferences with staff members for the purpose of analysis. When told of the purpose, caregivers are usually receptive, since they recognize that their supervisor is striving to become a more effective leader. Supervisors usually find this experience quite revealing. Videotaping a conference allows one to later analyze both verbal and non-verbal behavior, but individuals sometimes become overly conscious of the camera, and making arrangements for videotaping can be overwhelming.

When reviewing the audiotape of a conference, it is best to listen to the entire recording first to refresh one's memory and to get a holistic view of the meeting. Then, when playing the tape again, listen for specific purposes:

- In what ways and to what extent did you achieve your goals for the conference?
- In what ways were you successful in practicing the specific communication skills that you had set as a priority?
- In what ways did the supervisee respond to the conference climate and to your communication behavior?
- What are your goals for yourself for your next supervisory conference with this individual?

Blumberg suggests that supervisors ask themselves the following questions as they think about their supervisory conferences:

> Am I communicating the desire to understand the teacher with whom I am conferencing? Am I helping the teacher to sharpen his thinking about a problem he is experiencing? Am I helping the teacher to focus on problems having to do with the intellectual and emotional development of students rather than on classroom maintenance problems?[15]

There are formal systems for analyzing conference behavior, such as those developed by Blumberg and by Kindsvatter and Wilen. Blumberg's system for studying supervisor-teacher interaction was used in his extensive research studies of communication between principals and teachers during conferences.[16] This system could be adapted by supervisors for their own purposes. His communication categories are useful ones to keep in mind while conferring with staff.

Richard Kindsvatter and William Wilen's conference category system (see Figure 10.1) enables one to record the presence of particular behaviors, feelings, and strategies and to make judgments about their effectiveness.[17] This system looks only at supervisory behavior but goes beyond communication skills by examining the context of the conference, including such methods as target setting. Issues such as the balance of talk and sensitivity are taken into consideration as well.

Supervisors can also develop their own instruments for analyzing conference behavior. For example, questioning skills could be examined by making a simple chart, checking each time a simple, clarifying, or probing question was asked, or directive, collaborative, and non-directive behaviors could be assessed. Other tools could be constructed to look at the supervisee's actions.

Scrutinizing one's supervisory behavior during conferences fosters one's own growth and development and advances the notion in staff members that all adults, including supervisors, are learners.

FIGURE 10.1 *Conference Category System Analysis Form*

SUPERVISOR _____

TEACHER _____

DATE _____

ANALYSIS SCALES

OCCURRENCE	EFFECTIVENESS
1. Not evident	1. Not effective
2. Slightly evident	2. Slightly effective
3. Moderately evident	3. Moderately effective
4. Quite evident	4. Quite effective
N. Not applicable	N. Not applicable

CATEGORIES (Parts A&B Correspond to Occurrence and Effectiveness in the Analysis Scale)	A. OCCURRENCE	B. EFFECTIVENESS
1. **Climate:** A. Supervisor makes comments specifically intended to affect the climate. B. Supervisor's statements release tension and contribute to productive communication. This includes expressions of support and encouragement, stated in a comfortable, relaxing tone.	—	—
2. **Target Setting:** A. Supervisor designates intended conference content. B. Supervisor explains the purpose of the conference, possible outcomes, and items to be included. The teacher is given the opportunity to approve these and suggest others. The resulting agenda is attended to in the conference.	—	—
3. **Questioning:** A. Supervisor employs questions as an essential means of pursuing conference targets. B. Supervisor uses a questioning strategy thoughtfully and purposefully to encourage the teacher to reflect, analyze, and evaluate. Questions which focus, probe, clarify, which transcend the obvious and mundane, are posed.	—	—
4. **Commentary:** A. Supervisor clarifies ideas and provides information and suggestions. B. Supervisor remarks are descriptive rather than judgmental. Pertinent information is provided incisively. Comments are appropriate and substantive.	—	—

5. **Praise:** A. Supervisor praises and encourages when opportune. B. Praise is used judiciously and authentically to commend teacher ideas and performance. Praise is specific in most instances.	―――	―――
6. **Nonverbal:** A. Communication other than through voice occurs. B. Supervisor has a pleasant facial expression, smiles as appropriate. Speech is accompanied by gestures. Nonverbal behavior communicates interest and enthusiasm. Touching may occur if appropriate.	―――	―――
7. **Balance:** A. Communication occurs in both directions. B. Supervisor is a patient and attentive listener. Supervisor elicits ample teacher involvement, usually talks less than the teacher.	―――	―――
8. **Sensitivity:** A. Supervisor acts on the teacher's behalf. B. Supervisor is alert to emotional and conditional factors, to verbal and nonverbal cues, and responds appropriately, often with climate building comments. Supervisor avoids self-serving behavior.	―――	―――
9. **Closure:** A. Supervisor uses a culminating technique. B. Supervisor reviews, or causes the teacher to review, the major outcomes of the conference: under-standings, solutions, plans, and especially commitment.	―――	―――

Reprinted from Richard Kindsvatter and William W. Wilen, "A Systematic Approach to Improving Conference Skills, *Educational Leadership* 38 (April 1981): 527, with permission of the Association for Supervision and Curriculum Development. Copyright © 1981 by the Association for Supervision and Curriculum Development. All rights reserved.

THREE-WAY CONFERENCE

Although most conferences include just a supervisor and a staff member, there is need on occasion to have a third party participate. Student teachers, job trainees, or CDA candidates are often supervised by a representative of an outside program, who works in cooperation with the coordinator or head teacher. Although the caregiver may spend more time in the field setting and receive most supervision there, he or she must meet the requirements of both organizations and the expectations of both supervisors.

As the two programs and their representatives interface, it is critical that the staff member being supervised and both supervisors meet on a regular basis. Without ongoing communication among the three individuals, splits can develop whereby two develop mutual trust and common goals to the exclusion of the third. There is, therefore, the potential for misunderstanding and conflicting expectations.

Three-way conferences are also useful with individuals within a program. They can be especially effective in handling conflicts among staff members, in resolving contractual issues and negotiations with board members, and in dealing with parental concerns.

Conferences about grievances usually have clear and well-defined step-by-step procedures that directors must follow. Conferences about serious interstaff conflicts, even if they have not reached that official level, are particularly troublesome and should be carefully planned as well. Marjorie Kostelnik recommends a multi-step problem-solving approach for these encounters.[18]

She suggests that when directors initiate the mediation process, they should take the preliminary step of meeting with the individuals privately, before bringing them together in a face-to-face meeting. During the private sessions, the supervisor's skill of active listening is critical, for the supervisee needs that opportunity to present his or her view of the situation and express feelings openly and fully.

Once this step is taken, both parties should be brought together for mutual clarification. The role of the supervisor in this step is to be neutral and to manage the conference so that each party has an opportunity to present views and to state his or her ultimate desire with respect to the problem being discussed. By paraphrasing or reflecting what each supervisee has said, without evaluating, the supervisor can assist each caregiver in clarifying his or her own thinking, as well as ensuring that each person has an accurate perception of the other's notion of the problem.

Kostelnik elaborates on the supervisory role during mutual clarification.

The supervisor should solicit from each person in turn a statement of the situation from that individual's point of view. The ground rule here is that the situation must be described in terms of personal aims rather than phrased as an accusation about another person. An acceptable statement might be, "I wish I spent less time on classroom maintenance." An inappropriate remark would be, "She makes me do all the clean-up and saves the fun things for herself."[19]

Once each person has had an opportunity to state and clarify her or his position and the supervisor understands each worker's view of a desirable outcome, the supervisor needs to move both parties toward a resolution by defining the problem and making sure that each staff member accepts responsibility for the problem and its solution.

The parties then begin to generate possible alternative solutions to the problem, until one or more mutually beneficial solutions are agreed upon. The supervisor then praises each individual for his or her hard work in the problem-solving process and reminds them what the terms of the agreement are, including how the plan will be carried out and evaluated.

Kostelnik views this problem-solving process as one in which the supervisory role is that of a model and teacher, rather than a judge or disciplinarian.[20] Although sometimes time consuming, the problem-solving process does serve to reduce tension and create positive working relationships among staff.

Although it is often difficult to find and to arrange a time when all three individuals can meet, the three-way conference has several advantages. It builds relationships among individuals through a collaborative process where each individual has greater input. When more than one supervisor is involved, responsibility is divided, which is particularly appreciated when coping with serious problems. Goals or desired competencies are known to staff member(s) and supervisor(s) and are agreed upon at the beginning of a relationship. Each person involved has an opportunity to hear and to understand each other's point of view about a child, the teaching role, or a problem. Usually, during a three-way face-to-face conference, individuals use more careful descriptive language, which promotes greater respect and understanding. Three-way conferences that deal with conflict have the overall effect of reducing stress and anxiety among those participating.

CONCLUSION

A conference, whether two-way or three-way, provides a director the opportunity to practice the art of supervision. Planning, problem-solving, and evaluating can take place in conferences, and teachers can express themselves and get recognition and praise. Conferences are central to maintaining continued communication between supervisors and staff and to ensuring that caregiving and teaching are of high quality.

EXERCISES

As part of a staff training session in supervision, form small role-playing groups to consider the problem situations described below. Individuals take the roles of supervisor and caregiver. An observer whose primary function is to offer feedback to the supervisor should also be included. At the conclusion of an agreed-upon time segment of role-playing, individuals switch roles so that everyone has an opportunity to practice supervisory behavior. The observer might use the Kindsvatter or Blumberg category systems for analyzing conference behavior, or may create his or her own system to examine a particular type of communication skill such as questioning technique. Each role-playing sequence need not be long, and at the end the observer should report the results of the analysis to the supervisor. Practicing supervisors might write and discuss a hypothetical plan for resolving each dilemma.

TWO-WAY CONFERENCES

1. George is concerned that his kids aren't playing well together, particularly with Keith. Keith is an aggressive and active four-year-old. His parents have been separated for several months and are planning to finalize their divorce very soon. Keith does not see his father and has lots of baby sitters. He is at school from 9:00 A.M. to 5:30 P.M. Role play this conference with George.
2. Karen has come to you with a concern. She is very frustrated as the children are very sloppy with their food during snack time. She complains, "The kids don't stay seated like they're supposed to and milk gets spilled all over the place!" She explains that some of the children finish their snacks early and get bored and others never have a chance to finish. The kids who finish early get up to throw their containers away and bump into others, and the children who don't finish get up and go to their activities leaving their partly filled milk cartons on the floor to get kicked over. Role play this conference.
3. Diedre is an assistant teacher in your Head Start classroom. She is from a middle-class family and has a college degree. She has a hard time accepting and appreciating the lower-income children and families who are at the center. When her activities do not go well, she becomes angry and usually blames it on the children "who don't know anything," "never

learned manners," or "don't even speak the language." While she appears to be sweet with the children, you sense that there are a lot of feelings of anger and frustration underneath. Diedre is quite argumentative, and your suggestions have often been met with strong opposition. She feels that she is doing an excellent job and your criticisms are usually dismissed because "you didn't really see what was happening." The tension is mounting. You have decided that it is time to talk with her about the situation.

THREE-WAY CONFERENCES

1. You are a head teacher in a day care center in a large corporation. All the parents are employed by the corporation and tend to be quite conservative. Your assistant teacher, Cassandra, is very imaginative and has a unique and rather flamboyant style. She often wears sequined purple sneakers, brightly colored tights, and short skirts; other times, it is flowing Indian skirts and a headband (a la 1960s). Her activities with the children are age-appropriate and creative but represent a different life style from those of the parents (e.g., body painting, Yoga, Tai Chi, vegetarian cooking). She is wonderful with the children, and you feel that she offers a good balance to the daily businesslike atmosphere of the site. One day Diane, a parent, calls to say that she is distressed about the "crazy things" her child is learning and feels that Cassandra should dress and behave in a "more appropriate manner." You feel that both people would benefit from hearing the other's point of view. Role play that meeting.

2. You are a director of a day care center with a culturally diverse group of families and staff. You have recently hired an assistant teacher, Elena, who came from Russia last year. She is in her 40s and has the equivalent of a master's degree in education. Her head teacher is an American woman in her late 20s who has a bachelor's degree in education. Elena has had more years of teaching experience than Diane, her head teacher, but most of it was with older children. Elena is finding it difficult to take directions from a person with less education and experience, but at the same time she is not finding it easy working with three-year-olds. Diane, on the other hand, finds Elena to be somewhat intimidating and is having a hard time establishing a good working relationship with her. Both have come to speak with you about their frustrations in trying to work together. You have decided that it is time to have a three-way meeting. Role play that meeting.

11 Observation and Analysis

Observation provides the context for conferring in the clinical supervision cycle. When supervisors and supervisees talk about what is happening in the classroom, their discussion is based, not on speculation, but on what each has experienced directly, either through participation or observation. Through supervisory observations and follow-up conferences, staff members can receive accurate information and feedback on what they are doing, which enables them to compare it to what they think they are doing and what they would like to be doing. As Asa Hilliard has stated, "Two basic things help teachers to grow. One is relevant professional information, and the other is continuing feedback on what the teacher does."[1]

When observation is used within the cycle of clinical supervision, it can become part of "joint inquiry," which is so important for adult learning. Within this context, it has the following purposes:

- To provide a mirror for staff members' actions so they can have objective feedback on what they are doing.
- To provide a vehicle for working together with teachers to help them develop, improve, and maintain their skills in working with children.
- To provide information which supervisors and supervisees can use together to diagnose and solve teaching problems.
- To help teachers understand how the classroom/learning environment affects children's growth and development, and to enable them to act on this information.
- To help teachers assess the effectiveness of their program for children and of changes they have made in it.
- To collect data for evaluation based on shared criteria and standards.[2]

At its most basic level, observation is a way of gathering and recording data, yet it clearly involves more than entering a classroom, watching what is happening, and recording what is seen. The very complexity of the teaching/learning process makes effective observation difficult. The many interacting forces — teaching staff, children, the physical environment, the time of day, the activity — must be sorted out in some way. Observers have opinions and feelings about what is going on, and their prejudgments must be accounted for in planning accurate and reliable recording of data. The many layers and subtleties of social meanings, contexts, and feelings present in the classroom must be revealed but not confused with the "facts." Finally, the information collected must be conveyed to the persons observed in ways they can understand, accept, and use. Thus, supervisors who are helping teachers become active participants in their own learning will describe observation more as a *way of inquiring* than as a way of gathering data.

OBSERVATION
WITHIN THE CLINICAL SUPERVISION CYCLE

When using a clinical approach to supervision, most supervisors find it advantageous to use a variety of ways of observing and gathering information. In a study of the methods used by three hundred supervisors during observation and analysis, Noreen Garman found that they actually used five "modes of inquiry" at various stages in the cycle of supervision. At each stage there were different assumptions and, therefore, methods of collecting data. Each mode represents a particular "way of looking at the world. . . . Each has a different, yet vital, purpose in a comprehensive plan for supervision."[3]

The first mode, *discovery*, is an open-ended search to discover the reality of the classroom and "appropriate questions inherent in the classroom scenario."[4] Various systems of observation could be used at this stage. The data from these observations are usually analyzed by identifying the teacher's stated intent and comparing it with what has been observed.

In the second mode, *verification*, more objective and structured systems of observation are used. This is an important step, as this mode is used to verify the degree to which features or problems identified in the discovery stage do indeed exist.

The *explanation* mode puts to work both open and closed methods. At this time the supervisor and supervisee begin the analysis process, together trying to come to terms with their individual, and perhaps differing, perceptions of reality.

Interpretation is the search for meaning, the attempt "to get at what really matters."[5] The supervisor's knowledge, experience, and insights are used to help the supervisee find the deeper significance beneath the surface of literal descriptions and explanations.

It is in the *evaluation* mode that the supervisor and supervisee examine values and make judgments about specific aspects of the teacher's behavior to "determine the effectiveness of a particular action or the worthiness of the meaning."[6] In this phase, internal and external criteria become the basis for setting priorities.

As supervisors grow in the skills of inquiry and in knowledge of early childhood education and as they grow toward maturity as supervisors, they become increasingly able to understand and use the most appropriate mode for each particular situation.

APPROACHES TO OBSERVATION

Supervisors can approach observation in several ways: (1) informally, as a casual visitor to a classroom; (2) as a participant observer, having both involvement in the classroom and a systematic way of recording observations; and (3) formally, as one who is completely detached from the activities in the classroom, recording them in a systematic way.

Informal Observation

Because of the informality and open structure of most early childhood classrooms, adults who are not regular members of the classroom staff can usually move in and out without disrupting the children or the program. Children tend to ignore visitors or to welcome them as new sources of help, amusement, or interesting information. When a supervisor sits down with children during free play or pitches in with cleanup, teachers' apprehensions are often lessened. In fact, many teachers welcome informal visits from supervisors because they feel that the supervisor will have a clearer picture of what their classrooms are really like and will be able to better empathize with their problems.

Many directors and educational coordinators make casual visits to classrooms because they like to be with children, to break the routine of their office work, or, more deliberately, to get the flavor of day-to-day center activity. From such visits, supervisors can obtain a general sense of the tone of the room, a teacher's style, the ways staff work together, and the organization of the learning environment. This kind of information can add depth and dimension to a supervisor's knowledge and understanding of classroom life. It must not, however, be counted on as the major source of information, especially for evaluation purposes.

Because informal observations are usually unfocused and records, if any, are written after the fact, what is likely to emerge is only a general impression of the room and the teachers, or a record of events or factors that stand out or are unusual in some way. If such visits are made to all rooms on a relatively regular basis, however, they decrease the need for formal observation and round out the supervisor's picture of life in the center.

Participant Observation

Participant observation is a method used by ethnographers in which the inquirer has considerable involvement in the setting being studied. Anthropologists use this form of observation to become acquainted with a culture so that they will be able to see the world as the members of that culture see it.

True participant observation goes beyond informal observation. Observers must be consciously as aware as possible of their perceptions, because they really play two roles: as an observer who is responsible to the program as a whole, and as a member of the group, "a genuine participant," who thus "has a stake in the group's activity and the outcome of that activity."[7]

Supervisors with teaching responsibilities who wish to use observation as a supervisory tool are by definition participant observers of staff in their own rooms. When non-teaching supervisors function as participant observers, however, they must spend enough time in a classroom to immerse themselves in what is going on. Only then can they see the classroom through the eyes of the teachers and children and determine strategies for assistance from these viewpoints. This can be an especially valuable method for supervisors who work with staff or children whose cultural backgrounds differ from their own, or with teachers or programs whose early childhood goals or methods are very different from theirs. Teachers, too, can become participant observers. Their journals or other records can then be used as a basis for supervisory conferences or seminars.[8]

Formal Observation

Formal observation differs from participant observation in that the supervisor remains aloof from the situation, observing as objectively as possible. A great variety of recording systems can be used to observe in a formal way. These include open-ended systems, such as narrative descriptions of what is occurring, and closed systems, which limit what is recorded to a set number of behaviors or events that the observer checks off or tallies. When supervisors make formal observations, they record on the spot. Because they are not taking part in the classroom activity and presumably have no stake in it, their record should be the most accurate of any of the three approaches.

METHODS OF OBSERVATION

The methods used in observing are usually divided into two categories: quantitative or closed, and qualitative or open (also called naturalistic). They are based on different assumptions and points of view about the role of the observer. This becomes especially important in research, but supervisors can use both types. Each contributes breadth and depth to the supervisor's assistance to teachers.

Closed Systems

Quantitative or closed systems, which grow out of the "scientific" view of supervision, stress the use of methodology that limits the inferences that observers are required to make. Emphasis is placed on limiting the information collected to a predetermined set of behaviors, traits, or events that can be dealt with a few at a time — thus they are "closed" systems. Checklists and category systems using clearly defined terms are employed. The observer tallies or codes behaviors as they occur. From the "thin" or quantitative data generated by such an observation, a supervisor could determine, for example, that a teacher responded verbally to children six times and was unresponsive twice. The context, the exact words, and non-verbal nuances are not revealed, however. What does emerge is the frequency of certain behaviors and, with some systems, the duration and sequence of events.

Critics of quantitative methods contend that they obscure individuality because they use predetermined categories into which all teachers are expected to fit. Further, these methods do not lend themselves to interpreting the meaning of behavior. Closed systems can be quite useful, however, when there is a need to focus only on certain elements out of all that is going on in a classroom.

INSTRUMENTS

The following instruments are the most commonly used closed systems for observing in classrooms.

Rating scales consist of lists of traits or dimensions of behavior — for example, unresponsive/responsive, partial/fair — placed on a continuum against which teachers are measured. Or, on a scale from poor to excellent, the observer may rate the extent to which teachers demonstrate a particular behavior. Rating scales have been criticized as observation instruments because they usually require a high degree of observer inference. The statements that make up the scale generally refer to teacher characteristics rather than teaching behaviors, processes, or interactions.[9] For these reasons, they are best used as summaries of information derived from several observations and from other sources.

Checklists are lists of characteristics or behaviors that are simply checked off if they are present. See Figure 11.1 for an example of a checklist.

Category systems use a series of categories limited to the particular area of classroom life that supervisor and supervisee are interested in obtaining more information about. The observer tallies events or behaviors as they oc-

FIGURE 11.1   *Check List*

Teacher or aide available to talk to parent	
Teacher or aide greets each child	✔
Teachers encourage independence in taking off/hanging up coats	✔

cur or at specified intervals, sometimes using a coding system. The categories must be such that everything that takes place can be tallied. For example, the Flanders System of Interaction Analysis, the best known and most widely used example of this type of instrument, is designed to examine teacher and student verbal interaction. A code number is assigned to each of nine teacher and student verbal behaviors: (1) accepts feelings, (2) praises or encourages, and so forth. A tenth category, silence or confusion, ensures that everything that happens is accounted for. The observer records a number for the appropriate category every three seconds.[10]

Sign systems list behaviors that may or may not take place during a certain period of time. They differ from checklists in that the observer tallies each time they occur, either continuously or at time intervals. (Examples of the use of sign and category systems are given in the case study later in this chapter.)

There are a number of research-based instruments designed for observing in early childhood settings.[11] These instruments tend to be comprehensive in scope, and observers usually must have training and practice in their use. They have the advantage of reliability, but they may not be focused on the specific behaviors of concern at a particular time and thus are not generally practical in day-to-day supervision. It often makes the greatest sense for observers to construct their own instruments.

GUIDELINES FOR USING CLOSED SYSTEMS

Consider the following points when creating or selecting observational instruments:

1. Decide on a focus. It can be helpful to think of any situation in terms of actors, behaviors, context, and setting. Narrow the observation to the interaction of only two of these.

2. Determine whether there is a need to record everything that takes place (category system) or only certain behaviors or events (sign system).
3. Decide whether merely noting that something is present is sufficient (checklists) or whether you would gain from having information on the frequency or sequence of events (sign or category).
4. Make sure that behaviors do not overlap. For example, "asks question" and "makes statement" are clearly different behaviors. "Asks question" and "talks to child" are not, since asking a question is a kind of talking.
5. Define each category precisely and in writing. Two people should be expected to agree that the behavior in question fits the category. Very broad categories ("warm behavior") make agreement more difficult. Very narrow ones ("points," "motions with open hand") usually do not provide much meaningful information unless they represent specific behaviors a caregiver is trying to develop or eliminate.
6. Keep the instrument simple. Since behavior is complex and occurs rapidly, it is better to make two or three different instruments than to cram too much into one.

Open Systems

In recent years, there has been a growing interest in open or naturalistic inquiry both by practitioners and researchers. This form of observation and analysis makes use of the ethnographic techniques developed by anthropologists for use in field studies. These systems are based on the assumption that different people see events from different perspectives, and thus they focus on "multiple realities that, like layers of an onion, nest within or complement one another."[12] The observer tries to see the world from these differing points of view and to understand their relationships. Whereas scientific observers try to screen out human judgment from the process, naturalistic observers seek to sharpen and refine their judgment skills in order to become "more personally and environmentally sensitive" to what is unique in the situation and its meaning to the participants.[13] For these reasons, the information generated in open systems is sometimes referred to as "thick" or qualitative data.

One naturalistic approach is the "connoisseurship," or artistic approach espoused by Elliot Eisner and modeled after the methods used in art criticism. Eisner compares the role of the supervisor to that of the teacher of a master class — like a Heifitz observing, listening, and responding to students of the violin. He stresses the importance of recognizing each person's characteristic style, which should be developed and strengthened rather than molded into a particular "good teacher" model. Artistic methods differ from other open systems in that supervisors are urged to develop the ability to use expressive, "artistic language" to convey their observations to supervisees. Thus, the supervisor acts as an educational critic — not as a person who gives negative feedback, but as one who helps teachers see their own performances in a new light.[14]

Critics of open approaches note that because observers are free to record anything that occurs, they are more likely to be biased in what they focus on and in how they convey and interpret events to staff members. In addition, when using expressive language, supervisors may unconsciously lead caregivers to conclusions that are based on the supervisor's values rather than their own.

Advocates of naturalistic methods, on the other hand, point to the flexibility of such systems and their ability to help observers discover what is happening below the surface. Observations are described in detail, instead of simply counting the number of times a limited number of behaviors have occurred. Teachers and supervisors are thus free to examine, interpret, and re-examine the descriptions in various ways, as a basis for making plans to improve performance.

NARRATIVES

The major method used by naturalistic observers is the narrative, that is, writing down in a continuous fashion everything that happens within a chosen focus. One of the concerns when this method is used, however, is that judgments and interpretations can become confused with accurate descriptions. A way to ensure that these two types of information are kept separate is to use a two-column format:

Description	*Comments*
Four children in house corner. Justin enters. Others continue with dialogue. J. gets down on floor.	
Marie (teacher) walks over, sits down.	M. is casual; doesn't intrude.
M: "I like the way you're playing. . . . Who's the daddy?"	
Beth: "I'm the dog."	Has M. misinterpreted their theme?
J: "I'm the big dog."	

This system helps observers stay alert to the difference between description and interpretation, while making it possible to include feelings, thoughts, inferences from non-verbal cues, or questions to be followed up in the post-observation conference.

1. Develop an understandable shorthand system so you can get on paper as much as possible of what is taking place.
2. As soon as possible after the observation, while your memory is fresh, fill in whole words and details that you were not able to write down during the observation itself. Edit the narrative where the language is imprecise or ambiguous, and rewrite it for greater specificity.

   As you become experienced in recording observations, you can begin to use more descriptive language so that nuances can be conveyed more accurately. For example, instead of "T. goes over to Fred," use "strolls" or "strides with long deliberate steps" to convey the feeling tone of her actions.[15]
3. Verbatim recordings can help teachers become sensitized to the impact of their words on others and become aware of their own verbal style. Accuracy is especially important here, as paraphrasing can change or make ambiguous the meaning of what was said. "Tells children to stop throwing sand" could have been "Stop that!" or "It's not nice to throw sand" or "Sand stays in the sandbox," each of which conveys a different message to the children.
4. Separate inferences, conclusions, and judgments from the descriptive data. Avoid judgmental labeling such as "She was inflexible about that rule." Describe the behavior ("Immediately put child in chair") and perhaps add an interpretive comment ("Seemed to feel the rule must be upheld at all cost"). Recheck at the editing stage to ensure the objectivity of the narrative.
5. Note the time periodically in the margin to assist interpretation. If the observer becomes distracted or tired and loses some data, time checks alert the reader. Time checks also help portray the stream of events more accurately. They show that in one three-minute interval a great deal happened, while in another very little took place.
6. Finally, analyze the narrative for patterns of behavior or specific areas to be discussed in the post-observation conference or to be verified during subsequent observations. If the observation is made at the *discovery* stage of the clinical supervision cycle and with an open-ended agenda, you may have noted areas of concern or special interest during the observation itself for follow up. If a specific focus was agreed upon during the pre-observation conference, analysis should be made on the basis of that

concern. A copy of the narrative can be shared with the supervisee to foster cooperative analysis.

Combined Systems

Supervisors have wide latitude in developing observation forms for specific purposes or situations, using any combination of closed and open systems. The specific needs or interests of the caregiver, the characteristics of the situation, and the supervisor's and caregiver's creativity are the only limitations beyond following the guidelines for reliable observation construction.

A system that combines tallying and description can be a very useful teaching tool. For example, a listing of behaviors that support a child's self-concept could include space for the exact language used by the teacher or a description of the specific incident (see Figure 11.2). Because both the specific behavior and the outcome are described, caregivers are able to see exactly what they do and how this behavior affects children. In this case, only positive behaviors are listed; the supervisor is reinforcing what is desirable and not emphasizing that which is not. This technique is especially useful with staff members who have had little experience with field supervision or training, and for whom positive feedback and confidence building are very important.

Another method is to use a narrative but limit the focus to a few categories of behavior. In the example in Figure 11.3, used by a CDA advisor, some of the descriptors for the CDA Functional Area Communication have been

FIGURE 11.2   *Check List with Comments*

Gets down to child's level	✓ Ch. tugs on T's skirt. T. squats down, asks ch. to tell her what she wants. Ch. does.
Uses extended praise	✓ "You did a good job wiping up the spilled paint!" Ch. grins. Carefully puts sponge where it belongs.

FIGURE 11.3   *Focused Narrative*

FUNCTIONAL AREA: COMMUNICATION

Name   Chris G.   Date   3/5

Listens patiently to each child, tries to understand what
they want to communicate, and helps them to express themselves in whatever modes they have available.

Timmy pulls at Chris's jeans. C:Yes,Tim,what
is it? T. points. C:You'll have to tell me, Tim. T: Mark...
C:Yes—Mark...? T: Mark playing with my truck.

Encourages children to talk about experiences that are
special to their homes and personal lives.

Sees Su looking at Guinea pig. Picks it up and
gives to S. to hold. S: It's soft — like my kitty.
C: Oh, you have a kitty? S: Yes. His name is
Tommy. He gets lost sometimes. (Continues story.)

listed.[16] Since candidates for the CDA credential must show that they are
competent in each of thirteen Functional Areas, such a system provides a
way for supervisors to observe and record only behaviors relevant to that
area.

Videotapes and Audiotapes.   Observations do not always have to be
recorded in written form. Videotaping and audiotaping also have valuable
places in supervisory observation. Audiovisual equipment makes available
a permanent, credible record of what actually took place. The record is not
limited by the observer's attentiveness, ability to write fast enough, or un-
conscious biases. Non-verbal as well as verbal nuances are captured revealing the "feel" of classroom interaction. Such material can be reviewed over
and over and analyzed in a variety of ways.

A most important benefit of using such equipment is that caregivers are
able to assess their own behavior, becoming less dependent on the supervisor, and thus increasing the mutuality of the supervisory process. Because
both supervisor and supervisee are examining the same information at the
same time, real problem solving can result. The supervisor's role is to assist
the supervisee in identifying and analyzing what is significant and to comment on and question the events both are seeing. The strength of this medium — as with all types of observation — comes from the sensitive use of this
follow-up time.

SPECIAL CONCERNS FOR SUPERVISORS

Observer Bias

At several points in our discussion of observation we have emphasized the importance of discovering the meanings underlying the situations that are observed. An attempt to interpret meaning, of course, brings with it the possibility of misinterpretation, based on the limits of what an observer can perceive and on biases stemming from values and preconceptions. While these biases are natural and even legitimate at times, they must be brought to a conscious level or they will limit the ability to make accurate and meaningful observations.

Clearly, two people can see the same thing and interpret it differently: the parent who sees "just playing" and the caregiver who sees what the children are learning when they play; the teacher who sees Easter baskets for the children to take home and the supervisor who sees children who are bored or close to tears because the project is not developmentally appropriate; and the supervisor who is concerned because a Vietnamese caregiver does not use children's names while the caregiver is actually functioning in a culturally appropriate way.[17]

One source of bias, as we noted earlier, is the complexity of the observational field, which can cause observers consciously or unconsciously to attend to some features and ignore others. One way to overcome this is to take time before recording to look around a room and take into account all that is going on and all the kinds of things that could be observed. Another is to practice recording with a colleague, noting differences in what you record. Reviewing your own observations periodically can also reveal patterns you may not have been aware of.

Another source of bias is preconceived expectations about a person or situation. Previous experience with a teacher as a fractious participant in staff meetings or a report on an aide indicating that she is lazy can influence what a supervisor looks for and the interpretation of what is seen. Conversely, when observing a person known to have especially good qualities, a supervisor may take more time to try to understand a problem situation. Using a variety of observation tools, both closed and open, makes it more likely that situations will be viewed and interpreted accurately, since they can be seen from different perspectives.

Personal and Cultural Differences

Courtney Cazden cites two examples to illustrate differences in teaching styles due to cultural values. A study of Amish classrooms by R. W. McDermott indicated that teachers used a very directive, even controlling, style of teaching. Because the teachers were from the same background as the children in this closed community, children understood this style quite differently than would children (or adults) who were not attuned to the expectations built up through a similar home and community environment. This directive style made sense for them within the context of everyday routines and was supported by an underlying trust, accountability, and warmth that outside observers may not have perceived or understood.[18]

In Cazden's own study (with Frederick Erickson, Robert Carraso, and Arthur Vera) of two bilingual first-grade classrooms, where children and teachers were all of Mexican-American background, the teachers' styles of classroom control were quite similar, although their teaching styles (one open, one structured) differed. Both teachers used endearments, other "in-group identity markers," and behaviors characteristic of parents, such as kissing and holding children in their laps when working with them individually.[19]

Supervisors unfamiliar with adult-child interactional patterns in either of these cultures might have judged the behavior of these teachers inappropriate. Conversely, the absence of such behaviors might seem problematic to an Amish or Chicano supervisor.

Observers in classrooms in which there are cultural or social class differences must be especially concerned with looking for clues to the meaning of events (both to children and to adults). In such situations, both "thin" and "thick" data from observations of children and adults aid in interpretation. Discussions with supervisees about the meaning of events during the verification and explanation phases of supervision are especially important when differences in cultural values are present.

GENERAL GUIDELINES FOR OBSERVATION

The following points relate to observing in classrooms in general. They can be helpful in making the act of observing a positive experience for supervisors and supervisees and in making records both reliable and useful.

1. When beginning an observation, especially if it is in an unfamiliar room, it is helpful to "map" the setting. This "de-focusing" or "immersion" process helps the observer to become part of the world of the teachers and children so that the interrelatedness of its various aspects can be understood. Such a map should include a record of all of the people present; physical features, equipment, or materials that might affect what takes place, with perhaps a simple sketch of the room arrangements; the adult-to-child ratio; the number of males and females, minorities, handicapped

children, adults, and any other information that might assist in interpreting events.

2. If an inconspicuous place can be found to sit while observing, it decreases the pressure on the caregiver and lessens the disruption of the class as a whole. Curious children feel honored when told that someone is writing about what they are doing.

3. When one member of a classroom team is being observed, particularly if that person is an aide, there may be a strain on staff relations. If a teacher is visited often for written observations, other staff members may feel inhibited, perhaps suspecting that they are being judged. When schedules are disrupted, even in a minor way, for conferences, the change in normal routine can be unsettling and lead to hard feelings, especially when another caregiver has to take over in the staff member's absence.

    Much stress can be avoided or alleviated if the supervisor takes time to make frequent contact with the teacher or other classroom staff members, with an explanation of the purpose of the observations. Giving positive feedback from time to time to all classroom staff members and unobtrusively pitching in at busy times can temper many uneasy feelings. Staff members will often say that they do not mind these intrusions, but over a period of time, resentment can build if there are too frequent changes in patterns of responsibility or if communication is not maintained.

4. Planning with individual caregivers or with the classroom team when formal written observations are to be made is basic to making them part of a cooperative learning experience, rather than subjects of an examination. Dropping in for a written observation without notice or planning is seldom effective or necessary, except when there are serious concerns that cannot be documented in any other way.

5. By making several short observations, patterns of behavior can be discovered and verified. This avoids the problem of drawing conclusions based on a single observation.

6. When time for observing and conferencing is built into a supervisor's weekly schedule, there is a greater likelihood that such activities will take place. Remember that even 10 percent of a thirty-five-hour week is three-and-a-half hours — a substantial amount if regularly planned.

PUTTING OBSERVATION TO WORK:
A CASE STUDY

For the purpose of the following illustration, put yourself in the role of supervisor working with a teacher who has been with your program for about two years. You will note that, in addition to a variety of observation methods, all the modes of inquiry described in Garman's study are present. As supervisor you use a *discovery* mode in the early stages of observing the teacher. You then *verify* your hypothesis, *explain* by sharing points of view, *interpret* the meaning of events and behaviors, and *evaluate* in relation to what you and the supervisee feel ought to be occurring.

Sequence of Observations

As a result of her evaluation at the end of last year, you and your supervisee, Pat, have agreed that she needs to work on involving children in a greater variety of activities during free play. You have made informal visits to Pat's room in the last few weeks, sitting in with children during the free play period. Your general impression was that she is warm with children and has a wonderful sense of humor. You observed that she has some interesting group activities that children are free to take part in during this time. The period is by no means chaotic, but a number of the children do a good deal of aimless wandering and occasional mild roughhousing. Not all areas of the room are used.

In your initial meeting with Pat to plan how you will work together, Pat seems unsure about the purpose of the free play period. She knows that children "learn through play," but has never been quite sure what this means or what the teacher's role is in it. Her main concern about free play is that certain children "don't make use of their time effectively." You suggest that by observing what is actually happening, you may be able to find ways to help her restructure the program so that these children become more involved. She agrees to begin some participant observations herself, jotting down at approximately ten-minute intervals what goes on in the room.

Your first observation is a naturalistic, open-ended one. Your mapping of the room indicates that there are a limited number of learning centers. The block area seems small, the house area quite open, and there is a large open area in the middle of the room. Four to six children at a time were finger painting at one table. The others were involved at one time or another in water play, in the house corner, or at the easel. There was again some wandering and tussling.

In analyzing your narrative description, you note that Pat and her assistant seemed to function in two ways. Either they were in a kind of "rescuing" role, constantly responding to what wasn't going right, finding things for wandering children to do, cleaning up a spill, or stopping roughhousing; or they were "waiting on" children, responding to a child's request by getting materials, putting names on papers, hanging up wet paintings, telling children to let others have a turn, and even drawing a cat for a child who said he didn't know how.

During your next conference, Pat said she was pleased with the finger painting activity and that the children liked water play. She had noticed that Roberto and Jared often seemed to run out of things to do and that the block area of the room was not used much. She had recently seen a film on blocks and was interested in working on this area. When you discussed what she thought about the teacher's role in free play, she stated, "To make sure children have what they need, and to prevent and solve problems."

Although you are concerned about the overall picture of free play and Pat's limited perception of her role, you agree to work with Pat on the block area, using observation as a tool. It is something she is interested in, and by working in this limited area, you may be able to help her develop techniques that will help her with free play as a whole. It is also a logical place to involve the restless children.

FOCUS ON THE CHILDREN

You and Pat decide that your first focused observations will be used to verify what children do in the block corner and in the room as a whole during free play. There are several advantages to beginning with observations of children. First, it is often easier for teachers to look at children's behavior than at their own, especially if they have not been observed before. Second, observing children can serve as a means of verification and explanation of what actually is happening. Third, it puts the teaching role into perspective by looking at children first, focusing on learning rather than teaching.

The major disadvantage to an initial focus on children's behavior is that it may divert attention from the caregiver's behavior at a time when changes need to be made. Nevertheless, focusing on the children first can create a strong back-up for further steps.

In order to develop a set of categories, you and Pat brainstorm about what could or should take place in the block corner. You discuss what kinds of behaviors she would like to see there, what might go on that is inappropriate, and how categories can be defined with as little ambiguity as possible.

A list of many possible behaviors is eventually whittled down to a few. They are described and defined as you construct a manageable observation tool. The discussion that leads to this point helps Pat — and you as supervisor — think more specifically about goals for children in the block area and in free play in general.

You choose the following categories:

- *Building* — Interacting with blocks in any constructive way, or with accessories related to blocks; knocking buildings over if clearly acceptable to those involved
- *Other constructive play* — Using materials from another area; playing ex-

clusively with accessories (trucks, people) without involving blocks
- *Watching* — Observing; passive behavior; not actively part of block play but present in the area
- *Non-constructive play* — Interfering with others, non-constructive block play, unrelated rough play in area
- *Other* — All other behavior (where possible, note specific behavior)

Since you want to make sure to capture all of what goes on, you use a *category* system, thus, the "other" listing. The instrument can be refined if in actual use you find many tallies in the "other" category, or that a category is too limited or too broad. You further decide to use a *time sample* and to tally behavior at three-minute intervals. This sampling is enough to reveal patterns of activity within one free play period (see Figure 11.4). By doing several ten- to fifteen-minute observations over a period of days, you will be able to see day-to-day patterns as well and to use your time to best advantage.

You also decide to construct an instrument to use in observing the free play period as a whole. This observation tool lists the areas of the room and will also be used at time intervals. This enables you to tally on both forms during the same observation period. Figure 11.5 shows the patterns of play on a different day from the block observation above.

On examining the free play observations, Pat discovers that they confirm the low use not only of blocks but also of manipulatives and books. At the same time, she is uncomfortable about the number of tallies in the "uninvolved" category. For Pat, the use of this form has seemed more objective than your initial narrative.

Pat goes to the center library and reads *The Block Book* and *The Block Corner* to discover new ideas about what children can learn from block play, to formulate clear goals for that area, and to identify ways to arrange the area for greater involvement.[20] Pat decides to rearrange the entire room to make the block area larger. Since this affects the other areas as well, Pat and her assistant rethink the goals of all the underused areas in the room as a whole. Over the next several weeks, things begin to change and Pat is excited! She is now concerned, however, that although children use the block area more, they are not building as elaborately as she would like.

FOCUS ON THE TEACHER

As you and Pat discuss ways to enhance the children's play, you bring up your original concern that she and her assistant seem to spend much of their time rescuing things and waiting on children. She agrees that although the children are functioning more independently and she has more time, she still does not spend much time sitting in with children while they play.

FIGURE 11.4   *First Instrument*

BLOCK AREA   Room __Pat__   Date __10/20__

Time Begun __9:15__   Time Ended __9:30__

Interval __3-minute__

BEHAVIOR	9:15	18	21	24	27	30
Building					2	2
Other Constructive Play		1	1*			
Watching						
Non-constructive Play						
Other						

Comments: *Lenny takes out a truck, wheels it around for awhile, then "drives" it out to central area.

You suggest that she read the article, "Teaching Children as They Play," which provides examples of language caregivers can use to enhance play and learning in the block area.[21]

Based on the examples in the article, you develop categories for another observation (see Figure 11.6). This instrument uses a *sign* system, since the focus is only on specific behaviors, not all those that could occur. It is also an *event* sample, rather than a time sample, since time is not an important factor.

As a result of this observation you discover that Pat has relied heavily on direct questions and suggestions rather than on the indirect behaviors illustrated in the article. Asking convergent questions like "What shape is it?" is hard to change, and your discussion with Pat reveals that she isn't completely convinced that the children will learn as much if she uses indirect

FIGURE 11.5   *Second Instrument*

FREE PLAY   Room **Pat**   Date **10/21**

                   No. of Children **14**   No. of Adults **2**

                   Time begun **9:20**   Time ended **9:35**

                   Interval **3-minute**

ACTIVITY	TIME 9:20	:23	:26	:29	:32	:35
Directed	5	5	4	2	3	3
Manipulatives	2		1			
Blocks		1	2			
Easel	2	2		2	1	1
House			3	3	3	2
Books					1	1
Water Play	5	4	3	2	3	4
Uninvolved		2	2	4	3	3

Comments: **Children in finger paint area changed. Water + house had same core of children — same ones as yesterday.**

behaviors. She needs a chance to come to terms with this idea, to practice new skills, and to find a balance that makes sense to her. You feel comfortable that she is now looking at free play in a different way and will continue to find ways to make it a positive experience for the children. You leave her with the suggestion that she observe children's responses to her statements and questions, evaluating which kinds encourage more elaborate building, problem solving, and experimentation. She can call on you to observe her or the children again when she feels ready to do so.

This hypothetical sequence of observations illustrates some of the ways supervisors and supervisees can work together to improve teaching and learning. Many of these observations could have been made using a naturalistic mode, providing a more holistic, but less focused, view. Another alternative would be to have the supervisee do the observations of the children, which would allow her more direct knowledge of what is happening. This has the disadvantage, however, of removing the supervisee's own influence from the dynamics of the situation.

Since there are a number of problems or situations that tend to recur with different teachers over the years, instruments that you have developed for one situation can be used with little alteration in a number of others. The free

FIGURE 11.6   *Third Instrument*

TEACHER'S VERBAL ENCOURAGEMENT: BLOCK PLAY

Labels what child does	/	/
Asks "What if" questions	/ / /	3
Asks child to label	ᵀᴴᴸ /	6
Makes direct suggestion	/ / /	3

Definitions:

Labels: "You've used a <u>square</u> block." "The truck
    went right <u>through</u> the building instead of going
    <u>around</u>.
<u>"What if" questions</u>: "What would happen if you used
    a bigger one?" "Would it fall if you used a
    different block?"
<u>Asks child to label</u>: "What shape is this?" "Is this
    taller or shorter than your block?"
<u>Direct Suggestion</u>: "It won't fall if you put a bigger
    one on the bottom." "This one would work better."

play form, for example, could also be used to examine teachers' activities during free play. By writing in staff members' initials at periodic intervals, a classroom team could have their own behavior mapped to help them plan strategies for cooperating more effectively.

CONCLUSION

The information obtained by observing staff is the major source of the content of supervisory conferences. Observation enables supervisors to provide feedback on what actually goes on in classrooms, thus providing a basis for supervisee growth and change. As a result of regular observations, both supervisors and supervisees can become inquirers about classroom life.

Supervisor and supervisee will find many advantages to planning together what is to be observed, jointly analyzing the data, and discussing how they will follow up:

- Supervisors gain first-hand, reliable knowledge about what is happening in their programs.
- Teachers get attention and feedback.
- Supervisor-staff communication gaps are narrowed.
- Problem areas become focused rather than diffused.
- Change becomes visible to both caregiver and supervisor.
- Trust increases because staff and supervisor are dealing with the same information.

EXERCISES

1. Develop a category system for observing during circle time. Make sure that the categories are mutually exclusive, mutually exhaustive, and precisely defined. Try your system out and refine it.
2. Choose a specific teacher behavior that a caregiver might want to improve. Develop a sign system, using either only the behaviors you want to encourage or examples of both positive and negative behaviors. Check for mutually exclusive categories. Try your system out and refine it.
3. Do a naturalistic observation using the *Exploring Childhood* film "Little Blocks."[22] Use the two-column system — one for description, the other for comments. Role-play a conference with the student in the film to identify a specific focus for another observation.
4. If you are teaching, become a participant observer of your own classroom by setting aside a few minutes each day to focus on one dimension of

classroom life. Use this technique to analyze your own program or as a way to assess strengths and needs of assistants or volunteers to work with you. (See David Strahan, "The Teacher and Ethnography," for more details on methodology.[23])

5. Have two groups observe the same situation, focusing on the same concern, for example, a teacher's use of encouraging behaviors. Have one group use a naturalistic system and the other a closed system. Compare the information and discuss it in terms of the usefulness of each for ongoing staff development or evaluation.

12 Evaluating Staff

Probably no other single aspect of supervision creates as much discomfort and distrust, raises such emotion and controversy, and is carried out as ineffectively as the process by which staff members are evaluated. Evaluating, judging, examining, appraising, and rating connote behaviors that seem contrary to the humanistic ideals dear to early childhood educators. Yet probably no other supervisory process has the potential to affect the quality of learning experiences for children as much as the assessment of staff members by themselves and by supervisors.

Evaluation takes on special importance when one considers that the field of early childhood education has not achieved true professional recognition. Standards for entry into the profession vary greatly from state to state, and those providing services to children, especially at the pre-kindergarten level, have easy access to jobs. There is no universally accepted standard of success or empirical evidence defining good teaching in preschools or excellent caregiving in infant-toddler centers.

The great variability in experience and education among the professional and paraprofessional staff within a program suggests a strong need for evaluation. It also places great demands on the director who must do the evaluating while struggling with the dual roles of (1) fostering the growth of staff members at different points in their professional development and (2) making personnel decisions about them, keeping in mind the priority of providing quality care to children.

WHY EVALUATE?

If the evaluation process is so complex and controversial or, as some individuals believe, so unrefined and subjective, then why evaluate at all?

Through evaluation, a supervisor acquires information about his or her program and staff. Supervisors and supervisees can use this information to make better decisions as they plan for the future. The diagnostic component of evaluation gives staff members feedback and thus can foster their professional development. An informal survey of early childhood program directors yielded the following purposes for evaluation:

144

- To recommend that staff be rehired, fired, promoted, or reassigned
- To ensure that program goals are being met
- To judge staff so they can obtain college credits or certification
- To determine merit salary increases
- To meet requirements of outside funding agencies
- To improve teaching by analyzing teaching styles, teaching strategies, curriculum, and learning environments
- To improve the quality of overall services provided to children
- To motivate staff
- To note the progress of staff members

There is overlap among the stated reasons for evaluating staff and among the implied tasks, but the major purposes of evaluation remain: (1) to foster the professional development of staff members in order to improve care and instruction; and (2) to provide a data base for making decisions about personnel.

WHO EVALUATES?

Should the supervisor have the sole responsibility for evaluating, or should the supervisee, other staff members, parents, and children be involved?

Supervisors

Whether director, educational coordinator, or head teacher, the supervisor by virtue of position has the authority and responsibility for evaluating staff. The supervisor is accountable for the program and therefore must be interested in its quality.

Supervisors have the experience and expertise to make judgments. Most likely, they have observed and conferred with staff members over time and have conducted training sessions with them as well. This ongoing process enables them to assess the professional development of individuals and to have a sound data base for evaluation. Supervisors are also familiar with the children, parents, and community so they understand the context in which staff members work. Supervisors may also have developed the procedures for evaluating staff in cooperation with the staff as well as with board members.

For all these reasons, supervisors are the ones who evaluate supervisees. But supervisors need not be the only individuals who evaluate. In fact, supervisees can evaluate themselves, peers can evaluate each other, and parents can participate in the process, creating a significant opportunity to gain a broader perspective of a staff member's progress, to enable staff members to learn and grow from the process, and to permit other relevant parties to offer input. The views of each, taken alone, have limitations. Used together, they form a more complete portrait of the individual being evaluated.

Supervisee

Self-evaluation requires that an individual take the time to reflect about the growth that he or she has made. This can be an insightful and rewarding experience, enabling an individual to "take stock," to note gains and setbacks, and to set personal goals for the future.

Although all staff members benefit by evaluating themselves, our experience suggests that self-evaluation is easier for supervisees who are already analytical and reflective. Staff members may need ideas and structure to help them think about themselves; that is, evaluation criteria can serve as organizers for their thinking. Readings such as Katz's "Stages of Pre-School Teachers" and Caruso's "Phases in Student Teaching" can help them to think about their progress.[1]

The supervisory conference lays the groundwork for self-evaluation, for it is through the conference that the staff member practices reflecting, predicting, judging, and suggesting alternatives to caregiving and teaching behaviors. Through practice, patience, and hard work on the part of supervisor and supervisee, most staff members can learn to become skilled self-evaluators.

A drawback to self-evaluation is that supervisees sometimes underrate or overrate themselves but individuals usually know themselves and the quality of their work better than anyone else. An advantage of self-evaluation is that it is free from external threat and that it empowers staff members. They have an opportunity to judge themselves and to respect their own judgments.

Peers

Peers can become part of a support system to help staff members improve their performance. Teachers in early childhood programs work in classrooms with other teachers, aides, and volunteers and thus have a knowledge of each other's classroom practice. Although a head teacher often has supervisory responsibilities for others in a program, it is not unusual for colleagues to engage in supportive activities such as sharing frustration, offering specific suggestions, and assisting each other when the work of the day seems overwhelming.

Directors may be able to establish a structure within programs to enable peers to assess each other's work. Less threatening than the official supervisor, colleagues can be particularly helpful to each other in working on areas that supervisor and supervisee have agreed need improvement. When colleagues participate in peer supervision, a program gains the advantage of their expertise, and staff members gain further opportunities for growth. Peer supervision can build colleagueship and allow the director more time to engage in other important tasks.

Although we believe that peers should be involved in ongoing assessment, we question whether peers should participate in decisions that may lead to the termination of an individual from a program. Given the small size of many programs, summative judgments by peers could create divisiveness and reduce the climate of trust and respect that supervisors work so hard to create. The notion of judgment by peers is, however, an admirable one.

Parents

Parents informally evaluate early childhood programs. They judge staff members and programs by continuing to send their children to a center or withdrawing them. Parents can be asked to evaluate staff more formally by completing rating forms cooperatively developed by supervisor, staff, and parents; by being interviewed after they have visited a program; and/or by observing and rating staff in a center. These are practices that are a part of the CDA assessment system. (See chapter 15.)

Soliciting the views of parents can increase their support and enthusiasm for a program and can enhance its climate. Critical to their successful participation, however, is the method used to involve parents as well as the ways in which staff members are prepared for the involvement. Parents need to be informed about why their help is requested, to understand the nature of the actual power they have, and to know appropriate protocol and behavior for participating in the evaluation process.

APPROACHES TO EVALUATION

Formative Evaluation

Formative evaluation is an ongoing process that provides teachers, curriculum designers, and others with regular feedback about their programs and performance to create a formative effect on the educational environment. Staff members do not have to wait until the conclusion of a program or the end of a year to receive constructive suggestions or to know what a supervisor thinks about their work. Evaluation with a formative focus tends to be informal and diagnostic in nature. Supervisors collect data in a variety of ways, including conferences with supervisees, audiotapes and videotapes, observation schedules, and checklists. This information reflects specific strengths and weaknesses of a staff member and can be used to promote continuous growth; it therefore has a developmental focus. Formative evaluation is closely linked with clinical supervision. It occurs throughout the cycle of clinical supervision. In some programs, formative evaluation may take place at designated points, between summative evaluation periods.

Summative Evaluation

Summative evaluation usually takes place at the end of a specified time span, when an administrator or supervisor "sums up" the effectiveness of a staff member's performance, letting that person know where he or she stands against certain predetermined standards. The time established for summative evaluation may be set by the board, institution, or funding source.

Summative evaluation is a formal, legal process. Evaluation procedures may be mutually developed by supervisor and staff, or may be described in a contract and approved by a board of directors. The evaluation criteria, tools used, and people to be involved are usually described in a program's personnel policy.

In contrast to formative evaluation, which may focus on particular problems, issues, or teaching episodes, the summative evaluation examines the staff member's overall performance and helps supervisors make decisions about that individual's place in the program. The supervisor often collects data by the same methods used in formative evaluation, but the consequences of summative evaluation may be that a staff member is disciplined, terminated, promoted, or recommended for a teaching credential. A specific plan for assistance or the establishment of the general direction of the future work that supervisor and supervisee will pursue can be an outcome of summative evaluation as well.

In practice, it is sometimes difficult to separate formative and summative evaluation activities and practices, particularly since one supervisor often is responsible for both of them. Supervisors might find it useful, however, to keep in mind the different emphases of each type of evaluation.

METHODS OF EVALUATION

Present evaluation practices appear to be rooted in either of two basic viewpoints about supervision. One is characterized by a scientific or quantitative frame of reference; the other, by a naturalistic or qualitative one, analogous to the methods of observation described in the previous chapter.

Scientific Evaluation

The scientific method emphasizes objectivity and precision in measuring particular staff behavioral characteristics predetermined to be desirable and effective. Supervisory rating scales, which are based on specific traits or categories of behavior, are commonly used tools by those who have a scientific orientation to evaluation. Another scientifically based technique for evaluating the effectiveness of teachers is testing the achievement levels of their students, but this method is not especially relevant or appropriate to early childhood education.

One of the major tasks of the scientific evaluator is to determine the criteria that will form the basis of the evaluation. Appropriate criteria often lie within these general areas:

- *Physical characteristics* — the physical health and vitality conducive to effective performance of the duties the position demands
- *Mental ability* — the ability to conceptualize the philosophy of the program, the employee's role, and the roles of others as they relate to the position
- *Professional qualifications* — knowledge of the methods and materials used in the position
- *Personal attributes* — enthusiasm, poise, the ability to adjust to frustrations, and a cooperative attitude toward colleagues[2]

One source of specific evaluation criteria is research on what makes effective teaching and caregiving. Two examples of such research studies are those by Greta Fein and Alison Clarke-Stewart and by Elizabeth Phyfe-Perkins.

Fein and Clarke-Stewart, in their survey of the research on effective early childhood teaching, cited emotional warmth, creativity, high teacher interest and involvement, the intensity of the teacher's involvement, active teacher intervention and deliberate stimulation, sensitivity, responsiveness, and understanding as factors that have been consistently shown to have positive effects on children.[3]

Phyfe-Perkins reports that successful teachers were those who had the ability to be

> Encouraging, warm and friendly, involved with individuals and small groups, and attentive to two issues simultaneously. Adults need to keep the momentum going, effect smooth transitions, use positively worded instructions, minimize direct leadership of large groups, and maximize a child-centered approach as opposed to one in which adults make most of the decisions. . . .[4]

The research on effective teaching and caregiving, however, is scarce and offers practitioners a mixed bag. In discussing the research on teaching in general, James Popham sadly reports "a review of the teacher effectiveness research during the first three-quarters of this century reveals a woeful record of unfilled hopes and unrejected null hypothesis. . . . "[5] Bernard Spodek and Olivia Saracho report "there is little that we know about what constitutes effective teaching at the kindergarten level or prekindergarten level."[6]

In addition to criteria based on teacher characteristics and teaching behaviors, criteria based on pupil behavior change can also be tied to the appraisal of teacher performance.[7] Responding to the idea of assessing children as a means of appraising teacher effectiveness, Spodek and Saracho point out that the valued outcomes of early childhood programs include goals in the affective, social, and psychomotor domains, areas that are problematic to assess in young children.[8] These areas receive less research attention in favor of the cognitive area in which it is easier to measure outcomes, especially for older children.

Given this state of affairs, early childhood supervisors need to look to what practitioners believe are important caregiver qualities and competencies, less scientific but based on common sense, and at criteria developed by early childhood professional organizations.

The competencies developed by the Child Development Associate Program (see Appendix A) and the evaluation criteria developed by the Bank Street Follow-Through Program provide practitioners with comprehensive lists of criteria to use in evaluating staff. The early childhood literature on teacher evaluation, although limited, is another source. For example, Anne Willis and Henry Ricciuti have reviewed the qualities necessary for working in a day care program and for working with babies and adults; Alice Sterling Honig has developed questions directors can ask about staff members to assess their programs.[9]

Job descriptions of the various positions within a program, if already developed, can be useful in determining evaluation criteria. Probably the best resources for identifying criteria are the administrators and staff members of the program itself, as well as parents who support and are served by the program. The very process of developing evaluation criteria by asking staff members to keep track of their time, to describe their daily activities and their perceptions of the role, and to identify the qualities, knowledge, and skills they believe important can be an extremely worthwhile staff development endeavor.

The use of rating scales, teacher tests, and student achievement scores are technical, rational approaches to evaluating staff members, especially teachers. Supervisors using these methods identify specific outcomes, such as teacher and/or student behaviors, ahead of time, the assumption being that the existence of such characteristics indicates effective teaching. The popularity of these approaches may have to do with the psychological sense of security they provide to supervisors and supervisees who prefer quantitative methods, the clarity of stated objectives, and knowing ahead of time the specific outcomes upon which evaluation will be based.

Naturalistic Evaluation

A naturalistic approach to evaluation places greater emphasis on the meaning and quality of the experiences that children and staff members have in the classroom. Rather than rate a teacher on specific competencies, the supervisor is more concerned with context and setting, with understanding how teacher and child engage each other, and with discovering the assumptions that underlie classroom practices.

As inquirer, the supervisor works in the natural setting over time, developing detailed descriptions of what occurs in classrooms. Supervisors using the naturalistic method need to be perceptive and sensitive and to have strong analytic thinking skills so that they can infer meaning and appreciate the subtleties of classroom life. They also need facility with language in order to interpret, describe, and reconstruct events.

When a supervisor uses an "artistic" approach to naturalistic evaluation, she or he takes on the roles of critic and connoisseur, as described in the previous chapter. As critic, the evaluator's job is to construct artistically what has been observed, to help others, often through expressive or artistic use of language, understand what has transpired.[10] Eisner explains, "It is through the art of connoisseurship that one is able to appreciate and internalize meanings in classrooms, and through the skill of criticism that one is able to share or disclose the meaning to others."[11] This approach to evaluation demands that supervisors become highly skilled in developing representations of classroom events for analysis and interpretation. Videotaping and assembling the artifacts of teaching are other ways of developing such representations.

Integrating Methods

Although scientific approaches to evaluation have not fulfilled their promise and the application of the art of description and interpretation to "discover and create the meaning" of teaching needs further development, both approaches contribute in their unique ways to evaluation. Through the process of clinical supervision, supervisors and supervisees can bring both the scientific and the naturalistic aspects of evaluation together to create a more complete picture and deeper understanding of life in the classroom.

Thomas Sergiovanni[12] makes a case for not dismissing scientific evaluation strategies and their power to provide supervisors and supervisees with factual descriptions of classroom events. Yet the quantitative data that such instruments provide are not enough. We want to examine not only what is but also what events mean and what should be happening. That is the advantage of combining the strengths of both the scientific and the naturalistic approaches to the tasks of supervision and evaluation.

EVALUATION TOOLS

Two of the most common tools used in evaluating staff are narratives and rating scales. Portfolios, used in CDA, are becoming more recognized in the field of education as a useful means of collecting information and evaluating the work of staff members.

Narratives

A narrative summative report is a statement that describes what the supervisor has observed over a period of time and includes the supervisor's judgments and recommendations with regard to the staff member's performance. The format of this report can be completely open-ended, but some narrative instruments provide evaluators with more structure or restrictions by asking for comments on such general areas as knowledge of subject matter, planning, physical management, social management, teacher-child interaction, interpersonal communication, professional development, personal qualities, relations with parents and community, and non-teaching responsibilities.

The advantages of a narrative evaluation are several: It gives the evaluator(s) space to set a context and to describe and illustrate with examples. It can be very thorough, offering the reader a substantial amount of specific information. Summative evaluation reports provide a lasting record, support future evaluator(s), highlight patterns of behavior, and encourage evaluators to be thoughtful. On the other hand, writing a narrative report is time consuming. Its open-endedness may not provide enough structure for the evaluator(s), who may overemphasize some areas and leave out others just as critical. The narrative report is compatible with a naturalistic view of evaluation, but some believe that it is simply too open-ended and relies on the evaluator's values to a greater extent than need be.

Following is an example of a narrative summative evaluation report written by a college supervisor of a student teacher:

> Diane completed her junior student teaching in the class of three- and four-year-olds at the ABC Child Care Center. The classroom, which contained approximately 16 children, was in a large partitioned area within a very large space which houses the center's two classrooms. In addition to her cooperating

teacher, there were several other full and part-time teachers and aides with whom Diane worked.

I observed Diane on five occasions from January to June for approximately forty-five minutes each time. I saw her work with individual and small groups of children in the cooking, blockbuilding, and dramatic play areas and on two occasions, I observed her in charge of all the children in the class. After each observation, I met with her for a conference.

Diane worked well with her cooperating teacher and the other adults in the classroom. By the end of the semester she was fully a part of the teaching team, participating in planning and evaluation meetings and in decision making throughout the day. Other adults valued her ideas and often made changes in the classroom based on her suggestions. Diane also worked well with the children. She learned a great deal about the development of four- and five-year-olds, which helped her interpret their behavior and social and emotional needs. She seemed to genuinely care about the children and conveyed this as she worked with them. They came to rely on her as their teacher. Diane learned a lot about meeting the needs of a few children who seemed to have emotional problems.

With respect to program planning and curriculum development, Diane learned a great deal throughout the semester. She began by working with another teacher on planning small group activities for a regularly assigned group of children. The activities included a wide range of topics, subject areas, and activities. Increasingly as she did her planning, Diane was able to utilize her knowledge of individual children as well as build onto what had happened with the group the day before. She became clearer in her goals and better able to evaluate and modify her plans as she went along. Diane gradually took responsibility for group times, setting up the activities for the entire classroom and orchestrating transitions. She planned many appropriate activities for these times. She also gained a growing sense of how various subject areas and activities could be interrelated to foster greater continuity in the children's learning. For instance, she did a curriculum unit on cooking during which she made snacks with the children for several days. She incorporated art, language arts, math, science, and social studies into the activities and also helped the children gain a sense of responsibility in helping to meet their needs in the classroom. Her cooperating teacher was impressed with how she managed to weave this theme of cooking into the curriculum throughout the day.

In the courses which accompany student teaching, Diane was an active class member. She worked on applying child development theory and course content to classroom practice. She contributed to class discussions and shared her classroom experiences openly. She utilized suggestions from others and myself in building onto and modifying her views and revealed a growing appreciation of the complexities of the teaching process and the teacher's role in the classroom.

Diane has developed the skills required to be a competent and caring person in the lives of children. She has the confidence and commitment to continue to grow and develop in the profession.

Robert Fraser offers the following principles and suggestions for writing summative evaluation reports:[13]

1. Focus on strengths; be specific in citing what it is you thought was good and why.
2. Try to be positive and supportive but be judicious about the use of superlatives.
3. Focus on specific behaviors; simply stating that someone is well organized is insufficient. Be specific about the facts that have led you to make that inference.
4. Set forth any and all areas of concern. State exactly what you have observed which concerns you, why it concerns you, and what you expect to be done about it.
5. After you have written a statement, ask yourself how you would prove it to be true if you had to.
6. Use the written evaluation reports as a means of focusing on "growing edges."
7. Don't be afraid to set expectations relative to the next evaluation cycle or school year.
8. Avoid the use of "professional jargon"; write so that a third party who knows nothing about the situation will get a clearer picture of the teacher you are describing.
9. Don't use qualifying or equivocal terms. "Hedge words" have no place in an evaluation. You are presumably an expert rendering an informed opinion about what you know.
10. Don't be apologetic if something is unsatisfactory; say it.
11. Have another qualified administrator read your evaluations in "draft form" before you present them to the teacher involved.

Rating Scales

Another type of evaluation instrument is one that asks the evaluator(s) to rate the extent to which a staff member manifests certain discrete behaviors. Figure 12.1 shows a sample page from a rating scale.

Rating scales can be administered with relative ease, depending on their length. Unlike the narrative, the competencies to be evaluated are explicit and available to supervisor and supervisee at the beginning of the evaluation period. Rating scales with numerous competency statements can seem overwhelming and perhaps a bit unrealistic to the supervisee, yet they can be useful as both formative and summative evaluation tools. They should not, however, be used as observation instruments. Rating scales do not provide the reader with personal or specific examples and illustrations of a staff member's behavior.

Some programs have made successful attempts at combining some form

FIGURE 12.1   *Evaluation Rating Scale*

UNDERSTANDING BEHAVIOR: CHILDREN

1.   Is able to make natural, spontaneous conversation with
     children; appears to gain satisfaction and pleasure from
     interacting with them

0	1	2	3	4	5
serious problems	limited	adequate	good	superior	outstanding

2.   Understands what is developmentally appropriate behavior
     for children of a given age (i.e., nature of play,
     interest spans, social relationships, and so forth)

0	1	2	3	4	5
serious problems	limited	adequate	good	superior	outstanding

3.   Is aware of children's feelings and able to identify a
     range of affective behaviors such as fear, jealousy,
     anger, joy

0	1	2	3	4	5
serious problems	limited	adequate	good	superior	outstanding

4.   Interacts with children with sensitivity to the possible
     causes of behavior; exercises an understanding of
     individuality

0	1	2	3	4	5
serious problems	limited	adequate	good	superior	outstanding

5.   Actively seeks to understand and implement change in his
     or her own behavior as it affects working with children
     (i.e., issues of authority, anger, competition,
     insecurity, and so forth)

0	1	2	3	4	5
serious problems	limited	adequate	good	superior	outstanding

SOURCE: Department of Child Study, Tufts University, Medford, Mass.

of rating scale with adequate space for descriptive comments by supervisor and supervisee. These instruments incorporate some of the major advantages of the narrative and rating scale.

Portfolio Development

Portfolio development is based on naturalistic assumptions about evaluation. It is a means of studying classrooms as an anthropologist might to obtain a more complete representation of teaching and learning. In chapter 11, we described ethnographic techniques for observing in classrooms. Using anthropological methods, evaluators too can learn about the culture of classrooms by examining the artifacts assembled by staff members to form a portfolio.

As an evaluation strategy, portfolio development is somewhat similar to artifacts analysis done by the anthropologist. The portfolio is a collection of photographs, records, and other materials designed to represent some aspect of the classroom program and teaching activities. The teacher or teaching team has the responsibility for assembling the portfolio. The materials collected, or artifacts, reflect a sense of purpose and highlight key issues or concerns that the teachers wish to represent.[14]

An examination of the artifacts of the portfolio should enable supervisor and staff member to raise questions and to draw inferences about the teacher's assumptions of how young children learn, what the teacher values, how children spend their time, and the ways in which teacher and children interact.

Sergiovanni suggests that issues could also be raised about the role of the children in classroom decision making; the match between what the teacher does and his or her philosophy; the compatibility of teacher's goals and supervisor's goals; the type of thinking that activities in the classroom promote; the extent to which teacher preparation is evidenced; and the teacher's knowledge of subject matter.[15]

After analysis and discussion of what the artifacts represent, the supervisor's role is to test out the inferences generated by observing in classrooms and conducting follow-up conferences with supervisees. The portfolio offers rich possibilities for dialogue on the quality of classroom events and experiences.

Guidelines for Developing Evaluation Tools

In developing an evaluation tool for your program, consider the following questions:

1. Does the instrument encourage growth on the part of the staff member?
2. Does it encourage serious thinking on the part of supervisor and supervisee?
3. Does the instrument provide enough structure so that it helps the evaluator to focus?
4. Does the instrument allow adequate space for general comments, concrete examples, and/or specific recommendations?
5. Are the competency statements clear and understandable? Is there a need for definitions of terms or examples?
6. Is the format of the instrument free from clutter? Is the readability level appropriate?
7. Does the instrument enable the evaluator to comment on or describe the context and setting?
8. Are the time requirements for completing the form reasonable and appropriate?
9. Are the stated competencies reasonable and attainable?
10. Does the instrument and the process by which it is used encourage honesty on the part of evaluator and evaluatee?
11. Does the instrument and the process by which it is used encourage and offer guidance and direction for the future?

A SPECIAL CONCERN: THE MARGINAL PERFORMER

As a result of formative or summative evaluation, supervisors will occasionally have to deal with a staff member whose performance is marginal. According to Lawrence Steinmetz, a marginal performer may be defined as "any employee who recurringly, although infrequently, fails to produce a reasonable quantity of acceptable work in line with his capabilities and management's expectations."[16] Marginal performers may be tardy or absent from their work; they may be moody or aggressive; they may have many "blue Mondays" on the job; and they may offer many excuses for not performing up to par.

Reprimanding

When the need arises to reprimand an individual, Kenneth Blanchard and Spencer Johnson make a very strong case for reprimanding the *behavior* and never attacking a person's worth or value. They offer a number of worthwhile tips to keep in mind when reprimanding:

1. Intervene early. Provide immediate feedback by getting to the individual as soon as you observe "the misbehavior." Don't store up observations of poor behavior and release them in an end of year evaluation conference.
2. Eliminate the behavior and keep the person. The staff member has to know that the behavior is not O.K. but that they are O.K.
3. Never give a reprimand based on hearsay. Be certain that you see the behavior yourself.

Blanchard and Johnson believe that significant improvement in people's behavior will occur if you tell them what they did wrong, tell them how you feel about it, and remind them that they are valuable and worthwhile.[17]

In working with such individuals, determine the seriousness and the source of the individual's unsatisfactory performance. If the source is job-related, then it may be possible to spend more time with the staff member and alter certain job conditions to improve the situation. Supervisors may need to correct or change their own behavior if they are the source of the problem, for example, if they do not give complete and clear directions for accomplishing a task. Sometimes, a direct, take-charge approach is needed, whereby the supervisor sets up a very structured schedule for the individual or moves the staff member from one team to another. If the source of the program is outside the program, the supervisor may have little control over its solution but may be of some help by listening to the supervisee and offering suggestions.

Firing

As every supervisor knows, it is sometimes necessary to fire an employee. This is a very difficult and unpleasant supervisory responsibility. The decision to fire someone should come after careful thought, after the collection of solid data over time, and after a sincere effort has been made to examine the problem from different angles and to solve it. The collection of descriptive and relevant data is essential not only to make the reasons for the decision clear to the employee but as backup in case of a grievance or legal challenge to the firing.

There are many reasons why it may be necessary to terminate the employment of a staff member. These include lack of competence, attitudinal problems, and the existence of interpersonal conflict with others in the program. Steinmetz recommends these guidelines for supervisors to follow in discharging an employee:[18]

1. Check and consult with trusted people in the organization who are knowledgeable about the circumstances, concerned, and likely to be objective in their advice.
2. Get into a relaxed frame of mind before making the decision. Do not make the decision while under stress.
3. Never make the decision to discharge an individual under conditions of crisis.
4. Don't try to anticipate all the eventualities that could occur as a result of the dismissal. Assume that the decision is the right one.
5. Don't expect that everyone else in the program will consider the decision to fire someone to be the right one.
6. Don't overdo in planning for the discharge.
7. Once the decision is made, carry it out in a simple, forthright, and clear fashion. Make it very clear to the staff member that he or she is being dismissed, why, and when the discharge is to become effective.
8. To avoid embarrassment and possible eavesdropping, carry out the discharge at the end of the day in a thoroughly private place.
9. Once the decision is made, carry it out. Don't wait several days or weeks.
10. Have all the facts relevant to the decision at hand.
11. Allow ample opportunity for the employee to offer explanations and to ask questions.
12. Have at your disposal information with respect to contract and program policy so that you can answer questions about procedures, final payment, transferring medical benefits, and so forth.
13. Make a record of what transpires during the final conference and note unfinished tasks or projects that will need to be completed by another staff member.

In many cases, although certainly not all, firing someone can be in that person's best interest. Sometimes, an employee who is unhappy, frustrated, or unfulfilled in the job simply cannot make the decision to "get out of a rut" and into a new job, routine, or lifestyle. In those cases, supervisors actually relieve pain by making the decision for the individual.

Staff members in programs with good systems for self-evaluation and frequent communication between supervisor and supervisee are usually not surprised by such actions, as they have been working with their supervisors to address problems over time. Suggesting ways that the person might find another job, redirecting the person to another career, and reminding the individual of the skills that he or she does have can be helpful. This is especially important for low-income persons who have few alternatives.

Firing an employee can be almost as painful for the supervisor as the staff member. You should assume, however, that you are in a supervisory position because you have expertise and sound judgment and that your decision, not taken lightly, is in the best interest of the program and the people in it.

CONCLUSION

The following principles can serve as a guide to supervisors developing programs for evaluating staff:

1. The development of a system and policy for evaluating staff should be a cooperative endeavor including staff, board members, and parents.
2. Job expectations for a supervisee should be made explicit from the beginning. The competencies upon which an individual is being evaluated should be clearly stated and public. Staff members should have advance knowledge that evaluation will take place based on these competencies.
3. Evaluation is not an unilateral act performed by a supervisor. Peers and parents may be part of the process; supervisees should definitely be included.
4. Staff members should have the right to disagree with an evaluation report and to note their disagreement.
5. Although one purpose of evaluation is to make judgments about a staff member's performance, evaluation should also be diagnostic, to assist the supervisee in improving performance. Thus a supervisee should receive ongoing feedback.
6. Assessing the context in which an individual is working is an important ingredient in the process of evaluation. Studying the elements in the environment, such as the resources available, space, and so forth, which influence program quality helps pinpoint factors that affect a staff member's performance.
7. The evaluation process employed should help the supervisee and supervisor maintain and build personal and professional self-respect and self-image, as well as respect for each other.
8. The process should foster self-evaluation on the part of all involved, including supervisors who need to understand how they influence a situation.
9. The nature of evaluation should encourage experimentation, creativity, and variation. Good supervisors create programs that encourage supervisees to test ideas and try new approaches, rather than to conform to someone else's conception of what is good teaching.
10. The evaluation program should result in raising the quality of the care,

instruction, and experiences that children receive in classrooms. Unless evaluation makes a difference, then it may not be justified at all.[19]

EXERCISES

1. Discuss the notion of the teacher portfolio with your staff members. Ask if one or two teachers would be interested in experimenting with the idea by developing a portfolio and discussing its artifacts with you. After reasonable time intervals, confer with the staff members using the portfolios as a basis for discussion. You and the teachers can practice analyzing the material in terms of their goals for young children and their values.
2. Review your program's evaluation policy and procedures in the light of the principles discussed in this chapter. If revisions are needed, begin by involving your staff members in a process of describing the competencies they believe are necessary to do the job effectively.
3. Experiment with the idea of peer supervision by establishing a structure whereby staff members could observe each other at work and then confer with one another about the observation.

Part IV

STAFF DEVELOPMENT IN PRACTICE

13 Supervisory Problems

. . . I have a situation where I'm living rent-free. I live with one of the parents from the center in exchange for room and board. I bring their child back and forth as a back-up service so if one parent can't bring the child, I do it. But I'm just making it. I've got loan payments every month. If I had to pay rent as well as my other bills, I wouldn't be able to survive in this city. And it gets me angry because I think it's society's outlook — their attitude toward child care; yet, there's a great demand for child care. In this program, they won't hire you unless you have a college degree, which means this is a professional job. Yet I don't consider $8,000 per year professional wages. So it's very maddening because I want to do what I want to do. I enjoy what I do. . . .

The frustration of this college-educated woman in her mid-twenties embodies some of the major issues facing early childhood supervisors and teachers, as well as the field itself. Minimal salaries and benefits, the lack of professional status, and public misunderstanding and undervaluing of child care are among the factors that lead to low morale and staff turnover — two significant concerns that early childhood supervisors contend with on a daily basis. These problems, as well as those associated with diversity of culture and class, can create feelings of discouragement in supervisors.

The purpose of this chapter is to clarify some of the factors that underlie these problem areas, to establish a basis for managing them, and to suggest methods for ameliorating their negative effects. We want to show that these problems are not insurmountable.

STAFF MORALE

Employee morale is a major issue for any supervisor, whether in business and industry or in the human services professions. When morale is high, people are motivated to do exciting, innovative, and growth-oriented work. When it is low, they do their work in a routine fashion at best. They often withdraw, complain, and become cynical.

Morale is of particular concern in programs for young children because it affects children as well as staff. In their discussion of infant centers, Willis

165

and Ricciuti maintain that the quality of a program is affected as much by staff morale as it is by staff competence.

> A well-trained caregiver who is unhappy with working conditions or is not getting along with another staff member or who feels powerless to affect decisions about her job is not likely to do a good job caring for babies. A caregiver cannot focus on meeting babies' needs when her own are not being met.[1]

Exhaustion and Tedium

Watching children grow, creating successful learning experiences, and being warmly responded to by children are the kinds of rewards that attract people to the field of early childhood education. But the very humanness of children, which makes them loving and joyful, can be difficult to manage in group settings. Even with the warmest, most skilled caregiving efforts, children don't always respond positively, and handling one or more difficult children on a daily basis can be exhausting.

Daily routines, especially in centers for infants or toddlers, can become tedious: such chores as getting children dressed for outdoors, washing bottles, changing diapers, and cleaning up can easily cause caregivers to lose sight of the importance and meaningfulness of what they are doing. With preschool children too, when teachers feel as though they know every puzzle by heart; have said, "Tell me about your painting," too many times; and have had their fortieth cup of coffee in the house corner, they also need support and opportunities for change.

Isolation

A great deal of the caregiver's time is spent immersed in the world of children, where isolation from other adults is commonplace. In family day care settings providers may have little contact with adults at all, and none with others doing the same job unless they are part of a support network or training program. In group settings, although two or three adults often work together, their focus is mainly on children and classroom concerns. Sometimes teachers solve this problem in their own way by engaging in personal talk when they should be interacting with children. It is easy to label this as lazy or irresponsible behavior, but if feelings of isolation are involved, addressing the problem requires an analysis of factors that lead to those feelings.

Teachers are really dealing with isolation on two fronts — personal and professional. Both are supervisory concerns. Times set aside for open discussion of daily problems in the context of professional sharing can help teachers deal with their feelings about themselves and their children. At the same time, purely social situations, from coffee breaks to staff parties, can provide opportunities for adult, non-work-centered interaction.

Inadequate Pay and Poor Working Conditions

The problem of inadequate pay is a familiar one to those who have worked in preschool programs. The average salary of the *highest* paid classroom staff in day care, when extrapolated to a fifty-week year, is barely more than half of the average public school teacher's salary.[2] Although day care teachers rank over the 50th percentile in terms of their educational qualifications compared to workers in other professions, they rank below the 5th percentile in terms of their rate of pay.[3] The income of nursery school teachers and assistants, who work only half-days and no summers, can seldom be classified as more than supplemental. Fee rates for family day care providers are truly appalling.

Further, fringe benefits such as paid vacations, health insurance, and even sick leave, which have become standard in almost every other work place, are unavailable to many staff members, as Table 13.1 indicates. A recent survey revealed that only a very small percentage of caregivers in Illinois and California received maternity benefits, despite the fact that so many of the workers polled were of child-bearing age.[4] Even breaks, which are

TABLE 13.1 *Fringe Benefits of AEYC Respondents*

BENEFIT	YES	NO	NO ANSWER
Paid vacation	61	34	5
Sick days	85	11	4
Health insurance	60	37	4
Automatic salary increase for college earned credit	16	77	7
Regular in-service education	41	53	6
Agency contribution to college costs	28	65	7
Longevity raises	64	32	5
Merit raises	25	70	5

NOTE: Reprinted, with permission of the publisher, from Lana Hoestetler and Edgar Klugman, "Early Childhood Job Titles: One Step Toward Professional Status," *Young Children* 37 (September 1982), p. 17.

mandated by law in some states, are unavailable to as many as three-fifths of caregivers, either because they are not allowed, or because a shortage of time and staff makes them difficult to take.[5]

It is not unusual for administrators, sponsoring agencies, and boards of directors — especially in large multiservice organizations like YMCAs, family service, or community development agencies — to be inadequately informed about the merits of the services performed by the preschool programs they sponsor or about the skills needed by staff members. Few directors have had training in negotiating with boards or in methods of affecting public policy. Nor do many educational coordinators or head teachers have the necessary expertise to advocate for staff needs with their immediate superiors.

This situation is starting to change. Associations of day care directors and providers and public policy committees of local affiliates of NAEYC are becoming skilled at lobbying state legislators. Many have been successful in securing increased funding for day care, in part by stressing the need for better pay and benefits for staff. Some directors have found that one sympathetic board member may be willing to help interpret staff needs to others, to assist in developing strategies, and to become an advocate for center and staff concerns. Meetings of supervisor support groups are good places to explore and share these and other strategies. Sessions on negotiation or advocacy skills can also be planned through local early childhood associations.[6]

Although teachers and aides might appear to have the least power to influence change in working conditions, it is sometimes their efforts — especially when supported by supervisors — that have the greatest impact. A determined group of Colorado caregivers discovered that their attempts to influence government officials can have results: "You can call Welfare Department people a lot of dirty names, and that is exactly what we were doing at that time, but the political reality is that they need the community pressure. . . . because any kind of increase in their budget needs to be justified."[7]

Low Status

Almost everyone who works with young children has at some time, in one way or another, been given the feeling that their job requires few skills or that it is one that any woman can "naturally" do. Day care providers, especially those in home settings, are characterized as "just baby sitters," and nursery school teachers are often seen as "merely" supervisors of children's play.

It will take concerted, long-term efforts by professional groups and individuals to have an impact on the views of the public as a whole. Closer to home, however, parents can be educated through involvement in classrooms, by getting to know and respect staff members, and through infor-

national meetings at which the program for children is explained. Staff members will come to view themselves as professionals when their knowledge and skills are recognized and reinforced, when the difficulty of their job is acknowledged, and when their efforts to gain more knowledge and to improve their skills are supported.

Exclusion from Decision Making and Misleading Job Descriptions

Control over day-to-day decisions, the flexibility connected with the job, and the opportunity to learn and grow are high on the list of satisfactions of teachers of young children. This flexibility and autonomy, however, is often limited to classroom or curricular decisions. Marcy Whitebook and associates found that only 18 percent of teaching staff (aides, teachers, and head teachers/directors) were included in such major decisions as hiring and firing, budget, relations with parents and community, and working conditions. This was a source of dissatisfaction for many, because they felt that those who did make these decisions were not well informed and/or were insensitive to the ramifications of their decisions.[8]

The place of aides in this picture is of special concern. Early childhood educators often state with pride that all members of a classroom team are seen as "teachers," and job descriptions frequently reflect this view. This parity of role is one we generally support, and it is undoubtedly a source of real satisfaction to many aides. It can also, however, be a source of resentment. In spite of equal responsibility for day-to-day classroom decisions and sometimes for curriculum planning, aides' pay and benefits are lower — sometimes considerably so. In addition, they are often arbitrarily excluded from certain tasks and are even less likely to be included in major decision-making than teachers.[9]

Supervisors can help solve these problems. Opportunities for participation in decisions can be made available to all staff, including aides, through regular staff meetings and classroom team meetings. Job descriptions can be updated periodically with staff input so that they realistically reflect the expectations of each role. Pay scales can be reviewed and brought closer together where job expectations are substantially similar. And career ladders can be established so that the skills and knowledge obtained through in-service training, experience, and college courses are recognized.

Stress and Burnout

Seldom are all the conditions we have described present at the same time, and often they are balanced by the rewards of the job. At times, however, particularly for staff members who have been working in one center for many years, these concerns come together to create the condition commonly referred to as burnout.

Burnout has been described as "the depletion of [an individual's ordinary] resourcefulness, flexibility, and positive energy,"[10] and as "a syndrome of emotional exhaustion and cynicism that can occur in individuals who spend much of their time working closely with other people."[11] Conditions that lead to burnout are found in many of the human service professions, which require intensive involvement with others in emotionally demanding situations. In the early childhood field, caregivers in day care, Head Start, and hospital child life programs are particularly susceptible to burnout. Administrators and supervisors too, especially when they have little support for providing the kind of program they feel is necessary, are also prone to this type of emotional exhaustion.

Burnout does not arise exclusively from factors within the workplace, however. The National Day Care Study reported that fully 30 percent of caregivers were the sole income earners for their families and 69 percent provided more than half of their family's support.[12] Low salaries in the child care field create stress and strain on wage earners. When a caregiver is also confronted with major problems at home — a husband out of work, children in trouble at school, divorce — the daily task of caring for someone else's children can seem overwhelming. Even positive factors, such as an aide's growing confidence and competence on the job, can sometimes change his or her relationship with a spouse and family, creating tensions that can affect that person's work.

One study found that for low-income child care workers, life circumstances outside the job were much more anxiety producing than were job-related problems. Supervisors in programs where staff members are drawn from low-income or minority families should thus be especially alert to these concerns.[13]

Raising Morale

Individual and group morale can and will be low from time to time without leading inexorably to burnout. Supervisors who recognize that morale is a legitimate supervisory concern, and are alert to burnout symptoms at their early stages, can work out both long- and short-term strategies for dealing with it.

Several studies of burnout in early childhood settings have suggested guidelines for preventing this condition. Stanley Seiderman recommends recognizing the problem and developing an open communication system of which regular staff meetings are a key element. He found that lower rates of burnout and greater job satisfaction tended to result where there were staff meetings during which people were able to socialize informally, provide each other with support, receive advice and clarify goals, and exert some influence on the policies of the center.[14]

Other authors have recommended the following to prevent staff burnout:[15]

- Creating an atmosphere of trust, and inviting and giving honest feedback, especially in recognition of work well done
- Improving working conditions in whatever ways possible, including such things as stimulation through changes in routines and renewal experiences
- Setting short-term, reachable goals that provide opportunities for success
- Having flexible job responsibilities
- Allowing "responsible selfishness" — time off for a few minutes, hours, or even a day, when fatigue and stress are becoming overwhelming
- Implementing a break policy
- Hiring substitutes so staff members feel that they can take days off when they are ill

STAFF TURNOVER

It is a rare early childhood program that does not experience frequent changes in personnel from year to year. The lack of continuity resulting from these changes has an impact on the whole program. Supervisors are faced with the task of continually orienting and training new personnel. Maintaining and building support systems for a cohesive staff while attempting to counteract or ameliorate the forces that cause people to leave is one of the most difficult "balancing acts" for supervisors.

Regular Staff

Various sources place staff turnover in day care at between 15 percent and 30 percent or more, compared to a national average of 10 percent for other human service fields.[16] Whitebook and associates reported that two-thirds of staff in their San Francisco study had been at their present job for three years or less.[17] Gould, examining programs in New York state, found that only 21 percent of teachers and less than 1 percent of aides had been in the same program for more than five years.[18]

Many of the factors described in the previous section contribute to this high turnover rate. In Whitebook's study, centers with the greatest turnover tended to be those with the "highest adult-child ratios, the worst working conditions, the fewest benefits, and most stated tension." In interviews, staff cited low pay and lack of opportunity for advancement as major causes of turnover.[19]

Supplementary Staff

Frequent changes in personnel also occur among supplementary staff members. Parents, volunteers, students, Foster Grandparents, and job trainees contribute greatly to the life of many early childhood programs, but their presence can create special problems for on-site supervisors. Some may work for as little as a few hours per week. Often they have had little or no experience with small children in group settings. In addition, there is great variation in their educational backgrounds and in their motivations for becoming involved in early childhood programs.

These caregivers have specific training needs, but since most of them work in classrooms, much of this responsibility falls on teachers, who may have little experience or training in supervision. For some an outside program or agency may have specific training expectations and may provide some supervision, including periodic supervisory visits. These factors can contribute to potential misunderstandings between the parties involved.

Creating Stability

Although supervisors have only limited control over some of the factors that contribute to staff turnover, such as pay, benefits, and staff-to-child ratios, others can be addressed. A system for orienting all new personnel, paid or volunteer, ensures that newcomers have information about the program and its expectations of staff members. Practices that raise morale, such as those described earlier in this chapter, contribute greatly to a stable staff.

Working relationships with programs or agencies from which volunteers and trainees come will be smoother if there are agreements as to expectations, roles, and responsibilities of the parties involved. If standards and expectations for the selection of people who will work with children are established, temporary staff can be screened to ascertain whether they are truly interested in working with children, and alternative placements can then be arranged when appropriate. Written material describing the program's goals, philosophy, and daily schedule also aids in matching resources and needs. It facilitates the coordination of periods for placement of caregivers with visits by outside supervisors. A written contract between the agency and the center is recommended to clarify the commitment and expectations of each whether or not money is not involved. Such agreements have proven especially useful in CDA training programs, even when the candidate is a regular member of the staff.

Both permanent and temporary staff benefit when supervisors provide support and appreciation for teachers who take on supervisory responsibility of temporary staff. Recognition, along with training in supervisory skills, develops teachers' confidence as well as competence in carrying out these responsibilities.

It should be said that there are some positive aspects of staff turnover. Supervisors can be proud if they have supported the personal and professional growth of caregivers so that they continue their education, take advantage of promotions in the early childhood field, or move on to new careers in other fields. The involvement of parents, senior citizens, high school students, and volunteers brings diversity to the lives of both children and permanent staff. If a program has contributed to the training of student teachers and job trainees, it has contributed to the profession and to a better life for young children. Any program is healthier for having new people with new ideas periodically entering its life.

STAFF DIVERSITY

In recent years, the cultural and class makeup of children and staff members participating in early childhood programs has become increasingly diverse. Factors that contribute to the heterogeneity of people in early childhood settings include flexible educational qualifications for staff; the involvement of parents, senior citizens, and other volunteers; and requirements in programs such as Head Start and Chapter I that low-income community residents be hired as program staff members. Children and staff from immigrant and refugee families representing almost every region of the world add to the diversity found in many programs.

For supervisors and staff who work with people who differ from themselves in age, income, culture, or language, coming to terms with feelings about these differences and finding avenues for communication are major challenges. Writing about cultural pluralism in schools, John Carpenter makes two important points: First, both teachers and children must become "interculturally proficient," that is, knowledgeable about many cultures. Second, and even more essential is the development of "intercultural personal competence," that is, "openness, trust, and ability to communicate with persons, young and adult, from other cultures."[20] Supervisors can help staff members accomplish these goals through their own relationships with staff, through staff development and training, and through curriculum development. This process begins with supervisors' acknowledging and dealing with their own feelings and attitudes and becoming knowledgeable themselves about cultural differences and their significance.

Cultural and Class Barriers

When diversity of culture and class is considered an asset, it can bring a richness of experience to all involved in a program. Natural cultural barriers and preconceived perceptions about members of a particular group, however, can make valuing diversity more difficult. We do tend to make assumptions about people based upon group identities. Gordon Allport called this "the normality of prejudgment," stemming from the human need to mentally group things in order to make sense of them.[21]

There is a certain discomfort in focusing on differences. To say that someone is different seems to imply inferiority. Often this happens because, consciously or unconsciously, social status has become attached to perceptions of one or another particular group. The term "class" itself is one that Americans are not at all comfortable with. These feelings are sometimes reinforced when a supervisor or director is of the dominant culture or from a middle-income background and staff members, especially those in lower status jobs, are minorities or from low-income families. This is not uncommon in urban, community-based programs.[22]

When one feels uneasy about one's own possible prejudices, it often seems safer to rely on a basic sense of fairness and good will than to attend to differences and to examine their implications. But understanding and communication do not happen automatically. A true atmosphere of openness and trust is based on knowledge of another's life experiences and values and a sensitivity to the ways one is perceived. A middle-class Anglo head teacher, for example, may have developed a good understanding of Chicano culture and have been able to communicate well with her Spanish-speaking staff, but a new low-income Chicana aide who has experienced much discrimination has no way of knowing this. This aide's emotional survival *requires* that she proceed cautiously and perhaps defensively in her relationship with her supervisor. The head teacher's knowledge that the aide's previous experience could be the source of her defensiveness could allow a trust relationship to develop sooner.

Similarly, a supervisor's cultural background can also have a considerable effect on expectations of others and on interactions with them. The notion that anyone can succeed if he or she works hard enough may have been the key to one supervisor's experience. Another may regret that the only way she survived was by learning English on her own and suppressing her native language and heritage. These life experiences will probably be reflected in all aspects of a program for which that person has responsibility, in relationships with people, in the curriculum, and in the overall climate.

Often, the most difficult task for both supervisors and supervisees is accepting and understanding differences when they conflict with personal and professional values. Allport has described the powerful influence of values in our lives:

> The most important categories a man has are his own personal set of values. He lives by and for his values. Seldom does he think about them or weigh them; rather he feels, affirms, and defends them. . . . As partisans of our own way of life we cannot help thinking in a partisan manner. . . . Such partisan thinking is entirely natural, for our job in this world is to live in an integrated way as value-seekers. Prejudgments stemming from these values enable us to do so.[23]

Supervisors are also faced with the task of working with staff members' feelings about other center personnel. A middle-class teacher, for example, may have difficulty working with a low-income aide whose attitude toward children seems overly restrictive. Another teacher may feel that a college student's apparent permissiveness indicates that she doesn't understand poor children.

Adult expectations of children's behavior are also strongly tied to class and cultural values, and "partisan" attachment to these values may lead to conflict among members of a preschool staff. Since the work of teaching or caring for young children is so closely related to parenting, a consideration of some differences in child-rearing practices may be useful. For example, research indicates that working-class and lower-class parents are likely to believe that they should act as limit-setting authorities and should direct and guide children. Thus autonomy is not usually a goal of these parents. Middle-class parents, on the other hand, are likely to see themselves as supportive and accepting, yet helping the child to become self-disciplined and autonomous.[24] Since the goals of a developmental early childhood program often include autonomy and independence, supervisors may find that middle-class caregivers are more comfortable with those goals because they do not conflict with their values. On the other hand, a teacher's or aide's reluctance to follow a recommended way of working with children may represent a legitimate concern about the children based on personal knowledge of the child's culture. In such an instance, a supervisor will do well to listen, learn, and consider changes in program implementation.

Language Barriers

With an increased number of immigrants in some areas, and long established communities of Spanish-speaking or Native American people in others, the place and use of languages other than English in early childhood settings is another value-laden issue that cannot be ignored. Many people are uneasy about using a child's native language in school. Some fear that it will interfere with his or her learning English. Others believe that speaking English is a symbol of being, or wanting to be, truly American and that the use of another language emphasizes what is different about each child and leads to divisiveness rather than unity.

When teachers come to understand that a multilingual/multicultural approach to working with children is a way of developing self-esteem and that there is little evidence that use of the native language interferes with learning English, they begin to feel more comfortable with it. A multicultural framework then becomes a means of learning about and appreciating what is special about each person, adult and child alike. Program staff can begin by valuing differences in culture on a small scale, for example, by learning and using some words of one child's home language and preparing the native food of another. In programs in which there are many bilingual children, having staff members who speak the home language can be a way of providing connecting links between home and school. Some supervisors may wish to require all staff to be bilingual, and directors of all types of programs may want to consider including the sharing of culture and language as a central part of the curriculum.

Building a Multicultural Program

Research on child-rearing attitudes reveals at least as many similarities as differences in people's behavioral expectations for children.

> Evidence suggests that there is a common core of basic human values that all subcultural groups embrace. Happiness, honesty, consideration, obedience, dependability, manners, self-control, popularity, neatness, cleanliness are all valued to a greater or lesser extent in all social classes. . . . [25]

Thus, many of the basic goals of parenting are held in common by people in all cultures and classes with differences only in emphasis or in the means of attaining these goals.

Yet the differences are complex and often subtle. The problems they create can be relatively small ones, such as how to celebrate Christmas when some children are Jewish, Muslim, or Jehovah's Witnesses, or they can be large and difficult, as when outright racism occurs. A supervisor's attitudes and willingness to deal openly with differences are crucial to the creation of an atmosphere of real understanding and trust.

Having training sessions or staff meetings that focus on understanding parents or children may be an effective way to help staff begin to learn about people as individuals and about their cultural backgrounds. They can then move to personal sharing of their own backgrounds, life experiences, and values.

Parents are valuable resources. They can share their own cultural heritage with children or with staff in a variety of ways, and can also be involved in helping to solve problems stemming from differences. As a supervisor from a program with a strong multicultural emphasis said, "So *many* things are solved by including parents."

When staff members are representative of the culture or class of families served by the center, their opinions, as well as those of the parents, should carry considerable weight where values are involved. If cultural values are at odds with the principles of child development, however, the supervisor's task is to find ways to help people understand and adjust to change.

We encourage supervisors to build multicultural programs. Even when children and staff are relatively homogeneous, this can be an exciting way to begin to initiate children into a world of diversity.

CONCLUSION

The problems discussed in this chapter can be frustrating to supervisors and staff alike but most, as we have shown, can be overcome or ameliorated by thoughtful supervisory and staff development practices. We believe that staff development is an essential element of the supervisory process not only for improving staff skills but also for its positive effect on morale. In chapter 14 we present a framework for planning a staff development program, and in chapter 15 we describe some specific suggestions for implementation.

Many of the most difficult problems grow out of the history of early childhood education in the United States, but the circumstances that affect them are changing. As research about the importance of children's early years continues to be publicized in the popular press, parents will become better informed, and early childhood professionals will be able to interpret to them the implications of this knowledge for better training and compensation of caregivers.

EXERCISES

1. Discuss the differences between what was expected of children in your family as you grew up and what is expected of children in your center.
2. Use some of the materials from the Education Development Center's "Exploring Childhood" program, Module III, to help the staff explore their values in relation to child rearing.[26]

3. Develop strategies for advocating for higher pay, increased benefits, or lower staff-to-child ratios with the person or group that has control over funds for your program.

4. *A Problem for Discussion*: Rosa is a new aide in the Head Start program in which you are the educational coordinator. She is a Portuguese immigrant who has been in this country for about three years and speaks English fairly well, though with an accent. She has had no previous experience in group care, though she has two children of her own. She appears to need help in understanding which activities are appropriate for children and in interacting with them without doing things for them. She has a nice way with children and is a hard worker and eager to learn.

   Joanne, the teacher in whose room Rosa works, recently remarked to you that she just couldn't seem to communicate with Rosa. Then one day Joanne came stalking into the coffee room saying, "These Portuguese, they think they know everything." A couple of the other teachers seemed to nod in assent, with one adding an incident about a "greenhorn," concluding, "And why don't they learn English?" You are surprised by the vehemence of this discussion, because Joanne is usually understanding of children's differences and the other teacher is of Portuguese descent herself. ·

   What supervisory issues are apparent here? What kind of training might you plan for the staff in response to what you have observed and for Joanne as an individual?

14 A Framework for Staff Development and Training

Staff development is a term that can be applied to all experiences that aid staff in improving their work with children. The concept of staff development is a growth-oriented one. It is based on the assumption that all staff, including directors, can benefit from opportunities for renewal and that the quality of early childhood programs can only be maintained and improved through a well-planned and continuing program of experiences designed to foster the personal and professional development of staff members. A staff development program that accomplishes these purposes includes individual supervisory observations and conferences, but it has many other dimensions as well. It is these that are the focus of this chapter.

Staff training is one dimension of staff development. We are aware that *training* is a term that some readers may find offensive, feeling that it connotes limited goals, rote learning, or emphasis on skills and methods alone without an understanding of the reasons behind what is done. However, we view the term, as does Milly Almy, as one that is useful in describing a concentration on the particular skills needed to fit a person for a specified role:

> As trainer the early childhood educator assumes responsibility for the preparation of competent workers for early childhood programs. . . . The trainer role does not exclude approaches that are broadly educative as compared with those that are more narrowly focused.[1]

The discussion that follows is divided into descriptions of four areas of focus for training and staff development: orientation for new staff; on-the-job training for those with little or no training in early childhood education; career development available to but not required for all staff; and fine tuning for those who have worked in a program for some time and are skilled

179

at what they do. In the next chapter, we will describe the tools that can be put to use in many of these areas.

ORIENTATION FOR NEW STAFF

Many a supervisor has had the experience of accepting with eagerness parent volunteers, students, or extra staff from funded programs, only to find after a few weeks or months that these individuals have misperceptions about their place in the program or that they act inappropriately with children or parents. Trained and experienced staff members too bring with them expectations and preconceptions from their previous experience that affect their adjustment to a new setting.

Many problems, misunderstandings, and disruptions of well-established child care practices can be avoided by having an effective set of orientation experiences. The quality of an individual's first few days on the job can have a lasting effect on the program, the children, and the staff. The advantages to both the individual and the center of using this initial period to set the stage for a new person's involvement cannot be overestimated.

Content and Structure

The orientation need not be elaborate. The goal is to provide enough information so that a new person will feel welcome and will develop a sense of the structure and goals of the program and his or her place within it. Since much of this knowledge is needed by all new people, flexibility in design allows the special needs of volunteers and other untrained staff to be attended to along with those of trained and experienced personnel.

An overview of the goals and philosophy of the program, briefly and simply addressed, sets the context within which the new person will be working. This introduction might include a review of some foundations of a good developmental program for young children as well as certain key ideas that often require continued emphasis and reinforcement — for example, the place of play in young children's lives, respect for children, the importance of communicating positively with parents, and the need for objectivity and confidentiality.

Basic information regarding organizational aspects of the program is also valuable. For example:

- Daily schedules for children in which the times for arrival and departure, meals and snacks, naps, and so forth are noted
- Locations of rooms, personnel, and supplies

- Descriptions of the administrative structure and the names of staff and their roles
- Ground rules for children and adults about use of space, outdoor procedures, field trips, non-sleepers at nap time, rules for parent pick-up, and so forth
- Hours of work, including break and lunch, along with other expectations of staff or volunteers (e.g., what to do in case of illness)
- Safety precautions and health rules
- Information about the community
- Personnel policies for permanent employees

It is advantageous too to set forth clearly and simply the program's point of view about discipline right from the start. Very specific examples — even explicit do's and don't's — are more effective than general statements that can be misinterpreted. The reasons behind these procedures can be explored later when time is available and the new person has had a variety of experiences to build upon.

Volunteers, students, and job trainees who work only a few hours a week are often not aware that their roles in the classroom are important and affect other members of the staff as well as the children. Clarification of responsibilities, presented in a positive way, enhances the individual's role, while at the same time making clear that the expectations are real.

New staff members or volunteers do not always begin their employment at the start of the school year, even in large organizations. It can be most useful, therefore, to design a set of individual and group experiences that can be put into place for any new person at any time. During this phase of training a handbook is an especially valuable tool for presenting organizational information that is uninteresting, hard to retain, or requires special emphasis.

Personal Introductions

A major objective of the orientation period is to help each new person feel comfortable as a member of the staff. Dorothy Sciarra and A. G. Dorsey suggest that all staff members see themselves as having "an obligation to become involved with making the new employee's transition to the staff position as smooth and satisfying as possible."[2] Introductions to all staff, including secretaries and custodians, should not be overlooked. The staff member assigned to do this becomes a key person in facilitating the new person's transition to becoming a member of the staff.

An introduction to parents can take place informally, when parents leave their children and pick them up, and through a newsletter or announcement on a bulletin board. Such a notice could include brief background information about the new caregiver and his or her special interests and role at the center. Job trainees, students, and Foster Grandparents, as well as permanent staff, should also be introduced. When supplemental staff members begin as a group at the same time, parents can be given a list of their names, the times they will be working, and the rooms to which they are assigned, along with some information about how their presence helps the program.

If possible, have new people take part in setting up the rooms and in planning at the beginning of the school year. This gives them a stake in what will be happening with children and helps them understand what is needed to make it work.

Other Activities

Having new caregivers observe in classrooms is an especially effective means for helping them understand what a program for young children is all about. This technique helps them get to know children, staff, and the "personality" of the particular program. At this stage, observations can focus on such things as getting to know children's names, identifying areas of the room and what goes on in each, and noting some aspects of the roles of staff who are teaching.

Group sessions provide opportunities for sharing perceptions and for getting to know others with whom they will be working. When more formal workshops are held, information should be concrete and not far removed from the experiences the new person will be involved in during their first few weeks at the center.

Figure 14.1 illustrates the kinds of administrative and curricular topics that can be addressed in a week-long orientation preceeding the opening of a center.

As we noted earlier, in many instances the orientation will need to be designed so that it can be carried out on an individualized basis. Such a program can combine independent experiences with conferences with the supervisor. Figure 14.2 illustrates a sequence of activities used in a small program to which student volunteers are regularly assigned.

Supervisors often become aware of particular areas that cause problems for new staff members. One Head Start supervisor, who noticed that the paper work in her program can become confusing, has developed a packet of forms she finds useful in orienting new staff members. As she "walks through" each form with the staff member, different facets of Head Start's components and regulations, and their implications for children and staff, are revealed. Such creative solutions to specific problems can make the supervisor's job more interesting and provide important learnings for new staff members.

FIGURE 14.1   *Agenda for Orientation and Getting-Ready Week*

```
FIRST DAY
Morning Session (9:00-12:30)
     Topic:  An overview of the Child Care and Learning
     Program and the Related Staff Growth Program
Afternoon Session (1:30-5:30)
     Topic:  Getting acquainted with the materials we will
     be using

SECOND DAY
Morning Session
     Topic:  Planning the initial experiences parents and
     children have with your program
Afternoon Session
     Topic:  Continuing what we've started already, plus
     medical matters for staff

THIRD DAY
Morning Session
     Topic:  The Language Development Program; informal
     language development should permeate everything in
     all three threads of the program
Afternoon Session
     Topic:  The Number Concepts Program should also per-
     meate all aspects of the program; setting up learning
     centers

FOURTH DAY
Morning Session
     Topic:  Guiding children toward safety, happiness,
     and learning "preventive discipline"
Noon, Afternoon, or Evening (depending on how you're
scheduled--4 hours at one time or another)
     Parent meeting; home visits

FIFTH DAY
Morning Session
     Topic:  Visiting day (children visit school)
Afternoon Session
     Topic:  Completing readiness for center opening
```

Reprinted, with permission of the author, from Polly Greenberg, *Day Care Do-It-Yourself Staff Growth Program* (Winston-Salem, NC: Kaplan Press, 1975), p. 28.

There is sometimes a temptation to teach everything at orientation time. The purpose of an orientation, however, is to lay the foundation for a continuing process that builds as it goes on. With this goal in mind, it is usually most effective to be very specific and teach the most basic ideas, using examples wherever possible, even with sophisticated people if they are beginners. The general tone and, whenever possible, the methodology of this in-

FIGURE 14.2   *Orientation for Student Volunteers*

1. The student reads the handbook from cover to cover.
2. The supervisor discusses the information in the handbook with the student.
3. The student independently watches a slide/tape of the center and students at work in it.
4. The student observes the program. The assignment is to watch one learning center and learn the children's names.
5. The student discusses what was observed.

Used with permission of Elsa S. Grieder, Director, Barrington College Early Childhood Center, Barrington, RI.

itial training period should be a model of the kinds of attitudes and sometimes even the techniques that are to be used with children.

Taking time to orient new staff pays off, even if it places a burden on other staff members for awhile.

ON-THE-JOB TRAINING

On-the-job training is targeted toward those with little training or experience with young children in a group setting. It is more intensive than the ongoing staff development designed for all personnel. For the most part, those participating in this phase of training will be people who do not have the major responsibility for a group of children. However, lead teachers who lack a background in early childhood education may also need some training.

For staff members for whom on-the-job training is intended, learning about children and teaching begins with their experience in the classroom. The supervisor's role as teacher of these staff members is to make use of this experience not only to teach the skills of caregiving but to help trainees become self-directed learners — to help them learn how to learn about children and teaching.

Volunteers and new staff members alike come to their jobs with images of what it is they will be doing, but these views may or may not reflect the reality of a new situation. Classroom staff members may not have thought about how new volunteers or trainees will fit into the existing pattern of responsibilities. Added to this is the fact that those who are taking part in on-the-job training really have two roles: they are workers who are expected to carry out their jobs responsibly and with skill, but they are also learners whose skills are not expected to be perfect but who are open to change.

Clarification of roles and expectations for the training participants, the supervisor, and the classroom staff sets the stage for positive staff relations. Knowledge of what the training consists of, the extent of the lead teacher's and the supervisor's training responsibilities, and the role of the trainee as worker and learner is useful to everyone in a program. Most participants will welcome the opportunity for training, though perhaps with some apprehension. An emphasis on its supportive nature helps to alleviate some of their concerns.

Training objectives and methodology can be planned more effectively if the participants' strengths and needs are assessed at an early stage in the training. This should be done in the context of specific job descriptions and in the light of adult developmental issues. For example, a Foster Grandfather who has spent most of his life working as an accountant and whose assignment is to give one or two children special attention and love will have very different needs from a parent volunteer who eventually wants to move into a paid job in the program. Similarly, a student teacher who is familiar with child development theory but lacks experience will come with different skills and needs from a teenage Youth Corps worker who is not sure she even wants to work with children.

Such assessments make it possible to identify strengths and abilities so that caregivers can be involved in classroom activities in meaningful ways. They are then able to see themselves as necessary and competent staff members right from the beginning.

Content

There are many sources for the content of on-the-job training. The goals of the early childhood program itself, such as Head Start Performance Standards or Montessori principles, may serve as a guide. The CDA Competencies (see "The CDA Credential" later in this chapter), or a set of competencies specifically designed for a particular program may also furnish a basis for training. However, since the purposes of on-the-job training are to equip caregivers with basic skills and to help them *learn how to learn* about children and teaching, we suggest that four processes or skills be emphasized: (1) learning to see, (2) learning to listen, (3) learning to communicate, and (4) learning to understand and carry out group and individual activities with children.

Learning to see is probably one of the most valuable abilities that can be developed by anyone working with children. So much of good teaching and caregiving comes from being able to understand the subtle meanings of what children do and say — to see that for a four-year-old play is more than aimless activity or "merely" a time for fun; or to see what an eight-month-old is learning from crawling around the floor that she would not be learning in a play pen. As Alice Honig puts it, "Infants are the caregivers' teachers. Informed caregivers pace their teachings and their interactions depending on the responses of infants."[3] It is not easy to discern many of the small but important things that a good teacher does that make each day a positive one for children, or to see how the arrangement of the learning environment can affect life for children and adults in a center or day care home. It takes time and training to learn how to make sense of such things.

A skill that parallels learning to see is *learning to listen*. As teachers learn to listen to children during play — as the children talk to adults, to other children, to themselves, and even as they quarrel — they can understand the child's view of the world at a particular time. Caregivers can also learn to hear the underlying as well as surface messages of parents as they talk about their children and about their own concerns.

Caregivers can build on the above skills to *learn to communicate* appropriately with both children and adults in many kinds of situations. They will begin to understand the role of the teacher in enhancing a child's self-directed learning by learning to use effective language with children as they work and play — to use open-ended questions, to make non-directive statements, and to find ways that help rather than hinder the explorations of children. They can begin to develop a repertoire of positive ways to respond when children misbehave and to develop flexibility in their use. They can learn to use cues from their observations to help them decide how to respond.

Trainees can now also begin to acquire skills in communicating with parents, so they can share the child's daily joys and sorrows in informal contacts with them. They need to understand what is appropriate to discuss at such times and what should be saved for a parent conference. In all day care programs, but especially in family day care and infant/toddler programs, it is critical that caregivers build close and positive relationships with parents right from the beginning.

Finally, trainees can begin to develop skills for *carrying out group activities* and for *facilitating individual learning*. Caregivers can learn to view both group experiences and "free" play activities as means for developing children's confidence in themselves as individuals, along with their ability to solve problems, to express themselves, and to practice skills in their own ways. For many trainees, learning to allow children to make decisions and to use their own means of expression requires an entirely new way of viewing the teaching/learning process. Time as well as a variety of training approaches may be needed to help such caregivers feel comfortable with these teaching modes.

Structure

It is both practical and effective to take advantage of the classroom setting as much as possible for on-the-job training. Through observations of teachers and children, caregivers can now begin to examine the teaching/learning process in more varied ways. A focus on children enables them to see the marvelous capacity that children have for self-initiated learning. An examination of the learning environment reveals the ways that arrangement of space affects children's ability to be independent and to control their own behavior. And observations of teachers, either in natural or formal situations, provide opportunities to study the way disciplinary incidents are handled and the teacher's role in free play, transitions, and group situations.

A series of group meetings provides a setting for introducing trainees to basic child development principles, tying them in with the participants' observations and classroom experiences. Some time should also be made available to discuss concerns that a group of trainees may have in common. Foster Grandparents, for example, may need to talk about transportation to work, maintaining energy when working with active children, and understanding "modern" methods of discipline. Of course, many in-service training activities planned for the staff as a whole are equally valuable for new personnel and give them an opportunity to become part of the program.

CAREER DEVELOPMENT AND CDA TRAINING

In any program where there is concern for adults as well as children, career development should be considered as one of the training options for staff. Career development is simply a planned program designed to provide opportunities for upward mobility within an early childhood program and perhaps beyond. The opportunity for staff to obtain credentials that verify their acquired knowledge and skills is an important element of such programs.

Career development efforts are usually focused on staff members who are at the lower job levels and who have less than a bachelor's degree. These are the people who traditionally have the fewest options and can benefit most from credit-bearing course work or recognized credentials. Opportunities for career development are especially important in programs that employ or serve people from low-income families. Such training is a major goal in Head Start and other government funded programs.

The career development concept is not limited to such programs, however. In any program, staff members with degrees as well as those with little or no college background or without training in early childhood education

188

Staff Development in Practice

may be interested in preparing for a role such as educational coordinator or director, or in changing direction toward social services, parent education, or special needs.

Career development should be an option rather than a requirement. It has to do with life goals for the individual and calls for a commitment beyond what is ordinarily expected in order to do one's job effectively. When course work or a degree is required for promotion, however, this should be clearly stated in personnel policies.

There is a considerable range in the amount of involvement in career development that a supervisor will want to consider. In a large program with a commitment toward such training, it is best to have someone on the staff who has the major responsibility for coordinating contacts with educational institutions and keeping up with staff members who are taking part. Problems with finding transportation or baby sitters, choosing appropriate courses, or working through a college bureaucracy can quickly discourage a staff member whose self-confidence is low. The coordinator can field such problems and help trainees find ways to solve them.

In smaller programs, the involvement will be more informal, with supervisors acting as encouragers and facilitators for staff who wish to pursue career development goals. A third role for supervisors is to act as a field advisor or trainer for CDA candidates, supervising field experiences and taking part in the assessment of the candidates.

Training Institutions

The simplest and most helpful part supervisors can play is to gather and disseminate information about colleges that have early childhood courses, CDA training, and/or degree programs that are appropriate to the needs of their staff. A college or university that has provided CDA and other training for Head Start staff may also be able to serve staff from other early childhood programs. Institutions that show an understanding of the special strengths and needs of adult learners are preferable. Many now give credit for previous work or life experience. A few colleges have external degree programs, providing course work off campus or through independent studies.[4]

It is often possible to negotiate for courses on special topics and even for new degree programs if sufficient numbers of students can be guaranteed. On-site courses are also sometimes possible. Working together with other early childhood programs helps develop evidence that there will be a continued market for such courses or programs in that location.

In order to affect more than a few highly motivated staff members with enough money to pay for their own courses, every effort should be made to seek or provide some kind of subsidy toward tuition. Even without this, however, there are staff who will take advantage of any opportunity for training that can enable them to advance as professionals in the field.

Career Ladders

Any organization that has a commitment to career development should make an effort to couple it with job advancement based on training. Large programs can formalize this process through a career ladder or lattice that specifies job steps, including salary increases, relating the steps to years of experience and designated blocks of formal and informal training. It is discouraging for staff members to put extra time and effort into taking courses or preparing for a CDA assessment only to find that they can receive no recognition until they obtain a degree or must wait until there is a job opening at a higher level. Even a moderate salary increment and a change in title and responsibilities after completing a block of training experiences or courses can be encouraging. This also indicates that the program values professional growth.

The CDA Credential

The Child Development Associate credential has a number of advantages as a career development goal. This competency-based system allows people with varying amounts of formal education, with or without degrees, to focus on the same goals and reach them at their own pace and in a way that is most appropriate for them. The requirements are flexible, both in time and in the type of training needed. And, because the CDA Competencies are based on sound child development principles and the Credential is awarded on the basis of a caregiver's actual work with children, there is a direct relationship with the quality of teaching and care of children.[5]

The Child Development Associate assessment and credentialing system was developed in the early 1970s to provide a nationally recognized, validated standard of competence for early childhood caregivers. It is administered by the National Association for the Education of Young Children through a separate non-profit corporation entitled the Council for Early Childhood Professional Recognition, which is funded through a grant from the federal Administration for Children, Youth and Families. The policy board of the CDA Credentialing Program is made up of representatives of national early childhood professional organizations and other groups concerned with the health and well-being of young children.

At the heart of the CDA system are the six major Competencies, which are subdivided into thirteen Functional Areas (see Appendix A). These define the standards by which the individual is assessed and the credential awarded.

Thus arbitrary educational requirements, which may have little relationship to job performance, are not an issue, making the CDA an especially attractive alternative for those not working toward a degree.

A unique element in the CDA system is the assessment process, which is conducted by a four-member Local Assessment Team (LAT). This team consists of the caregiver (the candidate for the credential), an advisor, a parent or community representative, and a CDA representative (see Appendix B). Each contributes evidence as to the competence of the candidate in each of the Functional Areas, and each has an equal voice in making the final judgment. A "portfolio" prepared by the candidate to show evidence of her or his skill and understanding in working with young children, observations by the other three team members, and information from parents provide the data on which the assessment is made.

CDA candidates must have the equivalent of about a year's experience and some formal or informal training related to the age group and setting of the credential for which they are applying — for example, center-based three- to five-year olds, or bilingual-bicultural home visitor. Although no specific type of training is prescribed, guidelines have been developed for Head Start CDA training. These have proved useful to other programs that prepare people for the credential.[6] Many candidates do, however, prepare for assessment on their own.

All CDA training is really preparation for the assessment, focusing on the thirteen Functional Areas. Candidates who are competent in many areas when they begin may require little or no training; preparation for their assessment may take only a few months of intensive work. For others it can take up to two years or more, with any combination of college courses or seminars, self-directed learning modules, in-service training, and intensive field supervision.

Supervisors are often asked (or they volunteer) to be field advisors for CDA candidates, to help them prepare for the assessment, to serve as advisor at the LAT meeting, or to become training supervisors over a longer period of time. Any of these roles is significant. Advisors must be both advocates and critics for candidates, helping them see what areas need improvement and supporting their efforts to change. Much of the advisor's work involves helping candidates learn to assess their own competence and then finding ways to help them develop understandings and skills in the areas that need improvement. With those who need a longer period of training, the process is similar to the kind of on-the-job training we described earlier, with, if anything, a greater amount of in-classroom supervision.

Preparation for a CDA assessment, whether in a training program or not, takes a strong commitment of time and energy on the part of the candidate. The support and encouragement of a supervisor, even when not serving as an advisor, can contribute immeasurably to the staff member's experience with CDA. At its best, the process is one of self-affirmation, confidence building, and growth for the candidate — and often for others in the center as well.

Detailed information about the CDA assessment and credential system can be obtained from the CDA National Credentialing Program.[7]

Staff Resistance to Career Development Opportunities

Supervisors may be surprised to find that staff members do not always take advantage of career development opportunities. This can be discouraging to supervisors who have scrounged for tuition money or who are willing to offer their services as CDA field advisors. A number of factors contribute to this.

First, for many people, especially the poor, formal schooling has meant academic failure, negative experiences with teachers, and a lack of relevance to their lives. For such people, further schooling would be anticipated as a chore at best, and could easily be feared as a repetition of a painful experience.

Sometimes there is underlying peer pressure not to become involved in anything beyond what is required. This may come from those who feel they cannot or do not want to take part themselves or who see courses as an added burden when they are receiving very low pay. Such staff members do not understand how career development can benefit them or the children they teach.

Factors related to a staff member's personal life can also be a deterrent. A woman who is working and caring for a family may just not have the energy to do more or may not want to spend any more time away from her family. Husbands are not always supportive of their wives' furthering their education. Even a husband who is supportive may not be willing to help out with housework or babysitting, or a wife may not feel comfortable in asking him to do so. For single parents, there are added restrictions, since they may have only themselves to depend on for household chores and child care, as well as financial support.

Developmental issues, including life transitions, strongly affect a person's readiness for career development experiences. For example, young single adults might seem to be obvious candidates for career development, but if they did not finish high school or chose not to go to college, they may be too close to the school experience to want to begin again. Developmentally, their main interest outside of work is likely to be centered on their social life rather than work or school.

It is important to remember that those who do not respond to opportunities at one time may be candidates at another. Changes in their lives or a new comfort with their jobs may allow staff members to take on the challenge of one course, and this may be enough to start them on a path to a degree or a CDA credential.

Supervisors who have a watchful eye for staff with potential, who are sensitive to the factors that affect readiness to become involved, and who are able to find ways to help staff realize the advantages of career development will discover that many staff members blossom once they get going.

FINE TUNING

What kind of staff development and training is appropriate for experienced staff members and those who have degrees in early childhood and advanced training in the field?

The professional growth of these staff members should not come to a halt simply because they are already skilled at what they do or because they are "old timers." There is always a need to refine techniques, strategies, and skills and to take on new challenges. *Tuning* is a term that Bruce Joyce and Beverly Showers use to describe the act of working on the craft of teaching.[8]

Staff members who are at more advanced phases of their professional development need training oriented toward fine tuning their competence; such training will increase their effectiveness even more. Others who have been on a staff for many years but who have not developed beyond a minimum level of competence may also respond to an approach that focuses on sharpening their existing skills.

The following strategies are some that provide the kinds of challenge and stimulation that help prevent caregivers from becoming bored, unmotivated, or apathetic.

Taking part in workshops or seminars gives experienced staff opportunities to explore issues in depth. Topics for advanced training might include supervision, developing children's thinking, language development through block building, program models such as Montessori or the Cognitively-Oriented Curriculum, and the use of specific systems of assessment of children.

Leading workshops in areas of the curriculum in which they have particular strengths or interests gives skilled staff members a chance to receive recognition for their expertise. It also challenges them to develop the new skills necessary to make a presentation to a group of adults. Although some teachers may at first be reluctant to set themselves up as "experts" before their peers or may lack confidence in their ability to make effective presentations, supervisors can provide support by sharing in the planning or even co-leading the session. Acceptance by fellow teachers is more assured if workshop leaders are asked to present in an area in which they are generally recognized as having skill, in which they have recently received training, or in which others admit that they do not feel competent.

Developing and leading workshops for parents too might be an especially appropriate responsibility for these staff members. Some may want to become trained as leaders of specialized parent education programs such as Parent Effectiveness Training or Exploring Parenting.[9]

Visiting other programs in the area gives experienced caregivers a different perspective. Not only can it provide renewal and reinforcement for their own ideas, but it can also serve as a source of new ones.

Becoming active in local, regional, and national early childhood organizations helps advanced staff members gain a sense of professionalism and receive support from colleagues who have experience and expertise. Forming discussion groups around professional readings, developing descriptive research projects on topics of interest to them, and developing special curriculum or training materials also present challenges and contribute to teachers' sense of competence and professionalism.

In general, fine-tuning activities should recognize staff members' experience and training and, by putting them in new roles, stimulate them to continue to learn and grow as professionals.

BRINGING THE STAFF TOGETHER

So far, we have discussed staff development and training experiences for groups of people with different kinds of needs. It is essential that staff members also have opportunities to work together in groups that cut across roles, years of experience, and skills or abilities.

The teaching team of teacher and assistant, often including other full- and part-time staff, is the fundamental unit of most early childhood centers. Staff development at the team level strengthens the team as a unit and helps team members find ways to function better in the classroom. When team members are encouraged to clarify who does what in the classroom on a daily basis and to discuss and come to agreement about their expectations of children and of each other, they are able to function more harmoniously and productively.[10]

From time to time, supervisors may find it beneficial to act as consultants to teams to assist them in working on a project that they are particularly interested in, such as planning a new curriculum unit or changing the room environment. A team's autonomy and growth is enhanced when the supervisor acts as a facilitator of their efforts to evaluate their situation and to develop strategies for change. A social worker, psychologist, or special needs coordinator can function in a similar role, helping team members to develop strategies for working with one or several children. In these situations, staff members are developing skills that they can use on their own in the future.

Staff meetings that reach beyond the classroom team level serve as a means of communicating with the staff as a whole. As we noted in the previous chapter, staff meetings are an important element in combating burnout because they afford opportunities for increased participation in decisions by staff at all levels and the chance for social interaction and professional growth. Meetings can become support systems for staff when agendas include time for sharing information and feelings about current classroom projects, individual or team progress in putting to work something from the latest workshop, or problems on which staff members would like feedback and ideas.

Using different groupings for staff meetings from time to time can bring staff together within as well as across roles. At meetings where center-wide matters are discussed and decisions made, staff at all levels should usually be involved — including maintenance workers, cooks, or bus drivers if they are affected.

Role-related meetings can also be appropriate. When lead teachers meet without their assistants, they can share feelings about their role, work on leadership skills, and deal with administrative issues that are not of concern to assistants. Aides and assistants too gain from meeting on their own. They may need to discuss concerns about their roles within a team and to develop skills in communicating their ideas and feelings in a safe atmosphere. Groupings that cut across teams and roles can also be formed to work on curriculum or to plan workshops, parent meetings, or parties.

Morale is a significant factor in bringing the staff together. Injecting variety, stimulation, and fun into the work of teaching and caring for children, and showing concern for each staff member as an individual and a person, all contribute to high morale.

CONCLUSION

When staff development is viewed as a means for stimulating the continuing growth of all personnel, its dimensions are boundless. Growth-oriented staff development can take place through planned, ongoing, face-to-face supervision as well as through small- and large-group and other enriching experiences that occur on a regular basis. Programs that focus on the specific needs of staff members at different phases of their professional development will challenge them without being overwhelming. And when focused training is balanced with experiences that bring all staff together, supervisors can build relationships among individuals, increase communication, work on common problems and issues, and maintain high spirit and morale in a program.

EXERCISES

1. What problems are often encountered in your program when new staff or volunteers first begin? Plan a series of activities to deal with these problems.
2. Discuss staff development experiences that you could create to help your staff "stay alive" and not get bogged down by the routines of child care or overwhelmed when working conditions are not ideal.
3. Identify staff members who could benefit from on-the-job training or career development. Explore ways to accommodate their individual needs.
4. Share information with supervisors from other programs to define the levels of readiness for training. Expand the criteria given in this chapter.

15 Tools for Staff Development and Training

With a framework for staff development and training in place, the techniques and strategies for implementation can be designed. In this chapter we describe several that we believe are especially effective: handbooks, professional reading, observations of children and teachers, workshops and classroom follow-up, and morale builders.

Most of these methods and techniques can be used in more than one phase of training and for more than one purpose. When making decisions about which of several methods to use at a particular time or about content and form of training, supervisors may find it useful to consider the following questions:

- For which phase of training or staff development is this technique to be used?
- Who will the target audience be? Will it be limited to aides, volunteers, lead teachers, Foster Grandparents, social service staff, or staff in several roles?
- What issues related to personal or teacher development ought to be considered?
- What can this method accomplish better than some other method?
- How can this method be used in conjunction with other training tools so that each approach enhances and reinforces the other without being overly redundant?

HANDBOOKS

Written material in handbook form can be one of the most practical training tools. A handbook is especially beneficial when used as part of the orientation of new staff or volunteers, but it can also be used as a reference in other phases of training.

A handbook should include enough information so that the reader is able to obtain some understanding of the program's purposes, goals, and expectations for children, staff, and parents. A word of welcome and a statement about the goals and philosophy of the program, in language meaningful to a lay person, provide a good introduction. Headings like "Why Preschool?" "How Children Learn Best," or "Why So Much Play?" can stimulate interest in important goals such as the primacy of a child's self-esteem and the need for active learning and making choices.

An expanded version of the daily schedule is a useful way of presenting what goes on during each part of the day and the purposes of each period for the child. Some centers include a description of the learning areas typically found in preschools and the kinds of things children can learn in each. One program uses the daily schedule as a framework for illustrating all aspects of its goals and activities (see Figure 15.1).

Organizational information, such as that listed in the previous chapter, helps to make expectations clear. Statements about what to do in case of illness, and center rules, regulations, and procedures are especially useful.

Perhaps the most valuable section of a handbook is one that contains guidelines and suggestions—the do's and don't's—for the adult's role with children. It is best to avoid statements that are too general or words and phrases that have meaning mainly to professionals. Wording such as "respect for the child" or "positive ways of changing behavior" are not much help for a person who has had little experience with young children in a group setting. One program with many student volunteers begins a handbook section with "Students frequently ask WHAT DO I DO WHEN . . . ?" followed by simple statements and drawings illustrating ways of handling specific situations, and even words and phrases that can be used with children.[1]

A handbook for family day care training might include a greater emphasis on relationships with parents, suggestions for meal planning including sample menus, and information on representative fees, attendance policies, and accounting procedures.

The material in a handbook is most effective when it is direct, positive, and written in simple language without talking down to the reader. An attractive and lively format and a personal style make it easier to read and to absorb. Simple drawings, open space on the pages, and different colored paper for different sections can immeasurably enhance the readability and usefulness of such a booklet.

A handbook should not be expected to stand alone. It works best as a reinforcement for other aspects of training. Its greatest advantages are that it provides the same information to all readers and it can be referred to whenever necessary to refresh the memories of both supervisor and staff member.

FIGURE 15.1   *Daily Schedule*

```
8:30 A.M. - 9:00 A.M.
     Before the children arrive teachers are busy setting
up the classroom; tables are set up for breakfast, and
materials and supplies are gathered for the day's activi-
ties.   You can help by
     Setting the tables
     Asking the teachers if they need help preparing the
          activities they have planned
     Cleaning the classroom, being sure that materials and
          supplies are in their proper place and look neat
          --ask a teacher if you need suggestions

9:00 A.M. - 9:15 A.M.   HEADSTARTERS ARRIVE
     Five to ten minutes each day is devoted to a family
meeting to discuss the day's activities and share experi-
ences.   This is the time where all children, teachers and
volunteers are informed of the day's activity.   If you are
interested in a special activity and would like to be
involved, please inform a teacher.   Also, if you have any
questions, please feel free to ask.   During this time you
can help by
     Greeting the children as they arrive at the center
     Helping each child feel important by noticing some-
          thing special about him/her (i.e., "Jane, I love
          the flowers on your pants, they're beautiful!",
          "Can you run fast John in those new green
          sneakers?")
     Encouraging the children to hang their outerwear on
          the hooks (All cubbies and hooks are labeled
          with the children's names and a picture they
          have chosen)
     Participating freely in the family meeting
     Encouraging children to select a mat and sit on it in
          the large group discussion area
     Sitting with the children in the large group area (a
          loving arm around a restless child is always
          helpful)
```

Reprinted with permission from Woonsocket Head Start, *Let Us Tell You About Head Start* (Woonsocket, RI, no date).

The written words provide a degree of objectivity that is sometimes obscured in person-to-person interchanges.

PROFESSIONAL READING

A well-stocked library of professional materials is an essential supplement to the basic handbook. Finding ways to encourage its use, however, can be a challenge. Although books and magazines with specific project ideas are likely to be quite popular, it may be more difficult to stimulate regular professional reading by staff members. There are, however, both direct and indirect ways of working on this goal.

Polly Greenberg, in her interesting and detailed book, *Day Care Do-It-Yourself Staff Growth Program*, takes the direct approach. She suggests that staff be given a new recommended reading assignment every two weeks, with specified times during the day when staff members are *expected* to read.[2] In Greenberg's program, some of the times regularly scheduled for staff meetings are designated for reading, along with one or two nap times and "light hours" when volunteers and other staff can cover. She provides specific guidelines for reading and for discussing the material. On certain days, staff meetings are used for "imaginative problem solving" based on the readings. Greenberg's feeling about the importance of reading is so strong that she lists "Finding Time for Professional Reading" as one of the specific skills for staff members.[3]

Other less-direct methods can also be used to encourage staff in this most important medium for growth. If a place can be found where books, magazines, and an occasional photocopied article can be displayed, staff members can leaf through them in their spare time. This material should be changed periodically so that it does not get stale. Books and articles related to current in-service topics or background information on classroom themes are among those that can be highlighted. In preparation for a series of workshops on one subject, a variety of readings on the topic might be gathered, with specific chapters recommended or guide questions provided. These readings can then be reported on or discussed at the workshop sessions.

Supervisors serve as models when they share their own reading experiences in staff meetings on a regular basis. Staff members too can be invited to share books or articles they have recently read. Individual conferences and meetings with classroom teams also provide opportunities for supervisors to suggest readings related to a specific area of teaching or to problems with children or parents.

Some staff members may be interested in searching for books, articles, or magazines to recommend to parents. They could write short reviews for the center newsletter or create a special book-sharing area on the parent bulletin board.

In low-income areas, where it is not unusual to find caregivers who are not proficient readers, materials that are both appropriate and not too difficult must be searched out. An awareness of the readiness levels of all staff members and a sensitivity to differences in ability to read are important factors in making reading a successful training tool. When encouraged through enthusiasm and low-key persistence, staff may gradually become comfortable with the idea and discover its relevance to their day-to-day work.

OBSERVING TEACHING

Two observational techniques help both new and experienced caregivers "learn to see" what teachers do to create an environment where children can grow and learn. The first takes advantage of the incidental, day-to-day experiences of the classroom as they happen. For the second, supervisor and supervisee plan what is to be observed with specific goals in mind.

Informal Modeling

Modeling goes on all the time when there are two or more people working together in the same space with the same children. Sciarra and Dorsey emphasize that directors model behavior beginning with their first encounter with a new staff member. An attitude of trust and mutual respect for adults and children communicated at this early phase sets the stage for the way staff members are expected to interact with children, families, and colleagues.[4]

Caregivers are most likely to learn from modeling of teaching behaviors when they are helped to focus on significant aspects of what is taking place. It is not easy to recognize, for example, the importance of the ways in which a teacher reacts to small incidents during the day, spontaneously picking up on what a child says or does, preventing trouble by anticipating problems, and then keeping activities moving or changing pace.

Several supervisors have discovered methods of modeling that have proved effective. One nursery school director/teacher uses the technique of thinking out loud or of describing what she is doing as she does it. She might say, "It's beginning to cloud up outside. The children seem to be getting restless. Let's go sit with them for a minute." Or (to illustrate that few decisions are black and white) "Free play seems to be beginning to break down. I wonder, shall I wait a little to see if it will work out, or take a group and read a story?"

Non-teaching supervisors who visit a classroom during a free play period can model appropriate behaviors in the role of a temporary assistant on the classroom team. This technique, which Virginia Hatch calls "participatory supervision,"[5] is especially effective when the lead teacher or classroom team as a whole is the focus of training.

Lenore McCarthy and Elizabeth Landerholm used a similar method in their work as consultants to day care centers. They found that participating in planning and acting as a back-up for "first-time activities" were especially effective. They had particular success with initiating staff to field trips, both local walks and more extensive excursions. Teachers became eager to try trips on their own, as they were able to see the positive effects of planning.[6]

Trainees also benefit when teachers or supervisors talk about children —

their styles, likes and dislikes, and skills—as they work together in the classroom. This helps caregivers see the individuality of each child and to understand teachers' actions in relation to specific child behaviors.

Commenting when a child is misbehaving (or seems to be) can be especially instructive, since views about discipline are so bound by one's own experiences. The supervisor might say, "We're letting Tommy stay out of the group for the time being, since he becomes overwhelmed by sitting with so many people." Or "I wasn't sure whether to intervene in that little squabble or not. I'm glad to see they've worked it out themselves. It can be valuable when they do, but I try to keep an eye out."

These situations become a rich source of material for individual or group conferences. Recent incidents can be discussed and related to other experiences, to readings, or to other kinds of training in which caregivers have taken part.

Taking advantage of informal modeling opportunities helps new staff and volunteers to see that "teaching" includes everything that goes on in the classroom. These built-in strategies can in themselves make the difference between a person's passively accepting what goes on in the classroom and discovering that teaching involves an attitude of continually questioning and learning from one's experiences.

Planned Observations

Observations of teachers that are planned rather than spontaneous provide a different kind of learning opportunity. These observations can be based on a specific need identified by the supervisor or the supervisee. A specific setting, behavioral focus, or time of day can then be selected that can best accomplish that purpose. The caregiver thus takes part in the decision about what to observe and why.

During orientation or on-the-job training, trainees can be assigned to observe teachers during different parts of the day, especially times such as free play or transitions when "teaching" is not so clearly identifiable. A discussion beforehand about what to look for or an observation sheet with focus questions narrows what is to be examined to manageable proportions. For example, instead of suggesting that a caregiver "observe transitions," a series of observations might be set up: At one time the focus might be on how teachers prepare children for a change; at another, on what they do to make it easier for children who don't function well during transitions; and at a third, on how teachers work together to take care of stragglers. An observation sheet for free play might include this series of questions: "How do teachers help children make choices? What do they do when a child seems to be wandering around? What seems to help children learn from their play?

What seems to interfere?" Eventually, as caregivers develop their observation skills, they will be able to function with much more open-ended guidelines.

More experienced caregivers may respond better to ideas for changes in teaching strategies when they can examine alternatives in order to determine what method would work best for them. For example, in a supervisory conference a concern may be raised about keeping the children's attention while reading aloud. Through a problem-solving process, the teacher may be able to come up with some causes for their inattentiveness but still be unsure of what to do about it. It could then be suggested that she observe several other teachers as they read to children and identify some alternative strategies for keeping the children involved.

Frequently teachers are stimulated by workshops to try new teaching techniques or activities but do not feel confident enough to actually attempt to do them. In such situations, the supervisor or a skilled teacher can demonstrate the technique in the classroom. Art, cooking, and creative movement are types of experiences that lend themselves well to this type of demonstrating, since they are more easily shown than explained. If at all appropriate to the activity, classroom team members should take some part in it. These observations are most effective when they begin with a planning session in which all participants are actively involved and when they are followed by an evaluation session during which perceptions, questions, and opinions can be shared.

When opportunities for conferences are limited, a journal can be a means of structuring observations. A supervisor's response to a journal entry about a disruptive child might be, "I see Joey's difficulties in coping with change made the transition from snack very difficult the other day. Ms. R. has some effective ways of working with him. Why don't you observe her from time to time this week as she interacts with him. Keep notes in your journal, and we can discuss it next week."

Peer support and sharing can sometimes be engendered when staff members are encouraged to observe each other. One supervisor started a regular series of observations in which every staff member visited at least one other classroom in the center over a period of several weeks, recording impressions on a specially prepared observation sheet. Although the purpose was to find new ideas and to gain perspective on their own teaching, the teachers were asked to give some kind of feedback to the other teachers they observed. Not only did the project serve the purpose it was designed for, but because the teachers each received non-judgmental, mostly positive feedback and had seen their colleagues' teaching, they became more confident in sharing and in working together without the reluctance they had previously shown.

Even when models are less than ideal, they will have some teaching techniques worth examining. A highly structured experienced teacher may have excellent ways of planning for or of handling routines, while a teacher whose room seems somewhat chaotic may have interpersonal or creative skills worth observing. Learning also occurs from negative role models: "The process of comparing and contrasting philosophies and practices gives a stronger sense of what one's own program [or classroom] is like. Essentially, it defines it and increases the staff member's sense of identity with the program."[7]

There are some cautions about modeling, especially for supervisors who are not members of the classroom team. Sensitivity to the roles of other adults in the classroom, particularly in "participant supervision" situations, is essential. It is helpful when the supervisor is able to make clear to all members of the team, especially the lead teacher, that the supervisor's role is to fit in with the ongoing program, not to take over responsibilities that teachers, assistants, or volunteers see as their own. The message "You're really not doing it right; super-teacher will show you how" is less likely to be conveyed when supervisors respond in a natural way to children's real needs within the context of the particular activity.

The advantages of using modeling as a training tool are many. It is easily arranged and has a base in the reality of the classroom. And the consciousness-raising that occurs during its use, when combined with other training and staff development experiences, results in real learning for staff members.

OBSERVING CHILDREN

When teachers — whether they are new on the job or have been teaching for years — really begin to look at children, new worlds open up to them. Observing increases caregivers' understandings of developmental age/stage characteristics and of how children learn from their play. They gain insight into some of the very real differences children show in their interactions with adults, with other children, or with objects. And they develop an awareness of changes in individual children over time, an ability especially important for those who work with infants or handicapped children.

Objective observation of children is also, of course, a skill in itself, which should be acquired by anyone who works with young children. During the orientation phase of training, the focus of observation should be general. Developing specific techniques for observing is more appropriate for experienced teachers and on-the-job trainees. We suggest a review of the methods described in chapter 11, in addition to the techniques explained below.

Anecdotal records of one or two children over a period of several weeks help caregivers gain an understanding of children's behavior over time. Time for writing these can easily be found during rest periods or at the end of the day.

Ten-minute time samples or running records provide additional and different information. Because the recording is made on the spot, when the observer is not interacting with the child, a great deal is revealed about children's ability to be self-directing, to explore and learn from their explorations, and to learn through their play. With the use of a form that separates objective observations and comments (see chapter 11), staff become aware of the difference between *describing* exactly what they hear and see and *interpreting* that behavior.

Both time samples and anecdotal records have the added advantage of being able to be used as a working tool for the classroom team. Because the information is descriptive and not judgmental, it can be shared with other staff members to assist in making decisions about a child. Assignment of any observations of children, of course, must be accompanied by a discussion of professionalism and confidentiality.

Administering developmental checklists to a few children can also be an effective learning experience. Caregivers should, however, be trained in their use. Inexperienced caregivers sometimes see categories as absolute standards, compare children based on assumptions about their being "bright" or "slow," or try to push children beyond what is appropriate.

There are many sources for observational tools and methods for early childhood classrooms. Among these are Cohen and Stern's classic book, *Observing and Recording the Behavior of Young Children*, which provides guidelines and questions for looking at children's classroom behavior from several points of view; Lindberg and Swedlow's series of guide sheets for observing areas of the room and of the program; and Betty Rowen's *The Children We See*.[8] David Elkind has developed observation systems for students based on "frames," a concept he describes in *Child and Society*.[9]

Because young children's behavior reveals so much about their abilities and about how they learn, observation is an especially valuable tool for training. It makes available a reality base that is hard to find in any other way.

WORKSHOPS

We expect a lot from workshops. In one or a few sessions, participants are supposed to develop new skills or understandings, or to change attitudes toward children and parents. They are then presumed to be ready to demonstrate what they have learned on their return to the classroom. It's no wonder the results are often disappointing.

Successful workshops—those that are stimulating to participants and bring about change—result from a number of factors: staff readiness and motivation for what is to come, effective leadership, objectives and content responsive to staff needs, effective techniques for presenting the content, follow-up, and evaluation. Consideration of adult learning principles in planning, especially the need for active learning and links to real life and work, contributes to the effectiveness of each of these elements.

Assessing Needs and Interests

In order to present workshops that will have an impact on staff members, their needs and interests must be determined. Circulating checklists or questionnaires is probably the most common means for doing this. If carefully constructed with staff input, such instruments do provide a good base of information, but they are best used in combination with other methods.

One way to expand their effectiveness is to have staff members and supervisors fill out the same instrument. Staff members indicate what they feel their needs are, or what they would like to work on, and the supervisor rates each caregiver on what she or he perceives that person's needs to be. In addition to individual needs, an overview of needs of the staff as a whole emerges from this process.

Interviews of individuals or classroom teams are a more flexible and personal way of obtaining information on staff concerns and interests. This technique affords both the interviewer and caregivers a chance to clarify and explore issues at a deeper level. Classroom teams might also be asked to discuss their concerns on their own and then to submit a list of interests applicable to their classrooms. This encourages team self-evaluation that may in itself spur action toward change.

A method called "nominal grouping" can be used to develop a consensus on the content of workshops desired once the supervisor has obtained preliminary data.[10] Figure 15.2 illustrates the steps for this rather structured approach. The advantage of such a technique is that it assures opinions and reactions from every participant without their having to confront one another right away. Since discussion is allowed only after the ideas have been sifted and synthesized, and since ideas are presented anonymously, both ownership of ideas and inhibitions about participating are lessened.

Providing for a choice of workshops, where feasible, is another way of allowing for staff participation, making it possible for them to focus on their own concerns and interests. Getting together with other early childhood programs can increase the number of participants and thus allow for a greater variety of workshop offerings.

Finally, no matter how thorough or valid the assessment process, the plans

FIGURE 15.2   *Nominal Grouping*

1.   Listing--participants list their responses to the
     task; no interaction is permitted.
2.   Round-robin--participants present items from their
     lists, round-robin fashion, which are recorded for
     later use; no other interaction is permitted.
3.   Voting--using cards or ballots, each participant ranks
     the items on the group's master list to show his/her
     priorities for the items; again, no interaction is
     allowed.
4.   Discussion--voting results are tabulated and discussed.
5.   Final voting--each participant votes a final time,
     listing priorities from the master list. The results
     may then be tabulated and analyzed.

Reprinted from Frederick H. Wood, Steven R. Thompson, and Frances Russell, "Designing Effective Staff Development Programs," in Betty Dillon-Peterson, ed., *Staff Development/Organization Development*, pp. 69–70, with permission of the Association for Supervision and Curriculum Development. Copyright © 1981 by the Association for Supervision and Curriculum Development. All rights reserved.

resulting should not be considered immutable. As it has been aptly stated, "Today's need may become yesterday's problem by the time planning and implementation are complete."[11] Refinements and revisions can be made right up through the early stages of the workshop itself as staff members become better known or as their needs change.

Selecting Workshop Leaders

Once needs and interests have been determined, the goals and specific topics for one or a series of workshops can be developed and leaders selected. Resources for leadership, both from within or outside the program, are surprisingly varied, even when funds are limited. Supervisors often find it a good policy to lead some, but not all, sessions. The process of preparation, though time-consuming, is a way of keeping up-to-date in the field and adds to credibility with staff. Teachers from within a program are an additional source of leadership. Staff members from other components, such as health or social service, or consultants who work with the program on a regular basis also have much to offer.

From outside the program, community agencies are another resource. They are often happy to send someone to lead workshops on topics of mutual concern, frequently with no fee. Local and state early childhood organizations and nearby colleges, universities, or teacher centers can also supply names of effective leaders. Consultants who charge fees need not be overlooked. Parent fund-raisers and grants from charitable foundations or local industries are good sources of money to support a series of workshop sessions on a special topic.

It cannot be assumed that all experts on a particular subject will necessarily understand appropriate techniques for teaching adults. It is important, therefore, to ask the presenter, or someone who knows the person's work, about the kinds of methods that will be used. It may be necessary to recommend techniques actively involving the participants as opposed to straight lectures with lots of jargon. Workshop leaders will also benefit from having information about the staff and the program if they are not familiar with them.

Defining Objectives

When a program designs its own workshops, there are several steps to consider. The first is to prepare specific objectives based on the information gathered through the needs-assessment process. Writing objectives will aid both design and evaluation by helping to pinpoint the kinds of outcomes that are desired. There are advantages to stating objectives at three levels: knowledge or understandings, skills or behaviors, and attitudes. Thus for a series of workshops on discipline, an objective at the knowledge level might be to obtain a greater understanding of the social/emotional development of three- and four-year-olds; at the skill level, to practice a specific method of handling discipline problems; and at the attitude level, to be able to come to terms with feelings about children's behaviors that many would consider disrespectful but that are developmentally appropriate for young children.

The setting for a workshop should be considered in relation to its objectives. When the focus is on children's use of materials, changes in the learning environment, or trying out children's games, an actual classroom setting provides reference points for the experience. When adult problem solving is the goal or highly charged issues are to be considered, it may be more productive to be in a setting where participants can sit in adult-sized chairs and where visual and sound distractions are limited.

Pre-Workshop Activities

Pre-workshop activities that actively involve participants in preparing for the session increase their motivation and readiness for the experience. Among the methods that can be used are suggesting relevant readings, having staff observe a child or a learning area, or trying out a particular kind of activity. Filling out a self-assessment checklist about individual interests or classroom practices related to the workshop subject matter can also pique interest while contributing valuable information to the workshop leader.[12]

Starting Off

The way a workshop begins creates the climate for learning and sets the stage for what is to come. Providing time to relax beforehand, perhaps with coffee and doughnuts, and starting the workshop itself with a transition activity will help participants to feel comfortable with one another and to begin to focus on the workshop topics.

Warm-up or ice-breaker activities are transitional activities that are especially worthwhile when participants do not know each other well or have not met for some time, or if the topic is a difficult one. In a large organization with separate centers, these activities help to provide a sense of unity and mutuality of purpose. A simple warm-up activity is to have participants pair off with someone they do not know very well, interview each other, and introduce the partner to the group. Guidelines for the interviews may be open-ended or geared to the purpose of the workshop.

Recording information from pre-workshop assignments on newsprint or a blackboard focuses attention immediately on the workshop and reinforces the value of the participants' input. Forming pairs or small groups for discussion of these issues before they are considered by the whole group also builds increased interaction and sharing. Other methods are taking a problem census, brainstorming about the topic, and role-playing or simulations. A brief review of the workshop objectives, with revision of content or process if needed, can help to clarify just what the workshop can and cannot accomplish, lessening the expectation of a "quick fix."

Structuring the Body of the Workshop

It is useful to consider three elements in structuring the main part of a session: presentation of the central ideas, discussion, and practice/application activities. Each contributes to learning in a different way, and in combination they help to make connections between theory and "how-to." The following are some of the methods that have proven effective in workshop situations.[13]

Lectures. If used to present background information or theory, to provide a rationale for the activities to follow, or at the end to summarize what has taken place, a lecture can be quite effective. As the main body of a workshop, however, this method should be avoided. Even when presented in a lively style and geared to the participants' level and interests, listeners are passive recipients of information. When a lecture format is used, it is advisable to include films, charts, or other visuals to add to its accessibility.

Audiovisual Presentations. Slide/tapes, films, videotapes, or audiotapes can also serve as a way to present the central ideas of a workshop. These need not be limited to those that are commercially made. Slides of learning environments or videotapes of children or teaching situations, or of role plays of teacher-child interaction or parent conferences, can be made quite easily by staff members or parent volunteers.

Audiovisual materials should be introduced in a way that gives a focus to the discussion that follows. Providing questions to answer, a guide sheet with points to look for, or assigning topics from the presentation to different groups for discussion can make the viewing more productive.

Experiential Workshops. Workshops in which participants try out activities they will use with children are especially effective for creative activities such as movement, music, creative dramatics, making and using puppets, or using art materials, which many adults have not experienced themselves. In these process-oriented situations, the workshop leader models teaching behavior, and participants experience the process children might go through in response to open-ended direction. Participants in experiential workshops must make inferences about the meaning for children and about ways to translate their experiences into appropriate experiences for children. The discussion following the activities can be important in making explicit what was learned.

Role-Play and Simulation. These useful practice and application techniques make it possible for staff members to try out new behaviors in a safe situation and to gain insight into other people's behavior and feelings. Most interpersonal behaviors are appropriate for role-play: practicing parent conferences, working through a staff team problem, or trying out new ways of working with children, such as introducing an activity or using nondirective language during free play. Role-playing works best when the "players" are given guidelines for what they should say or a brief description of the background or motivations of the person whose role they are to take.

Discussions. A discussion period following the initial presentation sets a climate of inquiry and problem solving. It provides an opportunity for analysis of ideas or techniques and for questions about a concept or about how the content relates to participants' own situations. Careful planning for the discussion period helps the group to center on workshop objectives rather than peripheral concerns and provides the leaders with ways to stimulate discussion when responses seem to be lacking. Effective techniques for leading discussions include asking questions that provoke problem solving, creative thinking, and a personal response to a specific aspect of the presentation; putting some of the information on a blackboard or chart; seating participants in a circle; and breaking up into pairs or buzz groups followed by sharing with the whole group.

Exhibits and Handouts. Teacher and child-made materials, children's books, examples of learning materials, or wall charts can enhance workshop topics. They can be explored and examined during breaks or before and after the session. Handouts are also useful, but if they are too long they are seldom read. They are best presented in outline or graphic form to serve as a reinforcement of what has been covered or as worksheets to be used during the workshop.

Planning for Follow-Up

Too often, participants leave a workshop without any clear sense of how they will actually put the new ideas or skills to work in the classroom. The first step is to plan for implementation during the workshop. For example, participants can be asked to write down at least one thing they will do to try out a new technique or put to use new knowledge. Then several kinds of assistance can be suggested and participants invited to indicate which of these they would like to avail themselves of. One advantage of having a series of workshops leading to the same goal is that it is possible to make between-session assignments for trying out certain behaviors or activities, or for observing a child or a classroom situation. Staff members are more motivated to try these activities when they know that they will be able to discuss them and receive feedback on their efforts.

Providing support for follow-up activities in the classroom is the next step in ensuring that new ideas and skills will be implemented at more than a minimal level. Among the ways that a supervisor can be helpful are seeing that materials and resources are easily available, physically helping staff to rearrange their rooms, being available to assist in planning and trouble shooting, demonstrating new techniques, observing and giving feedback to staff as they try out new techniques, and joining in as a colleague when new methods are first being tried. Continued encouragement and support, through inviting staff members to share their experiences at staff meetings, reinforce and maintain continued growth.

Evaluating the Workshop

An evaluation of each workshop provides information for designing future sessions and is one more way of involving staff members in their own learning. For workshops taking place over several sessions, ongoing feedback is valuable, especially if the topic is one that requires considerable change in attitudes or practices. The supervisor can evaluate each workshop through observations of participants as they work in small groups, through brief questionnaires, or by having staff write concerns, problems, or insights on cards. The leader is then able to respond to this information by reflecting feelings, addressing problems, and sharing growth as the sessions progress.

For summative evaluation at the close of a workshop or series, it is useful to obtain information that pertains to the quality of the content, the process, and the leadership of the session. A question about the participants' interest in future workshops on the topic or on related topics can also be valuable.

MORALE BUILDERS

As we have noted previously, morale is a major factor in the growth of staff. We also believe that an early childhood center should be an enjoyable place for both staff and children. We conclude this book, therefore, with suggestions from many people in the field for experiences designed with staff morale in mind.

- "Make teaching fun," one supervisor suggests. Plan special days for the children built around a theme, a special guest, or a puppet show. Do it so it's fun for the *teachers* as well as the children, *not* so that it's so much work that the enjoyment is lost.
- Encourage teachers to try out things that are related to their special interests. Help them to use these areas as a focus while building a balanced curriculum.
- Promote caring and sharing. This is a phrase used by Clare Cherry, in an article entitled, "Promoting Harmonious Staff Relationships." At the first staff meeting of each new school year, she challenges each staff member to "see to it that each of the other teachers has the best year teaching they've ever had." Cherry has found that teachers who previously hoarded their ideas behind closed doors now get excited about sharing new ideas, resources, and materials.[14]
- Have social events periodically in which staff have a chance just to get to know each other as people. Tensions that begin to build over small things can be relieved and even dissipated when the people involved discover or rediscover that they can have fun together. Include spouses, friends, and children in some events and have others for staff alone. Plan them with sensitivity for financial and family needs, and help staff to accept lack of participation without resentment.
- Add food to a work session or staff meeting. It is a catalyst for informal talk and relaxation. If done only occasionally, it gives a meeting a bit of a party atmosphere. One staff found that getting together to make cookies and fill children's stockings for Christmas was fun in itself and also provided an opportunity to share perceptions of children on a professional level while enjoying the holiday spirit.
- Once in a while vary the place where meetings are held. This creates a

change of pace for a regular staff meeting but is especially effective if you must hold an extra one. Sometimes issues arise in one classroom or center that the staff themselves feel cannot be resolved during the regular course of the day. Perhaps tensions have developed, or time is needed just to think about a problem in a different way. Often these situations come up spontaneously, and the motivation needs to be capitalized upon before it is lost. A meeting at someone's house for pizza, for example, can supply the time and the atmosphere to permit staff to look at an issue as a problem to be solved rather than as a difficulty that creates hard feelings.

- Have "catch-up days" or "curriculum refreshers." Find blocks of uninterrupted time when the staff can work on renewing skills, rearranging the learning environment, or discussing special curriculum topics. Even day care centers can sometimes close down for two or three days, perhaps in late August, if parents know ahead that they will have to make other arrangements at that time. In the summer, when there are fewer children in attendance, several days to a week of full afternoons might also be arranged. Hire substitutes or use job trainees and supplementary staff where needed.
- Build a personal day or flexible time off into personnel policies. A half day off on a staggered basis for Christmas shopping can make a huge difference to staff who work long hours, as can "comp time" to make up for an evening meeting.
- Finally, be an advocate for better pay and working conditions for early childhood staff, both in your own program and in the profession as a whole.

EXERCISES

1. Design a handbook for new staff and volunteers at your center or form a committee of staff members for this purpose, serving as a facilitator as needed.
2. Develop ways to assess the needs and interests of staff members as a basis for planning staff development activities. Use a combination of means. Develop a plan for addressing one of those needs/interests through an integrated set of experiences.
3. Plan a workshop or series of workshops, using the criteria discussed in this chapter. Include specific plans for follow-up in the classroom.
4. Develop guidelines for observing children for staff members to use in different phases of training.

APPENDICES

NOTES

BIBLIOGRAPHY

INDEX

APPENDIX A

Child Development Associate Competency Structure

This chart outlines the Definition of a CDA, the Competency Goals, and the Functional Areas. It describes the settings for CDA assessment as well as the Infant/Toddler Endorsement, Preschool Endorsement, and Bilingual Specialization.

OFFICIAL DEFINITION OF THE CDA

The Child Development Associate or CDA is a person who is able to meet the specific needs of children and who, with parents and other adults, works to nurture children's physical, social, emotional and intellectual growth in a child development framework. The CDA conducts herself or himself in an ethical manner.

The CDA has demonstrated competence in the goals listed below through her or his work in one of the following *settings*:

1. In a center-based program (CDA-CB).
2. In a home visitor program (CDA-HV).
3. In a family day care program (CDA-FDC).

Within a center-based setting, a person who demonstrates competence working with children from birth to three is a Child Development Associate with an *Infant/Toddler Endorsement*; or,

A person who demonstrates competence working with children aged three

---

Reprinted with permission from *The Child Development Associate Credential* (Washington, DC: Child Development Associate National Credentialing Program, in press), p. 4.

through five is a Child Development Associate with a *Preschool Endorsement*.

Within any of the above settings, a person who works in a bilingual program and has demonstrated bilingual competence is a Child Development Associate with a *Bilingual Specialization*.

Competency Goals	Functional Areas
I. To establish and maintain a safe, healthy, learning environment	1. Safe 2. Healthy 3. Learning environment
II. To advance physical and intellectual competence	4. Physical 5. Cognitive 6. Communication 7. Creative
III. To support social and emotional development and provide positive guidance and discipline	8. Self 9. Social 10. Guidance and discipline
IV. To establish positive and productive relationships with families	11. Families
V. To ensure a well-run, purposeful program responsive to participant needs	12. Program management
VI. To maintain a commitment to professionalism	13. Professionalism

Roles of Local Assessment Team Members

1. *The Candidate.* A full member of the LAT, the Candidate has an equal voice in assessing her/his competence. To help do so, the Candidate compiles evidence to demonstrate competence in the 13 Functional Areas. This compiled material is in the form of a Portfolio.
2. *The Advisor.* This member of the LAT is selected by the Candidate. The Advisor is an early childhood professional who may be a college professor, CDA trainer, center director, or someone else. The Advisor establishes a professional relationship with the Candidate over time, observes the Candidate's classroom performance, provides assistance and feedback, and helps the Candidate decide when to be assessed.
3. *The Parent/Community Representative (P/C Rep).* Also selected by the Candidate, the P/C Rep must be or have been a parent or guardian of a child five years old or younger. The P/C Rep must have been recently involved with the Candidate's center as a parent or volunteer but must not be a current employee. Furthermore, the P/C Rep must not have a child currently in the Candidate's classroom. The P/C Rep serves as the spokesperson on the LAT for the parents and the community. To do this, the P/C Rep gets questionnaires filled out by the parents of children in the Candidate's room and observes the Candidate working with the children.
4. *The CDA Representative (CDA Rep).* Assigned by the CDA National Credentialing Program, the CDA Rep is a professional in early childhood

Reprinted from U.S. Department of Health and Human Services, Office of Human Development Services, *The Child Development Associate Credential*, DHHS Publication No. (OHDS) 82-31162-A, December 1980.

education who has worked with young children in a classroom setting. The CDA Rep has been trained to observe, interview, make fair judgments and verify that procedures are followed. The CDA Rep observes the Candidate in the classroom, interviews the Candidate, and conducts the LAT meeting at which the Candidate's competence is assessed.

Notes

CHAPTER 1. MYTHS ABOUT SUPERVISION

1. Herbert M. Greenberg, *Teaching with Feeling* (New York: Pegasus, 1969), pp. 24–37.

CHAPTER 2. EARLY CHILDHOOD PROGRAMS AND THEIR IMPLICATIONS FOR SUPERVISORS

1. Richard Ruopp, Jeffrey Travers, Frederic Glantz, and Craig Coelen, *Children at the Center*, vol. 1 of *Final Report of the National Day Care Study* (Cambridge, MA: Abt Associates, 1979), p. 36. This study reported that in 1976, 77 percent of children in day care came from families earning $15,000 or less, including incomes of two working parents.

2. Myron Magnet, "What Mass-Produced Child Care is Producing," *Fortune* (November 28, 1983): 157–58.

3. Studies by Jerome Kagan and Henry Ricciuti for the Federal Interagency Day Care Regulations Appropriateness Study recommend a ratio of 1 : 3 for infants and 1 : 5 for twos (see U.S. Department of Health, Education and Welfare, Office of the Assistant Secretary for Planning and Evaluation, *Policy Issues in Day Care: Summaries of 21 Papers* [November 1977], pp. 69, 75). State regulations average about 1 : 5 and 1 : 9, respectively (Ruopp, et al., p. 255). Observed ratios by National Day Care Study staff averaged 1 : 3.9 for children under 18 months and 1 : 5.9 for 18 to 24 months (Ruopp, et al., p. 252).

4. William Fowler, *Infant and Child Care: A Guide to Education in Group Settings* (Boston: Allyn and Bacon, 1980), p. 64.

5. Anne Willis and Henry Ricciuti, *A Good Beginning for Babies: Guidelines for Group Care* (Washington, DC: National Association for the Education of Young Children, 1975), pp. 20–21.

6. For a thoughtful discussion of this issue, see T. Berry Brazleton, "Cementing Family Relationships," in Laura L. Dittman, ed., *The Infants We Care For*, rev. ed. (Washington, DC: National Association for the Education of Young Children, 1984).

7. Andrea Genser and Clifford Baden, eds., *School-Age Child Care: Programs and Issues*, papers from a conference at Wheelock College (Urbana, IL: ERIC Clearinghouse on Elementary and Early Childhood Education, 1983).

8. Ibid.

9. Mary Bublin Keyserling, *Windows on Day Care: A Report on the Findings of Jewish Women on Day Care Needs and Services in Their Communities* (New York: National Council of Jewish Women, 1972), p. 147.

10. Alice H. Collins and Eunice L. Watson, *Family Day Care* (Boston: Beacon Press, 1976), p. 19.

11. Colorado State Board of Education, *Developing Training Support Systems for Home Day Care* (Denver, CO, 1973), p. 51ff.

12. Collins and Watson describe these arrangements in detail in chapters 5 and 6.

13. Keyserling, p. 155.

14. U.S. Department of Health and Human Services, Office of Human Development Services, "Project Head Start" (Washington, DC, 1984), mimeograph, p. 1.

15. U.S. Department of Health, Education, and Welfare, Office of Human Development, *Head Start Program Performance Standards* (Washington, DC, July 1975), p. 58.

16. Carolyn Harmon and Edward J. Harley, "Administrative Aspects of the Head Start Program," in Edward Zigler and Jeannette Valentine, eds., *Project Head Start* (New York: Free Press, 1979), p. 393.

17. Ibid.

18. The CDA is a nationally sponsored, competency-based credential for personnel in teaching roles in early childhood programs. For a description, see chapter 14 and Appendices A and B.

19. It is worth nothing here that, according to James Hymes, the half-day kindergarten is a relatively recent phenomenon, designed as a "two for the price of one" economy measure. Thus "five-year olds receive only 50 percent of the support given to the education of children six and older." *Teaching the Child Under Six*, 3d edition (Columbus, OH: Charles E. Merrill, 1981), p. 6.

CHAPTER 3. SUPERVISORS AND STAFF: ROLES AND RESPONSIBILITIES

1. "NAEYC Position Statement on Nomenclature, Salaries, Benefits, and the Status of the Early Childhood Profession," *Young Children* 40 (November 1984): 65.

2. Joseph J. Caruso, "Characteristics of 184 Early Childhood Supervisors and Their Settings" (Paper presented at the Rhode Island Early Childhood Conference, Providence, RI, April 1982), p. 18.

3. Ibid., p. 23.

4. Gwendolyn Morgan, unpublished paper, p. 1.

5. Bernard Spodek and Olivia N. Saracho, "The Preparation and Certification of Early Childhood Personnel," in Bernard Spodek, ed., *Handbook of Research in Early Childhood Education* (New York: Macmillan, 1982), chap. 17.

6. William Ade, "Professionalization and Its Implications for the Field of Early Childhood Education," *Young Children* 37 (March 1982): 27.

7. Mary Bublin Keyserling, *Windows on Day Care: A Report on the Findings of Jewish Women on Day Care Needs and Services in Their Communities* (New York: National Council of Jewish Women, 1972).

8. Roger Neugebauer, "Organizational Analysis of Day Care," (unpublished paper), 1975.

9. Nora Palmer Gould, "Caregivers in Day Care: Who Are They?" *Day Care and Early Education* (Summer 1983): p. 20.

10. Caruso, p. 52.

11. Richard Ruopp, Jeffrey Travers, Frederic Glantz, and Craig Coelen, *Children at the Center*, vol. 1 of *Final Report of the National Day Care Study* (Cambridge, MA: Abt Associates, 1979).

12. "Results of the NAEYC Survey of Child Care Salaries and Working Conditions," *Young Children* 30 (November 1984): 10.

13. Greta G. Fein and Alison Clarke-Stewart, *Day Care in Context* (New York: John Wiley and Sons, 1973), p. 241.

14. Ruopp, et al., p. 98.

15. Marcy Whitebook, Carollee Howes, Rory Darrah, and Jane Friedman, "Caring for the Caregivers: Staff Burn-Out in Child Care," in Lillian Katz, ed., *Current Topics in Early Childhood Education*, vol. 4. (Norwood, NJ: Ablex Publishing, 1982), p. 221.

16. Gould, p. 20.

CHAPTER 4. THE DEVELOPMENTAL DYNAMIC

1. Donald H. Brundage and Dorothy Mackeracher, *Adult Learning Principles and Their Application to Program Planning* (Toronto: Ontario Institute for Studies in Education, 1980), p. 58.

2. Ibid., p. 59.

3. Ibid., p. 60.

4. Carl D. Glickman, *Developmental Supervision: Alternative Practices for Helping Teachers* (Alexandria, VA: Association for Supervision and Curriculum Development, 1981).

5. Ibid., pp. 39–50.

6. Richard H. Bents and Kenneth R. Howey, "Staff Development — Change in the Individual," in Betty Dillon-Peterson, ed., *Staff Development/Organization Development* (Alexandria, VA: Association for Supervision and Curriculum Development, 1981), pp. 11–36. These authors provide an excellent description of behaviors of teachers as learners at various levels of conceptual functioning and strategies to use with them.

7. Sharon Nodie Oja, "Deriving Teacher Educational Objectives from Cognitive-Developmental Theories and Applying Them to the Practice of Teacher Education" (Paper presented at the annual meeting of the American Educational Research Association, Los Angeles, CA, April 1981).

8. Peter P. Grimmett, "'Effective' Clinical Supervision Conference Interventions: A Preliminary Investigation of Participants' Conceptual Functioning" (Paper presented at the annual meeting of the American Educational Research Association, Montreal, Canada, April 1983), p. 18.

9. Ibid., p. 19.

10. Lois Thies-Sprinthall, "Supervision: An Educative or Mis-Educative Process?" *Journal of Teacher Education* 31 (November 4, 1980): 17-20.

11. Oja; Sally Glassberg, "A View of the Beginning Teacher from a Developmental Perspective" (Paper presented at the annual meeting of the American Educational Research Association, Boston, MA, April 1980).

12. Frances F. Fuller and Oliver H. Bown, "Becoming a Teacher," in Kevin Ryan, ed., *Teacher Education: The 74th Yearbook of the National Society for the Study of Education*, part 2 (Chicago: University of Chicago Press, 1975), pp. 25-52.

13. Ibid., p. 39.

14. Lillian G. Katz, "Developmental Stages of Preschool Teachers," *Elementary School Journal* 73 (October 1972): 50-54.

15. Ibid.

16. Ibid.

CHAPTER 5. SUPERVISION AS ADULT EDUCATION

1. Donald H. Brundage and Dorothy Mackeracher, *Adult Learning Principles and Their Application to Program Planning* (Toronto: Ontario Institute for Studies in Education, 1980), pp. 11-12.

2. Gordon J. Klopf, *The Principal and Staff Development in the School* (New York: Bank Street College of Education, 1979).

3. Brundage and Mackeracher, pp. 24-26.

4. Robert C. Peck, "Psychological Development in the Second Half of Life," in Bernice L. Neugarten, ed., *Middle Age and Aging: A Reader in Social Psychology* (Chicago: University of Chicago Press, 1968), pp. 88-92.

5. Arthur W. Combs, Donald L. Avila, and William W. Purkey, *Helping Relationships*, 2d ed. (Boston: Allyn and Bacon, 1978), pp. 53-54.

6. Brundage and Mackeracher, p. 33.

7. Malcolm S. Knowles, *The Modern Practice of Adult Education: Andragogy vs. Pedagogy* (New York: Association Press, 1970), pp. 44-45.

8. Combs, Avila, and Purkey, p. 58.

9. Ibid., p. 51.

10. Knowles, pp. 44-45.

11. Jan M. Diamondstone, *Designing, Leading, and Evaluating Workshops for Teachers and Parents: A Manual for Trainers and Leadership Personnel in Early Childhood Education* (Ypsilanti, MI: High/Scope Educational Research Foundation, 1980), p. 27.

12. Knowles, p. 43.

13. Ibid., p. 48.

14. William Fibkins, "Ownership and Dialogue in Transforming Teachers'

Work," in Kathleen Devaney, ed., *Essays on Teachers' Centers* (San Francisco: Far West Laboratory for Educational Research and Development, no date).

15. J. R. Kidd, *How Adults Learn*, rev. ed. (New York: Association Press, 1973), p. 37.

16. Combs, Avila, and Purkey, p. 61.

17. Erik H. Erikson, *Childhood and Society*, 2d ed. (New York: W. W. Norton, 1963), pp. 247-74; Robert Havighurst, *Developmental Tasks and Education* (New York: David McKay, 1952); Daniel J. Levinson, Charlotte N. Darrow, Edward B. Klein, Marsha H. Levinson, and Braxton McKee, *The Seasons of a Man's Life* (New York: Alfred A. Knopf, 1978); Roger L. Gould, *Transformations* (New York: Simon and Schuster, 1978); Gail Sheehy, *Passages* (New York: E. P. Dutton, 1974).

18. Judy Arin-Krupp, *Adult Development: Implications for Staff Development* (Manchester, CT: Adult Development and Learning, 1981).

19. Levinson, et al., p. 100.

20. K. Patricia Cross, *Adults as Learners* (San Francisco: Jossey-Bass, 1981), pp. 129-30.

21. Combs, Avila, and Purkey, pp. 66-67.

22. Jerome Bruner, *Toward a Theory of Instruction* (Cambridge, MA: Harvard University Press, 1966), cited in Richard C. Sprinthall and Norman A. Sprinthall, *Educational Psychology: A Development Approach*, 3d ed. (Reading, MA: Addison-Wesley, 1981), p. 289.

23. Lillian G. Katz, *Talks with Teachers* (Washington, DC: National Association for the Education of Young Children, 1977), p. 63.

CHAPTER 9. THE FIVE STAGES OF CLINICAL SUPERVISION

1. Robert Goldhammer, Robert H. Anderson, Robert J. Krajewski, *Clinical Supervision: Special Methods for the Supervision of Teachers*, 2d edition (New York: Holt, Rinehart and Winston, 1980), pp. 32-44.

2. Ibid., p. 70.

3. Morris L. Cogan, *Clinical Supervision* (Boston: Houghton Mifflin, 1973), p. 197.

CHAPTER 10. THE SUPERVISORY CONFERENCE

1. Arthur Blumberg, *Supervisors and Teachers: A Private Cold War* (Berkeley: McCutchan, 1974), p. 3.

2. Noreen B. Garman, "The Clinical Approach to Supervision," in Thomas J. Sergiovanni, ed., *Supervision of Teaching, 1982 Yearbook* (Alexandria, VA: Association for Supervision and Curriculum Development, 1982), chap. 3.

3. Arthur L. Costa, "What Goes On In Your Head When You Teach?" (Paper presented to ASCD National Commission on Supervision, annual meeting of ASCD, New York, 1984).

4. Blumberg, p. 43.

5. Ibid.

6. Carl E. Pickhardt, "Supervisors and the Power of Help," *Educational Leadership* 38(7) (April 1981): 531.

7. Ibid.

8. Thomas J. Sergiovanni and Robert J. Starratt, "The Human Organization of Schools," Chapter 8 in *Supervision: Human Perspectives*, 2d ed. (New York: McGraw-Hill, 1979), pp. 150–73.

9. Carl E. Rogers, "The Interpersonal Relationship: The Core of Guidance," *Harvard Educational Review* 32 (1962): 417.

10. Charles M. Galloway, "Nonverbal Communication in Teaching," in Ronald T. Hyman, ed., *Teaching: Vantage Points for Study*, 2d ed. (Philadelphia: Lippincott, 1974), pp. 395–406.

11. Arthur Blumberg, "Supervisor-Teacher Relationships: A Look at the Supervisory Conference," *Administrator's Notebook* no. 1 (September 1970): 2.

12. Kiyo Morimoto, "Notes on the Context of Learning," *Harvard Educational Review* 43 (May 1973): 247–49.

13. Robert G. Johnson, *The Appraisal Interview Guide* (New York: Alpine Press, 1979), pp. 75–76.

14. Richard Kindsvatter and William W. Wilen, "A Systematic Approach to Improving Conference Skills," *Educational Leadership* 38 (April 1981): 527.

15. Blumberg, "Supervisor-Teacher Relationships," p. 3.

16. Arthur Blumberg, "A System for Analyzing Supervisor-Teacher Interaction," in Anita Simon and E. Gail Boyer, eds., *Mirrors for Behavior VIII: An Anthology of Classroom Observation Instruments* (Philadelphia: Research for Better Schools, 1970), pp. 34.1-1–34.1-15.

17. Kindsvatter and Wilen, p. 529.

18. Marjorie J. Kostelnik, "How to Mediate Staff Conflict," *Child Care Information Exchange* (September/October 1982): 1–5.

19. Ibid., p. 2.

20. Ibid., p. 5.

CHAPTER 11. OBSERVATION AND ANALYSIS

1. Asa G. Hilliard, III, "Moving from Abstract to Functional Teacher Education: Pruning and Planting," in Bernard Spodek, ed., *Teacher Education: Of the Teacher, By the Teacher, For the Child* (Washington, DC: National Association for the Education of Young Children, 1974), pp. 18–19.

2. These goals are based in part on the "Aims of Clinical Supervision," described in Keith A. Acheson and Meredith Gall, *Techniques in the Clinical Supervision of Teachers: Preservice and Inservice Applications* (New York, Longman, 1980), pp. 12–14.

3. Noreen B. Garman, "The Clinical Approach to Supervision," in Thomas J. Sergiovanni, ed., *Supervision of Teaching* (Alexandria, VA: Association for Supervision and Curriculum Development, 1982), p. 50.

4. Ibid.

5. Ibid., p. 51.

6. Ibid.

7. Egon G. Guba and Yvonne S. Lincoln, *Effective Evaluation* (San Francisco: Jossey-Bass, 1981), pp. 189–90.

8. For some ways to use this approach, see David B. Strahan, "The Teacher and Ethnography: Observational Sources of Information for Educators," *Elementary School Journal* 83 (January 1983): 196–203.

9. Michael J. Dunkin and Bruce J. Biddle, *The Study of Teaching* (New York: Holt, Rinehart and Winston, 1974), pp. 71–72.

10. Ned A. Flanders, *Analyzing Teacher Behavior* (Reading, MA: Addison-Wesley, 1970).

11. For examples, see Ira J. Gordon and R. Emile Jester, "Techniques of Observing in Early Childhood and Outcomes of Particular Procedures," in R. M. Travers, ed., *2nd Handbook of Research on Teaching* (Chicago: Rand McNally, 1973), p. 194; and David E. Day, Elizabeth Phyfe-Perkins, and Judith A. Weithalter, "Naturalistic Evaluation for Program Improvement," *Young Children* 34 (May 1979): 18.

12. Guba and Lincoln, p. 57.

13. Ibid., p. 129.

14. Elliott Eisner, "An Artistic Approach to Supervision" in Sergiovanni (ed.), pp. 60–65.

15. See Dorothy Cohen and Virginia Stern with Nancy Balaban, *Observing and Recording the Behavior of Young Children*, 3d ed. (New York: Teachers College Press, 1983), pp. 7–10.

16. *CDA Application Book* (Washington, DC: Child Development Associate National Credentialing Program, 1984), p. 15.

17. Duong Thanh Binh, *A Handbook for Teachers of Vietnamese Students* (Arlington, VA: Center for Applied Linguistics, 1975), pp. 8–9.

18. Courtney Cazden, "Language in Education: Variation in the Teacher-Talk Register" (Paper presented at the 30th Annual Georgetown University Round Table on Languages and Linguistics, *Language in Public Life*, 1979), p. 14.

19. Ibid.

20. Elizabeth Hirsh, *The Block Book*, 2d ed. (Washington, DC: National Association for the Education of Young Children, 1984); *The Block Corner: A Creative Curriculum for Early Childhood* (Washington, DC: Creative Associates, 1979).

21. Dorothy Anker, J. Foster, J. McClane, J. Sobel, and B. Weissbourd, "Teaching Children as They Play," *Young Children* 29 (May 1974): 203–13.

22. *Exploring Childhood*, EDC School and Society Program, 55 Chapel Street, Newton, MA 02160.

23. Strahan, pp. 196–203.

CHAPTER 12. EVALUATING STAFF

1. Lillian Katz, *Talks with Teachers* (Washington, DC: National Association for the Education of Young Children, 1977); Joseph J. Caruso, "Phases in Student Teaching," *Young Children* 33 (November 1977): 56–63.

226

2. C. A. Decker and J. R. Decker, *Planning and Administering Early Childhood Programs* (Columbus, OH: Bobbs Merrill, 1976), p. 52.

3. Greta G. Fein and Alison Clarke-Stewart, *Day Care in Context* (New York: John Wiley and Sons, 1973).

4. Elizabeth Phyfe-Perkins, *Effects of Teacher Behavior: A Review of the Research* (ERIC Clearinghouse, Elementary and Early Childhood Education, 1981), pp. 36–37.

5. James W. Popham, *Educational Evaluation* (Englewood Cliffs, NJ: Prentice-Hall, 1975), p. 283.

6. Bernard Spodek and Olivia N. Saracho, "The Preparation and Certification of Early Childhood Personnel," in Bernard Spodek, ed., *Handbook of Research in Early Childhood Education* (New York: Free Press, 1982), p. 414.

7. William H. Lucio and John D. McNeil, *Supervision: A Synthesis of Thought and Action* (New York: McGraw-Hill, 1969), p. 241.

8. Spodek and Saracho, pp. 412, 413.

9. Anne Willis and Henry Ricciuti, *A Good Beginning for Babies: Guidelines for Group Care* (Washington, DC: National Association for the Education of Young Children, 1975), p. 114; Alice Sterling Honig, "What You Need to Know to Select and Train Your Staff," *Child Care Quarterly* 8 (Spring 1979): 19–35.

10. Elliot W. Eisner, *The Educational Imagination* (New York: Macmillan, 1979), p. 241.

11. Ibid., p. 2.

12. Thomas J. Sergiovanni, "Toward a Theory of Supervisory Practice: Integrating Scientific, Clinical, and Artistic Views," Chapter 5 in Thomas J. Sergiovanni, ed., *Supervision of Teaching* (Alexandria, VA: Association for Supervision and Curriculum Development, 1982), pp. 67–78.

13. Robert G. Fraser, "Practical and Legal Aspects of Teacher Evaluation" (unpublished paper, 1982).

14. Thomas J. Sergiovanni, "Reforming Teacher Evaluation: Naturalistic Alternatives," *Educational Leadership* 34 (May 1977): 606.

15. Ibid., pp. 606–7.

16. Lawrence Steinmetz, *Managing the Marginal and Unsatisfactory Performer* (Reading, MA: Addison-Wesley, 1969), p. 88.

17. Kenneth H. Blanchard and Spencer Johnson, *The One-Minute Manager* (New York: William Morrow, 1982), pp. 86–92.

18. Steinmetz, pp. 145–48.

19. Harold J. McNally, "Teacher Evaluation That Makes A Difference," *Educational Leadership* 29 (1972): 353–57.

CHAPTER 13. SUPERVISORY PROBLEMS

1. Anne Willis and Henry Ricciuti, *A Good Beginning for Babies: Guidelines for Group Care* (Washington, DC: National Association for the Education of Young Children, 1975), p. 127.

2. Richard Ruopp, Jeffrey Travers, Frederic Glantz, and Craig Coelen, *Children at the Center*, vol. 1 of *Final Report of the National Day Care Study* (Cambridge, MA: Abt Associates, 1979), p. 224.

3. Richard Ruopp, as reported in *Child Care Information Exchange* (June 1980): 22.

4. Lana Hoestetler and Edgar Klugman, "Early Childhood Job Titles: One Step Toward Professional Status." *Young Children* 37 (September 1982): 13–22.

5. Marcy Whitebook, Carollee Howes, Rory Darrah, and Jane Friedman, "Caring for the Caregivers: Staff Burn-Out in Child Care," in Lillian Katz, ed., *Current Topics in Early Childhood Education*, vol. 4 (Norwood, NJ: Ablex Publishing, 1982), p. 221.

6. For suggestions about influencing public officials, see Lana Hoestetler, "How-To Guide for Advocates," *Child Care Information Exchange* (March/April 1983): 25–29.

7. Colorado State Board of Education, *Developing Training Support Systems for Home Day Care* (Denver, CO, 1973), p. 12.

8. Whitebook, et al., p. 222.

9. Ibid., pp. 221–22.

10. Stanley Seiderman, "Combating Staff Burn-Out," *Day Care and Early Education* 5 (Summer 1978): 6.

11. Ayala Pines and Christine Maslach, "Combating Staff Burn-Out in a Day Care Center: A Case Study," *Child Care Quarterly* 9 (Spring 1980): 6.

12. Ruopp, et al., p. 224.

13. Paul D. Wessen, "Off-Site Stress and the Disadvantaged Caregiver: A Neglected Factor," *Child Care Information Exchange* (November/December 1981): 10–12.

14. Seiderman, p. 6.

15. Whitebook, et al., pp. 226–33; Roger Neugebauer, "Techniques for Avoiding Director Burn-Out," *Child Care Information Exchange* (January 1980): 9–15; Pines and Maslach, p. 6.

16. Seiderman, p. 8.

17. Whitebook, et al., p. 224.

18. Nora Palmer Gould, "Caregivers in Day Care: Who Are They?" *Day Care and Early Education* (Summer 1983): 20.

19. Whitebook, et al., pp. 224–25.

20. John A. Carpenter, in Judith Herman, ed. *The Schools and Group Identity* (New York: Institute on Pluralism and Group Identity of the American Jewish Committee, 1974).

21. Gordon W. Allport, *The Nature of Prejudice* (Garden City, NY: Doubleday Anchor Books, 1958), p. 19.

22. Greta G. Fein and Alison Clarke-Stewart, *Day Care in Context* (New York: John Wiley and Sons, 1973). See Context III: "The Family," pp. 143–95 of this work, for an extensive review of research on class and cultural diversities and their relationship to day care issues.

23. Allport, p. 24.

24. Fein and Clarke-Stewart, pp. 171–73.

25. W. E. Lambert, "Portuguese Child Rearing Values: A Cross-National Analysis" (Paper presented at the Fifth National Portuguese Conference, "Bilingual Education in the 1980s," Providence, RI, June 1980).

26. *Exploring Childhood*. EDC School and Society Programs, 55 Chapel Street, Newton, MA 02160.

CHAPTER 14. A FRAMEWORK
FOR STAFF DEVELOPMENT AND TRAINING

1. Milly Almy, *The Early Childhood Educator at Work* (New York: Teachers College Press, 1975), p. 196.

2. Dorothy J. Sciarra and A. G. Dorsey, *Developing and Administering a Child Care Center* (Boston: Houghton Mifflin, 1979), p. 195.

3. Alice Sterling Honig, "Quality Training for Infant Caregivers," *Child Care Quarterly* 12 (Spring 1983): 131.

4. For information on early childhood degree programs, see *Directory of Educational Programs for Adults Who Work with Children* (Washington, DC: National Association for the Education of Young Children, 1979).

5. At this writing, the credential is available for center-based and family day care staff working with infants through five-year-old children, and home visitors, including those in bilingual/bicultural (Spanish) settings.

6. U.S. Department of Health and Human Services, Office of Human Development Services, *The CDA Program: The Child Development Associate, A Guide for Training*, 2d ed., DHHS Publication No. (OHDS) 82-31171, Fall 1981.

7. CDA National Credentialing Program, 1341 G Street, NW, Suite 802, Washington, DC 20005.

8. Bruce Joyce and Beverly Showers, "Improving In-Service Training: The Messages of Research," *Educational Leadership* 37 (February 1980): 379–85.

9. Thomas Gordon, *Parent Effectiveness Training: The Tested Way to Raise Responsible Children*. (New York: Peter H. Wyden, 1970); U.S. Department of Health, Education and Welfare, Office of Human Development, *Exploring Parenting*, DHEW Publication No. (OHOF) 79-3137, 1978.

10. For valuable guidelines to improve team functioning, see Mary Hohmann, Bernard Banet, and David Weikart, *Young Children in Action: A Manual for Preschool Educators* (Ypsilanti, MI: The High/Scope Press, 1979), p. 100ff.

CHAPTER 15. TOOLS
FOR STAFF DEVELOPMENT AND TRAINING

1. Barrington College Early Childhood Center, *Student Handbook* (Barrington, RI, no date).

2. Polly Greenberg, *Day Care Do-It-Yourself Staff Growth Program* (Winston-Salem, NC: Kaplan Press, 1975), p. 112.

3. Ibid., p. 305.

4. Dorothy Sciarra and A. G. Dorsey, *Developing and Administering a Child Care Center* (Boston: Houghton Mifflin, 1979), p. 3.

5. Virginia B. Hatch, "Creative Supervision of Head Start Centers," in Dorothy W. Hewes, ed., *Administration: Making Programs Work for Children and Families* (Washington, DC: National Association for the Education of Young Children, 1979), pp. 141–46.

6. Lenore B. McCarthy and Elizabeth Landerholm, "Classroom Interaction: A Field-Based Model for Improving Teaching in the Day Care Center," *Child Care Quarterly* 7 (Spring 1978): 35–44.

7. Anne Willis and Henry Ricciuti, *A Good Beginning for Babies: Guidelines for Group Care* (Washington, DC: National Association for the Education of Young Children, 1975), p. 119.

8. Dorothy H. Cohen and Virginia Stern with Nancy Balaban, *Observing and Recording the Behavior of Young Children*, 3d ed. (New York: Teachers College Press, 1983); Lucille Lindberg and Rita Swedlow, *Early Childhood Education: A Guide for Observation and Participation*, 2d ed. (Boston: Allyn and Bacon, 1979); Betty Rowen, *The Children We See: An Observational Approach to Child Study* (New York: Holt, Rinehart and Winston, 1973).

9. David Elkind, *The Child and Society: Essays in Applied Child Development* (New York: Oxford University Press, 1979), Chapter 6, "Cognitive Frames and Family Interactions," pp. 65–79, and Chapter 12, "Observing Classroom Frames," pp. 135–42.

10. Frederick H. Wood, Steven R. Thompson, and Frances Russell, "Designing Effective Staff Development Programs," in Betty Dillion-Peterson, ed., *Staff Development/Organization Development* (Alexandria, VA: Association for Supervision and Curriculum Development, 1981), pp. 69–70.

11. Linda Rubin and John H. Hansen, "Assessing Needs and Prioritizing Goals," in W. R. Houston and R. Pankratz, ed., *Staff Development and Educational Change* (Reston, VA: Association of Teacher Educators, 1980), p. 107.

12. Jan M. Diamondstone, *Designing, Leading, and Evaluating Workshops for Teachers and Parents: A Manual for Trainers and Leadership Personnel in Early Childhood Education* (Ypsilanti, MI: High/Scope Educational Research Foundation, 1980), p. 27.

13. These ideas are compiled from Diamondstone; Wood et al.; Gordon J. Klopf, *The Principal and Staff Development in the School* (New York: Bank Street College of Education, 1979); and the experience of the authors.

14. Clare Cherry, "Promoting Harmonious Staff Relationships," *Child Care Information Exchange* (July 1980): 25–28.

Bibliography

Acheson, Keith A., and Gall, Meredith D. *Techniques in the Clinical Supervision of Teachers: Preservice and Inservice Applications.* New York: Longman, 1980.

Ade, William. "Professionalization and Its Implications for the Field of Early Childhood Education." *Young Children* 37 (March 1982): 25–32.

Alfonso, Robert J. "Will Peer Supervision Work?" *Educational Leadership* 34 (May 1977): 594–601.

Allport, Gordon W. *The Nature of Prejudice.* Garden City, NY: Doubleday Anchor Books, 1958.

Almy, Milly. *The Early Childhood Educator at Work.* New York: Teachers College Press, 1975.

Anker, Dorothy; Foster, J.; McClane, J.; Sobel, J.; and Weissbourd, B. "Teaching Children as They Play." *Young Children* 29 (May 1974): 203–13.

Arin-Krupp, Judy. *Adult Development: Implications for Staff Development.* Manchester, CT: Adult Development and Learning, 1981.

———. "Sparking an Aging Staff Through Increased Awareness of Adult Developmental Changes." *SAANYS Journal* (Winter 1982–83): 9–13.

Barrington College Early Childhood Center. *Student Handbook.* Barrington, RI, no date.

Bents, Richard H., and Howey, Kenneth R. "Staff Development — Change in the Individual." In *Staff Development/Organization Development,* edited by Betty Dillon-Peterson. Alexandria, VA: Association for Supervision and Curriculum Development, 1981, pp. 11–36.

Blanchard, Kenneth, and Johnson, Spencer. *The One-Minute Manager.* New York: William Morrow, 1982.

The Block Corner: A Creative Curriculum for Early Childhood. Washington, DC: Creative Associates, 1979.

Blumberg, Arthur. *Supervisors and Teachers: A Private Cold War.* Berkeley: McCutchan, 1974.

———. "A System for Analyzing Supervisor-Teacher Interaction." In *Mirrors for Behavior VIII: An Anthology of Classroom Observation Instruments,* edited by Anita Simon and E. Gil Boyer. Philadelphia: Research for Better Schools, 1970, pp. 34.1-1–34.1-15.

———. "Supervisor-Teacher Relationships: A Look at the Supervisory Conference." *Administrator's Notebook, No. 1.* University of Chicago, September 1970. p. 104.

Brundage, Donald H., and Mackeracher, Dorothy. *Adult Learning Principles and Their Application to Program Planning.* Toronto: Ontario Institute for Studies in Education, 1980.

Bruner, Jerome. *Toward a Theory of Instruction.* Cambridge, MA: Harvard University Press, 1966.

Caruso, Joseph J. "Characteristics of 184 Early Childhood Supervisors and Their Settings." Paper presented at the Rhode Island Early Childhood Conference, Rhode Island College, Providence, RI, April 1982.

_____. "Phases in Student Teaching." *Young Children* 33 (November 1977): 56–63.

Cazden, Courtney. "Language in Education: Variation in the Teacher-Talk Register." Paper presented at the 30th Annual Georgetown University Round Table on Languages and Linguistics. *Language in Public Life,* 1979.

Cherry, Clare. "Promoting Harmonious Staff Relationships." *Child Care Information Exchange* (July 1980): 25–28.

Child Development Associate Credential, The. Washington, DC: Child Development Associate National Credentialing Program, in press.

Cogan, Morris. *Clinical Supervision.* Boston: Houghton Mifflin, 1973.

Cohen, Dorothy. *The Learning Child.* New York: Pantheon Books, 1972.

Cohen, Dorothy, and Stern, Virginia, with Balaban, Nancy. *Observing and Recording the Behavior of Young Children,* 3d ed. New York: Teachers College Press, 1983.

Collins, Alice H., and Watson, Eunice L. *Family Day Care.* Boston: Beacon Press, 1976.

Colorado State Board of Education. *Developing Training Support Systems for Home Day Care.* Denver, CO, 1973.

Combs, Arthur W.; Avila, Donald L.; and Purkey, William W. *Helping Relationships,* 2d ed. Boston: Allyn and Bacon, 1978.

Costa, Arthur L. "Supervision: The State of the Art." Paper presented to the Association for Supervision and Curriculum Development, National Commission on Supervision, New York, 1984.

_____. "What Goes On In Your Head When You Teach?" Paper presented to the annual meeting of the Association for Supervision and Curriculum Development, New York, 1984.

Cross, K. Patricia. *Adults as Learners.* San Francisco: Jossey-Bass, 1981.

Day, David E. *Early Childhood Education: A Human Ecological Approach.* Glenview, IL: Scott, Foresman, 1983.

Day, David E.; Phyfe-Perkins, Elizabeth; and Weithaler, Judith A. "Naturalistic Evaluation for Program Improvement." *Young Children* 34 (May 1979): 12–24.

Decker, C. A., and Decker, J. R. *Planning and Administering Early Childhood Programs.* Columbus, OH: Bobbs Merrill, 1976.

Devaney, Kathleen, ed. *Essays on Teachers' Centers.* San Francisco: Far West Laboratory for Educational Research and Development, no date.

Diamondstone, Jan M. *Designing, Leading, and Evaluating Workshops for Teachers and Parents: A Manual for Trainers and Leadership Personnel in Early Childhood Education.* Ypsilanti, MI: High/Scope Educational Research Foundation, 1980.

Directory of Educational Programs for Adults Who Work with Children. Washington, DC: National Association for the Education of Young Children, 1979.

Dittman, Laura L. *The Infants We Care For*, rev. ed. Washington, DC: National Association for the Education of Young Children, 1984.

Dunkin, Michael J., and Biddle, Bruce J. *The Study of Teaching.* New York: Holt, Rinehart and Winston, 1974.

Duong Thanh Binh. *A Handbook for Teachers of Vietnamese Students.* Arlington, VA: Center for Applied Linguistics, 1975.

Eisner, Elliott. "An Artistic Approach to Supervision." In *Supervision of Teaching*, edited by Thomas J. Sergiovanni. Alexandria, VA: Association for Supervision and Curriculum Development, 1982, pp. 60–65.

––––––. *The Educational Imagination.* New York: Macmillan, 1979.

Elkind, David. *The Child and Society: Essays in Applied Child Development.* New York: Oxford University Press, 1979.

Erikson, Erik H. *Childhood and Society*, 2d ed. New York: W. W. Norton, 1963.

Exploring Childhood. EDC School and Society Programs, 55 Chapel Street, Newton, MA 02160.

Fein, Greta G., and Clarke-Stewart, Alison. *Day Care in Context.* New York: John Wiley and Sons, 1973.

Fibkins, William. "Ownership and Dialogue in Transforming Teachers' Work." In *Essays on Teachers' Centers*, edited by Kathleen Devaney. San Francisco: Far West Laboratory for Educational Research and Development, no date, pp. 49–56.

Flanders, Ned A. *Analyzing Teacher Behavior.* Reading, MA: Addison-Wesley, 1970.

Fowler, William. *Infant and Child Care: A Guide to Education in Group Settings.* Boston: Allyn and Bacon, 1980.

Fraser, Robert G. "Practical and Legal Aspects of Teacher Evaluation." Unpublished paper, 1982.

Fuller, Frances F., and Bown, Oliver H. "Becoming a Teacher." In *Teacher Education: The 74th Yearbook of the National Society for the Study of Education*, part II, edited by Kevin Ryan. Chicago: University of Chicago Press, 1975, pp. 25–32.

Galloway, Charles M. "Nonverbal Communication in Teaching." In *Teaching: Vantage Points for Study*, 2d ed., edited by Ronald T. Hyman. Philadelphia: J. B. Lippincott, 1974, chapter 32.

Garman, Noreen B. "The Clinical Approach to Supervision." In *Supervision of Teaching, 1982 Yearbook*, edited by Thomas J. Sergiovanni. Alexandria, VA: Association for Supervision and Curriculum Development, 1982, chapter 3.

Genser, Andrea and Bade, Clifford. *School-Age Child Care: Programs and Issues.* Urbana, IL: ERIC Clearinghouse on Elementary and Early Childhood Education, 1983.

Glassberg, Sally. "A View of the Beginning Teacher from a Developmental Perspective." Paper presented at the annual meeting of the American Educational Research Association, Boston, MA, April 1980.

Glickman, Carl. *Developmental Supervision: Alternative Practices for Helping Teachers.* Alexandria, VA: Association for Supervision and Curriculum Development, 1981.

Goldhammer, Robert; Anderson, Robert H.; Krajewski, Robert J. *Clinical Supervision: Special Methods for the Supervision of Teachers*, 2d ed. New York: Holt, Rinehart and Winston, 1980.

Goodwin, William L., and Driscoll, Laura A. "Evaluation of Individuals' Performance." In *Handbook on Measurement and Evaluation in Early Childhood Education*. San Francisco: Jossey-Bass, 1980, chapter 10.

Gordon, Ira J., and Jester, Emile. "Techniques of Observing in Early Childhood and Outcomes of Particular Procedures." In *2nd Handbook of Research on Teaching*, edited by R. N. Travers. Chicago: Rand McNally, 1973, pp. 184–217.

Gordon, Thomas. *Parent Effectiveness Training: The Tested Way to Raise Responsible Children*. New York: Peter H. Wyden, 1970.

Gould, Nora Palmer. "Caregivers in Day Care: Who Are They?" *Day Care and Early Education* (Summer 1983): 17–22.

Gould, Roger L. *Transformations*. New York: Simon and Schuster, 1978.

Greenberg, Polly. *Day Care Do-It-Yourself Staff Growth Program*. Winston-Salem, NC: Kaplan Press, 1975.

Greenburg, Herbert M. "Teacher or Myth." In *Teaching with Feeling*. New York: Pegasus, 1969, pp. 24–37.

Grimmett, Peter P. "Effective Clinical Supervision Conference Interventions: A Preliminary Investigation of Participants' Conceptual Functioning." Paper presented at the American Educational Research Association, Montreal, Canada, April 1983.

Guba, Egon G., and Lincoln, Yvonne S. *Effective Evaluation*. San Francisco: Jossey-Bass, 1981.

Harmon, Carolyn, and Harley, Edward J. "Administrative Aspects of the Head Start Program." In *Project Head Start*, edited by Edward Zigler and Jeannette Valentine. New York: Free Press, 1979, pp. 379–96.

Harvey, O. J.; Hunt, David E.; and Schroeder, Harold M. *Conceptual Systems and Personality Organization*. New York: John Wiley and Sons, 1961.

Hatch, Virginia B. "Creative Supervision of Head Start Centers." In *Administration: Making Programs Work for Children and Families*, edited by Dorothy W. Hewes. Washington, DC: National Association for the Education of Young Children, 1979, pp. 141–46.

Havighurst, Robert. *Developmental Tasks and Education*. New York: David McKay, 1952.

Herman, Judith, ed. *The Schools and Group Identity*. New York: Institute on Pluralism and Group Identity of the American Jewish Committee, 1974.

Hilliard, Asa G., III. "Moving from Abstract to Functional Teacher Education: Pruning and Planting." In *Teacher Education: Of the Teacher, By the Teacher, For the Child*, edited by Bernard Spodek. Washington, DC: National Association for the Education of Young Children, 1974.

Hirsch, Elizabeth, ed. *The Block Book*, 2d ed. Washington, DC: National Association for the Education of Young Children, 1974.

Hoestetler, Lana, "How-To Guide for Advocates." *Child Care Information Exchange* (March/April 1983): 25–29.

Hoestetler, Lana, and Klugman, Edgar. "Early Childhood Job Titles: One Step

Toward Professional Status." *Young Children* 37 (September 1982): 13–22.

Hohmann, Mary; Banet, Bernard; and Weikart, David. *Young Children in Action: A Manual for Preschool Educators*. Ypsilanti, MI: High/Scope Press, 1979.

Honig, Alice Sterling. "Quality Training for Infant Caregivers." *Child Care Quarterly* 12 (Spring 1983): 121–35.

_____. "What You Need to Know to Select and Train Your Staff." *Child Care Quarterly* 8 (Spring 1979): 19–35.

Hymes, James. *Teaching the Child Under Six*, 3d ed. Columbus, OH: Charles E. Merrill, 1981.

Johnson, Robert G. *The Appraisal Interview Guide*. New York: Alpine Press, 1979.

Joyce, Bruce, and Showers, Beverly. "Improving In-Service Training: The Messages of Research." *Educational Leadership* 37 (February 1980): 379–85.

Katz, Lillian G. "Developmental Stages of Preschool Teachers." *Elementary School Journal* 73 (October 1972): 50–54.

_____. *Talks with Teachers*. Washington, DC: National Association for the Education of Young Children, 1977.

Keyserling, Mary Dublin. *Windows on Day Care: A Report on the Findings of Jewish Women on Day Care Needs and Services in Their Communities*. New York: National Council of Jewish Women, 1972.

Kidd, J. R. *How Adults Learn*, rev. ed. New York: Association Press, 1973.

Kindsvatter, Richard, and Wilen, William W. "A Systematic Approach to Improving Conference Skills." *Educational Leadership* 38(7) (April 1981): 525–29.

Klopf, Gordon J. *The Principal and Staff Development in the School*. New York: Bank Street College of Education, 1979.

Knowles, Malcolm S. *The Modern Practice of Adult Education: Andragogy vs. Pedagogy*. New York: Association Press, 1970.

Kohlberg, Lawrence, and Turiel, Elliot. "Moral Development and Moral Education." In *Psychology and Education Practice*, edited by Gerald Lesser. Glenview, IL: Scott, Foresman, 1971.

Koral, Jacqueline. *Daycare Advisory: A Teacher Center Perspective on Staff Development*. New Haven, CT: The Teacher Center, no date.

Kostelnik, Marjorie J. "How to Mediate Staff Conflict." *Child Care Information Exchange* (September/October 1982): 1–5.

Lambert, W. E. "Portuguese Child Rearing Values: A Cross-National Analysis." Paper presented at the Fifth National Portuguese Conference: "Bilingual Education in the 1980s," Providence, RI, June 1980.

Levinson, Daniel J.; Darrow, Charlotte N.; Klein, Edward B.; Levinson, Marsha H.; and McKee, Braxton. *The Seasons of a Man's Life*. New York: Alfred A. Knopf, 1978.

Lindberg, Lucille, and Swedlow, Rita. *Early Childhood Education: A Guide for Observation and Participation*, 2d ed. Boston: Allyn and Bacon, 1979.

Loevinger, Jane. *Ego Development*. San Francisco: Jossey-Bass, 1976.

Lucio, William H., and McNeil, John D. *Supervision: A Synthesis of Thought and Action*. New York: McGraw-Hill, 1969.

McCarthy, Lenore B., and Landerholm, Elizabeth. "Classroom Interaction: A Field-

Based Model for Improving Teaching in the Day Care Center." *Child Care Quarterly* 7 (Spring 1978): 35–44.

McNally, Harold J. "Teacher Evaluation That Makes a Difference." *Educational Leadership* 29 (1972): 353–57.

Magnet, Myron. "What Mass-Produced Child Care is Producing." *Fortune* (November 28, 1983): 157–74.

Morgan, Gwendolyn. Unpublished paper, no date.

Morimoto, Kiyo. "Notes on the Context of Learning." *Harvard Educational Review* 43 (May 1973): 245–57.

Murphy, Lois B., and Leeper, Ethel M. *Caring for Children* series (stock #1790-00016). Superintendent of Documents, U.S. Government Printing Office, Washington, DC 20402, no date.

"NAEYC Position Statement on Nomenclature, Salaries, Benefits, and the Status of the Early Childhood Profession." *Young Children* 40 (November 1984): 9–14.

Neugebauer, Roger. *Organizational Analysis of Day Care.* Unpublished paper, 1975.

———. "Techniques for Avoiding Director Burn-Out." *Child Care Information Exchange* (January 1980): 9–15.

Oja, Sharon Nodie. "Adult Psychological Growth: A Goal of Inservice Education." Paper presented at the American Educational Research Association, Boston, MA, April 1980.

———. "Deriving Teacher Educational Objectives from Cognitive-Developmental Theories and Applying Them to the Practice of Teacher Education." Paper presented at the annual meeting of the American Educational Research Association, Los Angeles, April 1981.

Peck, Robert C. "Psychological Development in the Second Half of Life." In *Middle Age and Aging: A Reader in Social Psychology.* Edited by Bernice L. Neugarten. Chicago: University of Chicago Press, 1968.

Phyfe-Perkins, Elizabeth. *Effects of Teacher Behavior: A Review of Research.* Urbana, IL: ERIC Clearinghouse on Elementary and Early Childhood Education, 1981.

Pickhardt, Carl E. "Supervisors and the Power of Help." *Educational Leadership* 38 (April 1981): 530–33.

Pines, Ayala, and Maslach, Christine. "Combating Staff Burn-Out in a Day Care Center: A Case Study." *Child Care Quarterly* 9 (Spring 1980): 5–16.

Popham, James W. *Educational Evaluation.* Englewood Cliffs, NJ: Prentice-Hall, 1975.

Read, Katherine H., and Patterson, June. *The Nursery School and Kindergarten: Human Relations and Learning,* 7th ed. New York: Holt, Rinehart and Winston, 1980.

"Results of the NAEYC Survey of Child Care Salaries and Working Conditions." *Young Children* 39 (November 1984).

Rogers, Carl E. "The Interpersonal Relationship: The Core of Guidance." *Harvard Educational Review* 32 (1962): 416–29.

Rowen, Betty. *The Children We See: An Observational Approach to Child Study.* New York: Holt, Rinehart and Winston, 1973.

Rubin, Linda, and Hansen, John H. "Assessing Needs and Prioritizing Goals." In *Staff Development and Educational Change*, edited by W. Robert Houston and Roger Pankratz. Reston, VA: Association of Teacher Educators, 1980, pp. 105–24.

Ruopp, Richard; Travers, Jeffrey; Glantz, Frederic; and Coelen, Craig. *Children at the Center*, Vol. 1 of *Final Report of the National Day Care Study*. Cambridge, MA: Abt Associates, 1979.

Sciarra, Dorothy J., and Dorsey, A. G. *Developing and Administering a Child Care Center*. Boston: Houghton Mifflin, 1979.

Seiderman, Stanley. "Combating Staff Burn-Out." *Day Care and Early Education* 5 (Summer 1978): 6–9.

Sergiovanni, Thomas. "Reforming Teaching Evaluation: Naturalistic Alternatives." *Educational Leadership* 34 (May 1977): 602–07.

————. "Toward a Theory of Supervisory Practice: Integrating Scientific, Clinical, and Artistic Views." In Thomas Sergiovanni, ed., *Supervision of Teaching*. Alexandria, VA: Association for Supervision and Curriculum Development, 1982, pp. 67–78.

Sergiovanni, Thomas J., and Starratt, Robert J. *Supervision: Human Perspectives*, 2d ed. New York: McGraw-Hill, 1979.

Sheehy, Gail. *Passages*. New York: E. P. Dutton, 1974.

Spodek, Bernard, and Saracho, Olivia N. "The Preparation and Certification of Early Childhood Personnel." In *Handbook of Research in Early Childhood Education*, edited by Bernard Spodek. New York: Free Press, 1982.

Sprinthall, Richard C., and Sprinthall, Norman A. *Educational Psychology: A Developmental Approach*, 3d ed. Reading, MA: Addison-Wesley, 1981.

Steinmetz, Lawrence. *Managing the Marginal and Unsatisfactory Performer*. Reading, MA: Addison-Wesley, 1969.

Strahan, David B. "The Teacher and Ethnography: Observational Sources of Information for Educators." *Elementary School Journal* 83 (January 1983): 194–203.

Texas Department of Community Affairs. *CDA Instructional Materials: Training Counselor's Guide*. June 1977.

Thies-Sprinthall, Lois. "Supervision: An Educative or Mis-Educative Process?" *Journal of Teacher Education* 31 (November 4, 1980): 17–20.

U.S. Department of Health, Education and Welfare, Office of the Assistant Secretary for Planning and Evaluation. *Policy Issues in Day Care: Summaries of 21 Papers*. November 1977.

U.S. Department of Health, Education and Welfare, Office of Human Development. *Exploring Parenting*. DHEW Publication No. (OHOF) 79-3137, 1978.

U.S. Department of Health, Education and Welfare, Office of Human Development. *Head Start Program Performance Standards*. July 1975.

U.S. Department of Health and Human Services, Office of Human Development Services. *The Child Development Associate Credential*. DHHS Publication No. (OHDS) 82-31162-A, December 1980.

U.S. Department of Health and Human Services, Office of Human Development Services. *The CDA Program: The Child Development Associate, A Guide for Training*, 2d ed. DHHS Publication NO. (OHDS) 82-31171, Fall 1981.

U.S. Department of Health and Human Services, Office of Human Development Services. "Project Head Start." Mimeograph, 1984.

Wessen, Paul D. "Off-Site Stress and the Disadvantaged Caregiver: A Neglected Factor." *Child Care Information Exchange* (November/December 1981): 10–12.

Whitebook, Marcy; Howes, Carolla; Darrah, Rory; and Friedman, Jane. "Caring for the Caregivers: Staff Burn-Out in Child Care." In *Current Topics in Early Childhood Education*, vol. 4, edited by Lillian Katz. Norwood, NJ: Ablex Publishing Company, 1982.

Willis, Anne, and Ricciuti, Henry. *A Good Beginning for Babies: Guidelines for Group Care*. Washington, DC: National Association for the Education of Young Children, 1975.

Wood, Frederick H.; Thompson, Steven R.; and Russell, Frances. "Designing Effective Staff Development Programs." In *Staff Development/Organization Development*, edited by Betty Dillon-Peterson. Alexandria, VA: Association for Supervision and Curriculum Development, 1981, pp. 59–91.

Woonsocket Head Start. *Let Us Tell You About Head Start*. Woonsocket, RI, no date.

Zigler, Edward, and Valentine, Jeanette, eds. *Project Head Start*. New York: Free Press, 1979.

Index